Origins of

Christianity

From Genesis to Jesus

George A. Brinkmann

Published by Brinkmann Enterprises, Inc.

P.O. Box 1106, Rathdrum, Idaho 83858

www.BrinkmannEnterprises.com

Origins of Christianity – From Genesis to Jesus

Non-fiction

ISBN soft cover book 978-0-9824465-1-5

Copyright information on pages 282 – 286

Copy editor: Frances Leighty

Cover design: Kim Brinkmann

Printed in the United States of America

INTRODUCTION

Join me as I share with you an intriguing journey through the history of early Judaism, the Bible and Christianity.

This book offers you a better understanding of the people who gave us the Scriptures, both the Old and the New Testament.

The first five books of the Bible were written by the early Jewish people. Discover when they brought together the oral and written stories that had been handed down to them by their ancestors to create these Sacred Scriptures.

This book offers explanations for the conflicting information within several of the stories in the Bible. It also tells of some of the legends, political upheavals and wars that gave rise to many of the beliefs and traditions within early Judaism and Christianity, some of which continue to be major influences in our world today.

As you read this book you will gain a better understanding of the 'culture wars' between the Greeks and the Jews and between the Romans and the Jews and why at least some of the early followers of Jesus first began to distance themselves from their Jewish friends and neighbors.

The events that transpired during the last week of Jesus' life are central to Christianity. The gospels present several crimes that Jesus was accused of just before his crucifixion.

There were several key people involved in bringing this particular week to such a tragic ending. This book gives you critical information about these people and how their actions ultimately led to the crucifixion of Jesus. A closer look at historical records will show us just who was most responsible for those events which cost Jesus his life and resulted in such a dramatic change in the course of history.

ABOUT THE AUTHOR

For the past fifteen years I have made a concerted effort to study the history of Judaism and early Christianity and have gained a better understanding of the New Testament through a better understanding of the Old Testament.

My research for this book has been gathered from several Bibles, both Christian and Jewish, also from religious and non-religious history books, as well as from my own personal experiences.

ACKNOWLEDGEMENTS

I would like to thank those who helped me write this book, especially my wife Connie for her support over the years, even though this is not a subject of particular interest to her. I would also like to thank my sister Mary Beth for her having shared her own research with me, and my sister Frances for editing and for her professional literary advice. I appreciate my family and friends for their input and encouragement.

I would also like to thank the authors of the books that I have read whose research helped me so much in writing this book.

CONTENTS

PART ONE

The Hebrew nation prior to 539 B.C.E.
(the first Temple period and earlier)

PART TWO

The early second Temple period (539 B.C.E. to 4 B.C.E.)

PART THREE

The life and death of Jesus (4 B.C.E. to 33 C.E.)

PART FOUR

The early years of Christianity (33 C.E. and forward)

Part One

The Hebrew nation prior to 539 B.C.E.

(the first Temple period and earlier)

Chapter 1

The first story of creation has no Adam and Eve

During their early years, the Hebrew people struggled with their identity as a people apart from others. As a result, they adopted some of the customs and beliefs of the non-Hebrew people around them, including the belief in other gods. Then, at some point they collectively agreed to worship only one God. They then held to the belief that their God was the God above all other gods. He was mightier than the other gods and did not need to do battle with them for control of the universe or to determine the destiny of humans.

Several centuries later Jewish writers, descendants of the Hebrews, wrote the Torah – the first five books of the Bible. By this time, as is reflected in *Genesis*, the first book of the Bible, they were firmly committed to their belief in only one God.

Genesis begins with God creating the universe in six days and resting on the seventh day. On the <u>first day</u> God separated light from darkness. On the <u>second day</u> he separated the water above from the water below. On the <u>third day</u> he created the plants. On the <u>fourth day</u> he created the sun and the moon to separate day from night, and he created the stars. On the <u>fifth day</u> he created the birds, fish and great 'sea monsters'. On the <u>sixth day</u> he created animals, both domestic and wild. Also on the sixth day, <u>after he created the animals</u>, he created the first two people: "Then God said, *Let us make mankind in our image, in our likeness*" (Genesis 1.26).[1] On the <u>seventh day</u> God rested. There is no mention of any sin by either the man or the woman.

The first story of creation presents a somewhat impersonal God: "So God created mankind in his own image, in the image of God he created them; male and female he created them. God blessed them and said to them, *Be fruitful and increase in number*" (Genesis 1.27-28).[2] This story of creation ends within the next few verses without God giving names to the first man or the first woman.

Some people question the historical accuracy of this creation story because it refers to God in the plural. The Jewish writers very likely included this reference to God in the plural, which appears in only this one verse, as a way of saying that at least some of their ancestors believed that there were two Gods, one male and one female: "*Let us make mankind in our image, in our likeness* [one male God and one female God created one male human and one female human]" (Genesis 1.26).[3]

This use of God in the plural: "*Let us make mankind*" (Genesis 1.26)[4] has been used by Catholics and other Christians as one of the biblical references in support of the doctrine of the Trinity – the Father, Son and Holy Spirit. The Jewish people, the people who wrote the book of *Genesis*, do not interpret this verse in this way.

---

[1] Bible, *New International Version*, page 2
[2] Bible, *New International Version*, page 2
[3] Bible, *New International Version*, page 2
[4] Bible, *New International Version*, page 2

Because of similarities, the first story of creation in the Bible appears to be a redacted/rewritten version of an ancient Babylonian creation story. However, the Babylonians, as well as the Mesopotamians, Assyrians, and Persians believed in a wide variety of gods including Ratri, the spirit of the night; Agni, the god of fire; Parjanya, the god who shatters the trees; Mitra, god of the sun; Indra, the calmer of chaos; Baal, the god of thunder and rain (the primary male god of the non-Hebrew Canaanites); Dagon, a fish-god of the Philistines; Astarte, goddess of the Philistines; Shamash, the sun-god of Babylon; Mithras, the Persian god of light; Enlil, god of the wind; Asherah, the god of fertility; as well as many other gods.

Eight thousand years ago many of the people in the Mediterranean area were farmers. Their primary crops were grain and pastures. Most of the fields were dry farmed. That is, the farmers depended on the annual rainfall to produce their crops, not manual irrigation. However, some of the farmers built diversion ditches to direct water from small streams to irrigate their crops while others used water from springs.

Other people in the Mediterranean area were hunter-gatherers. As with many other nomadic tribes throughout the world, they moved from one area to another and back again, following the seasonal migration of the wild game they depended on for survival.

The major concerns of the hunter-gatherers, as well as the farmers, included dangers faced when hunting large animals, protection from weather extremes, deadly diseases and attacks from neighboring tribes.

People did not have access to scientific explanations for natural events such as violent storms, droughts, earthquakes, volcanic eruptions, terminal illnesses, birth defects, women's miscarriages and other dramatic events. As a result, they very likely attributed at least some of these tragic events, as well as their good fortune, to someone in their community making choices that displeased or pleased a particular god.

Superstition and the general lack of scientific knowledge often led people to believe in and seek the favor of a power greater than themselves, a being with supernatural power who would alleviate their misery, whether it was a god of fire, a goddess of fertility, a god of war or one of many other gods or goddesses. The myths and legends people developed through the course of time provided them an explanation for what they considered supernatural events. It also contributed to their tribal identity.

It was not unusual for people within a community to worship several gods, depending on the situation. At the same time, these same people would join in worship in a neighboring country or community where the people there believed in different gods. Sometimes the people in another community believed in the same gods but placed them in a different priority of importance. However, there was usually one god in any given community or country that was considered of greater importance or to have greater influence than the other gods.

Many of the beliefs that were held sacred by the people who lived thousands of years ago might seem quite foreign to us today. However, for them, these beliefs were acceptable and were often incorporated into their rituals and prayers.

In ancient times it was primarily through oral stories that people passed their beliefs down through the generations. It would have been natural for these stories to change as a community's circumstances changed and their collective knowledge increased. Also, given human nature, some of the details in these stories were almost certainly exaggerated, at least in some instances.

The Jewish writers did not present all of the stories in the Torah as what people today would typically refer to as historical documents. The distinction between Hebrew and Jew will be explained in a later chapter. The Jewish scribes (writers) wrote the Torah to memorialize the many oral stories passed down to them through many generations even though they must have realized that some of these stories had irreconcilable differences. It is doubtful that the Jewish writers considered this style of writing misleading or deceptive, just different.

Chapter 2

The second story of creation has no 'seven days'

The second story of creation begins in the second half of chapter two, immediately following the first story of creation. This second story describes God as more caring and compassionate, a God who interacted with the animals and the first two people.

God created the first man and named him Adam. Then, God created the animals. God brought all of the different kinds of animals to Adam. Adam named each of them.

Then God realized that not one of them was a suitable partner for Adam: "The LORD God said, *It is not good for the man to be alone. I will make a helper suitable for him*" (Genesis 2.18).[1] God put Adam into a deep sleep: "Then the LORD God made a woman from the rib he had taken out of the man" (Genesis 2.22).[2] God gave the woman a name – Eve.

Notice that this story has a different sequence for the creation of the animals and the first two people. In the first story God created the animals and then the first man and woman. In this second story of creation God created Adam, then the animals, and lastly he created Eve.

---

[1] Bible, *New International Version*, page 3
[2] Bible, *New International Version*, page 4

There are historians today, including Jewish biblical scholars, who acknowledge that the origins of the Bible's second creation story can be traced to a very similar non-Jewish story that originated in Mesopotamia many years or even centuries before the birth of Abraham, the first Hebrew/Jewish patriarch.

After the creation of Adam and Eve, the story continues with Eve and Adam eating fruit from the tree in the middle of the Garden of Eden even though God had told Eve not to eat it.

Many church leaders and teachers taught that Eve's decision to eat fruit from the 'forbidden tree' was a sin of a sexual nature even though the story clearly states that Eve's choice was to 'gain wisdom'. It was not a choice to engage in any actions of a sexual nature: "When the woman saw that the fruit of the tree was good for food and pleasing to the eye, and also desirable for gaining wisdom, she took some and ate it. She also gave some to her husband, who was with her, and he ate it" (Genesis 3.6).[1]

It appears that this sinful choice to eat fruit from the 'forbidden tree' had nothing to do with sex since God commanded Adam and Eve to have sexual intercourse: "God blessed them and said to them, *Be fruitful and increase in number* [*have many children* or *be fertile and increase* or *have a lot of children*, depending on which Bible is quoted]" (Genesis 1.28).[2] Also: "That is why a man leaves his father and mother and is

---

[1] Bible, *New International Version*, page 4
[2] Bible, *New International Version*, page 2

united to his wife, and they become one flesh. Adam and his wife were both naked, and they felt no shame" (Genesis 2.24-25).[1]

After Eve and Adam ate fruit from the 'forbidden tree', they were banished from paradise and forced to live a hard life: "To Adam he said, *Because you listened to your wife and ate fruit from the tree about which I commanded you, 'You must not eat from it', Cursed is the ground because of you; through painful toil you will eat food from it all the days of your life*" (Genesis 3.17).[2]

Supposedly, at this point in their lives, Adam and Eve were both mature adults: "Adam made love to his wife Eve, and she became pregnant and gave birth to Cain" (Genesis 4.1).[3] Cain was born and then Abel. Cain grew into adulthood and developed a farm while Abel became a shepherd. This is followed with offerings to God by Cain and Abel, envy and murder by Cain, and Cain's banishment.

Then, as the story goes, Adam and Eve had several other children, more than 100 years later: "When Adam had lived 130 years, he had a son in his own likeness, in his own image; and he named him Seth. After Seth was born, Adam lived 800 years and had other sons and daughters. Altogether, Adam lived a total of 930 years, and then he died" (Genesis 5.3-5).[4]

Many of the first people spoken of in *Genesis* are said to have lived hundreds of years – Adam 930, Seth 912, Enosh 905, Methuselah 969

---

[1] Bible, *New International Version*, page 4
[2] Bible, *New International Version*, page 5
[3] Bible, *New International Version*, page 6
[4] Bible, *New International Version*, pages 7-8

years. These stories also state that many of these same men were more than one hundred years old when they fathered their children: "When Jared had lived 162 years, he became the father of Enoch. After he became the father of Enoch, Jared lived 800 years and had other sons and daughters. Altogether, Jared lived a total of 962 years, and then he died" (Genesis 5.18-20).[1] "When Methuselah had lived 187 years, he became the father of Lamech. After he became the father of Lamech, Methuselah lived 782 years and had other sons and daughters. Altogether, Methuselah lived a total of 969 years, and then he died" (Genesis 5.25-27).[2] "After Noah was 500 years old, he became the father of Shem, Ham and Japheth" (Genesis 5.32).[3] However, later writings indicate that there was some doubt as to how old a person could be and still father a child: "Abraham fell facedown; he laughed and said to himself, *Will a son be born to a man a hundred years old? Will Sarah bear a child at the age of ninety?*" (Genesis 17.17).[4]

Those who wrote *Genesis* did not attribute as many years to their later patriarchs. According to *Genesis* Abraham lived 175 years (7 x 5 x 5), Isaac 180 years (5 x 6 x 6) and Jacob 147 years (3 x 7 x 7). This numerology motif was very important to the Hebrew people, as can be seen in many of their writings.

Today there are many people, including Jewish scholars, who believe that these numbers were never meant to be interpreted literally.

---

[1] Bible, *New International Version,* page 8
[2] Bible, *New International Version*, page 8
[3] Bible, *New International Version*, page 8
[4] Bible, *New International Version*, page 24

This literary style, with the exaggeration in the number of years, can be seen as a way for the Jewish writers to emphasize the importance of the lives of many of their patriarchs. Using this style of writing was apparently more important to them than writing unemotional matter-of-fact historical documents.

After the tribal leaders and the scribes completed the first five books of the Bible they tried to ascertain just how many years it had been since God created the universe. To accomplish this they added the number of years between all of the generations recorded in *Genesis* to the number of years that each of the Hebrew kings had ruled. Then they added the number of years after the rule of their last king up to the time of their writing. With these numbers they determined what they believed to be Year One, the year of the creation of the universe, including the earth and the first humans.

The following might place the second story of creation into a more historical perspective. This creation story describes how Adam and Eve (the tribe) lived comfortably in Paradise (the tried-and-true hunter-gatherer way of life). However, all of that changed when Eve (the women of the tribe) chose to eat the fruit of the tree (the produce from their agricultural enterprise) and thus replaced Adam (the men of the tribe) as the primary provider of food (or at least substantially supplemented their customary food source). It was Eve (the women of the tribe) who enticed Adam (the men of the tribe) to eat the forbidden fruit (to give up the long-established hunter-gatherer way of life and become farmers and herders).

The story of Cain and Abel is a mythical story that may have been written to illustrate ongoing conflicts between those tribes who raised sheep (Abel) and those who raised crops (Cain): "Later she gave birth to his brother Abel. Now Abel kept flocks, and Cain worked the soil" (Genesis 4.2).[1] Sheep and goats were domesticated between 9,000 and 11,000 years ago.

Before the domestication of animals, people survived as hunter-gatherers. The men and the women each had responsibilities in providing for their families and the tribe. The women gathered wild fruits, grains and roots while the men hunted wild game.

Over time, the women learned to store some of the grain for the upcoming winter. However, meat continued to be an essential staple in their diet, especially during winter months.

The development of agriculture was a natural progression of civilization. It would have been the women of the tribe, at least in some cases, who harvested fruits and vegetables while the men were hunting wild game.

It also would have been a natural progression for some of these women to realize that grain and other desirable plants thrived better and were easier to harvest when the undesirable plants were weeded out, thus establishing fields of crops. This was a major advance in agriculture. However, women have received little recognition for their extraordinary efforts in the development of agriculture and animal husbandry in those ancient times.

---

[1] Bible, *New International Version*, page 6

Sometime soon after 8,000 B.C.E. (Before the Common Era) the people living in the Fertile Crescent (a strip of land extending eastward from the Mediterranean Sea) became the first people in the Mediterranean area to cultivate plants and raise animals on a large scale. Canaan was within the Fertile Crescent.

The expansion of crops and the domestication of sheep, goats, pigs and cattle decreased people's dependency on wild animals. The downside to this change would have been that these tribes would then be increasingly exposed to the many hardships brought on by floods, droughts, wildfires and diseases, which are inherent in a sedentary lifestyle.

This dependence on agriculture brought with it some of the most dramatic social and health changes in human history. Those tribes who raised livestock and those who raised crops became increasingly dependent on each other for their food supply.

Centuries after this *date of creation* was first determined, Jewish scholars came to believe that the universe was older than their ancestors had calculated, possibly millions of years older. They then taught that the year previously believed to have been the *year of all creation* was the year of the creation of the first two people. Today, most Jews, Christians and others believe that not only animals, but also humans existed many thousands of years earlier than the date originally thought to have been *Year One.*

The Jewish Temple in Omaha, Nebraska was built in 2001. It has the year 5861 cast into the concrete cornerstone. Counting back 5861 years from 2001 reflects the year the Hebrew people originally believed to be the Beginning of Time: "Literally meaning the 'head of the year', Rosh Hashanah falls on 1 Tishri (usually in September) and marks the beginning of a period both solemn and joyous. On the one hand, this festival is *Yom ha-Zikaron / the Day of Remembrance.* But it is also the *Yom ha-Teru'ah / the day of the Shofar Blast* and the 'Birthday of the World,' the day on which, as Jewish lore has it, God created mankind and we symbolically re-enthrone him, an event that calls for an appropriate amount of celebration".[1]

The Day of Remembrance is the first day of the month in the first month of the year in the Jewish calendar. This month, Tishri, in the ancient Jewish calendar, is the second half of September through the first half of October in the calendar we use today. The rationale was that since the tree in the center of the Garden of Eden had 'forbidden fruit' on it when Adam and Eve were created it must have been fall, or at least late enough in the year for trees to have ripe fruit hanging on the branches.

The first Hebrews lived in Canaan. This was a relatively small country on the eastern shore of the Mediterranean Sea. For several centuries the Canaanites were under the rule of the Assyrians, their neighbors to the north. Years later the Canaanites were governed by the Mesopotamians, their neighbors to the east. In the sixth century B.C.E. Babylon, the country east of Mesopotamia, conquered Canaan, Mesopotamia and Assyria.

The Babylonians soon became oppressive. However, the Hebrew people continued to resist Babylonian rule. In 598 B.C.E. the Babylonians put down a Hebrew revolt. Many of the Hebrew people were killed.

---

[1] *Essential Judaism*, George Robinson, page 93

14

Others were forced into slavery. Some of the men, especially those who were skilled builders and knowledgeable businessmen, were placed in work camps in Assyrian and Babylonian cities: "… the skilled workers and the artisans had gone into exile from Jerusalem" (Jeremiah 29.2).[1] However, they were allowed to take their families with them.

During the following sixty years, the Hebrews who lived in the Babylonian cities completed several buildings for the royalty and numerous public-works projects. Many of them remained segregated from the general population and continued to live their Hebrew faith, as much as circumstances would allow. They also maintained their genealogy records.

While they were in this foreign land with no temple or other central place of worship, they built synagogues (synagogue is a Greek word meaning *assembly* or *to bring together*). Men, which included boys thirteen years of age and older, were allowed inside the sacred curtained area of the synagogue. Women, teenage girls and children were restricted to the outer portion of the room.

Eleven years later, in 587 B.C.E., the Babylonians put down another Hebrew revolt in Canaan. This time the Babylonians destroyed the city of Jerusalem, including the First Temple, the temple built by King Solomon.

Several decades later, in 539 B.C.E., Persia (today's Iran) conquered Babylon: "King Cyrus of Persia defeats Babylon and permits the Judean exiles to return to, and rebuild, Israel".[2] Also, "about forty thousand take

---

[1] Bible, *New International Version*, page 1321
[2] *Biblical Literacy*, Rabbi Joseph Telushkin, page 599

up his offer and reestablish a Jewish state under Persian rule".[1] However, as it turned out, the Persian war against the Babylonians was really not much of a war. As soon as the Persian army entered the country, King Nabonidus fled. Without their king's support and leadership, the Babylonian army immediately surrendered.

---

[1] *Jewish Literacy,* Rabbi Joseph Telushkin, page 106

Chapter 3

A literal interpretation of a few of the Bible stories presents problems

It is easy to read at least a few of the Bible stories with skepticism, especially when they are viewed from a logical or scientific perspective. However, we can never know the family environments and social struggles of those people long ago who gave us the first few stories in the Bible.

For many centuries the Catholic Church held that it was wrong to question the accuracy of any story in the Bible, sometimes under penalty of death, even though the Bible contains contradictory accounts of multiple events. Many of the Catholic Church leaders failed to understand the ancient form of writing and continued to demand a literal interpretation of biblical stories. This remains a stumbling block for many people even today, including some theologians and many Christian Church authorities.

Nicolas Copernicus, a Polish cleric, published the book *On the Revolutions of the Heavenly Spheres* in 1543. This book laid out his theory that the sun was the center of the universe. This contradicted more than a thousand years of teaching by European scholars and the Catholic Church leaders who held to the belief that the earth, not the sun, was the center of the universe.

Copernicus did not have the benefit of a telescope, only the recordings of many observations of astronomers in previous centuries and a few of his own observations. His conclusions were based primarily on mathematical calculations. Because he was a timid man, he delayed publishing his book until he was on his deathbed. By then it was too late for the Church authorities to punish him for teaching heresy. Heresy is a Greek word meaning *an alternate choice*.

Galileo Galilei was a scientist who lived in Italy. He was born in 1564 and died in 1642. His circle of friends included many university instructors, Catholic priests, bishops and Pope Urban VIII. Galileo had a heritage of physicians in his family. He studied medicine for two years at the University of Pisa before turning to the pursuit of mathematics and physics.

Galileo was a university instructor for many years. He is credited with many scientific discoveries and inventions. Galileo demonstrated that ice is lighter than water and that a ten pound cannon ball does not fall ten times faster than a one pound musket ball.

He dispelled many other common misconceptions of the time. With this new understanding of gravity, later scientists were able to plot out the elliptical path of the planets in our solar system. Scientists also came to realize that when the planets were nearer the sun their speed of travel was greater than when they were farther from the sun. Galileo is credited by many as being *the father of experimental physics*.

In 1609, with a little help from others, Galileo developed the first telescope. It had a magnification factor of twenty. For example, objects twenty miles away appear to be only one mile away.

His telescope was built on the new technology that was being used in Paris for the shaping of eyeglasses and the spyglass. With this telescope he was able to get a much closer look at the stars and the planets in our solar system. He discovered the four largest moons circling Jupiter. He plotted out the orbit of the earth, the moon, the five planets nearest the earth and Jupiter's four moons.

His calculations agreed with the discoveries of earlier scientists who had stated that the sun, not the earth, was the center of our solar system. He manufactured additional telescopes for other scholars, clerics and royalty in Italy and neighboring countries so they might share his exciting discoveries. His later telescopes had a magnification factor of thirty.

Galileo knew it was not acceptable to write his findings as any more than theory. He therefore wrote his book *Dialogue* in the format of a discussion to explain the merits of his findings. He did not intend to teach as fact anything the Church officials might interpret as heresy.

The Dominican friar Giordano Bruno was burned at the stake in Rome just nine years earlier for insisting that the earth was not stationary and was not the center of the universe.

To avoid the same fate, Galileo submitted a draft of his book to the appropriate Church authorities. With a few minor changes, his book was given the necessary approval to go to print. Galileo proceeded to have 1,000 copies printed, all of which sold very quickly.

Grand Duchess Madama Cristina (1565 C. E. – 1637 C. E.) of Lorraine, France was a devout Catholic with a circle of friends that included priests, cardinals and even the pope. Madama Cristina read

Dialogue. However, she did not agree with Galileo's theories. She reminded the Church court of a verse in Scriptures: "On the day the LORD gave the Amorites over to Israel, Joshua said to the LORD in the presence of Israel: *Sun, stand still over Gibeon, and you, moon, over the Valley of Aijalon.* So the sun stood still, and the moon stopped, till the nation avenged itself on its enemies" (Joshua 10.12-13).[1] Also: "He set the earth on its foundations; it can never be moved" (Psalms 104.5).[2]

Prior to writing *Dialogue*, Galileo had made a name for himself in Europe for his many writings on mathematical and scientific discoveries. However, for this writing, even though he was under the understanding that the book had the Church's final approval, he was called before the Holy Office of the Inquisition. Galileo had no intention of taking a stand against the Catholic Church. He tried to convince them that science and the Bible could be interpreted in harmony.

To compound the Church's problems and the repercussions for Galileo, the book had been written in Italian rather than the traditional Latin. This made the writings easily readable by anyone who was literate and could read Italian. However, the majority of the European population during that era was illiterate.

After a very long investigation and trial, *Dialogue* was placed on the Index, the list of books that Catholics were forbidden to read. All but a few copies were found, confiscated and destroyed. Galileo was placed under house-arrest for the remaining seven years of his life and forbidden to ever again teach or discuss publicly that the earth was not the center of

---

[1] Bible, *New International Version*, page 372
[2] Bible, *New International Version*, page 1007

the universe. *Dialogue* was not removed from the Index of Forbidden Books until 1835. Copernicus and Galileo had 'dropped pebbles into the water' that soon became 'tidal waves'.

Centuries earlier, the Catholic Church authorities declared that to teach heresy was a crime not only against the Church but against all of society. In the year 1209 the Church organized a group of institutions within their judicial system to combat heresy. Their efforts led to the torture and killing of thousands in what became known as <u>The Inquisition</u>.

The Office of the Inquisition was the group of Church officials who were well known for authorizing the torture and execution of those it chose to punish for what they determined were crimes against the Church, especially for teaching heresy. The Inquisition began in southern France because of an issue with Mary Magdalene and her child Sarah.

At that time, the Catholic Church had the authority to order the civil authorities to enforce Church law. This included the mandates of the Inquisition. The Catholic Church leaders today no longer have the authority to execute people who refuse to comply with the laws of the Church or those who contradict their 'official' interpretation of the Bible.

During the 500 years of the Inquisition, the Catholic Church was responsible for the murder and execution of more than 100,000 Catholics and non-Catholics as well as the torture and abuse of many more who did not accept the Church's teachings. Even though, most often, it was the civil authorities who actually tortured and executed people for heresy, it was the popes, cardinals and other Church authorities who were ultimately responsible for these crimes.

Galileo spent the last seven years of his life under house-arrest for teaching heresy. It was not until October 31, 1992, 350 years after his death, that Pope John Paul II officially rescinded Galileo's house-arrest orders. He stated that the Church officials of Galileo's time had not allowed enough latitude for scientific discoveries when interpreting stories in the Bible.

The categories of books that Catholics were or are forbidden to read can be found in the 1970 Bible *The New American Bible*, on page 36, in the Encyclopedic Dictionary.

Charles Darwin published his book *The Origin of the Species* in 1858. The Catholic Church considered much of the information in this book to be heresy. Prior to the era of Darwin, the European people's perception of the universe was very different from that of most people in Western societies today.

The creation stories in *Genesis* were generally interpreted as follows: the earth was flat, the center of God's creation; below the surface of the earth was the nether world, the place where evil spirits resided; the sun gave light and warmth for the day; the moon gave some light for the night and gave rise to a lunar calendar; the stars also gave light to the night and direction to the occasional night traveler; the heavens was all of the space between the earth and the blue above the vault or dome: "And God said, *Let there be a vault between the waters to separate water from water*. So God made the vault and separated the water under the vault from the water above it. And it was so. God called the vault *sky*" (Genesis 1.6-8).[1] Some Bibles use the word <u>dome</u> rather than <u>vault</u>.

Also, as recently as seven centuries ago, many European people still believed that the blue above the earth was not the sky but rather an ocean of water above the <u>vault</u> or <u>dome</u>. They also believed that the sun, all of the planets and all of the stars were between the earth's surface and that <u>vault</u> or <u>dome</u>. Today's science quite clearly contradicts that theory.

Today's science also shows that the earth's continents are not and were not floating on an ocean of water as the story of *Genesis* portrays: "... who spread out the earth upon the waters" (Psalms 136.6).[2]

Thousands of years before the Bible was written, some of the people in the Middle Eastern countries had access to water from natural springs. Others dug shallow wells for drinking water and for irrigation. This water that was found a short distance below the surface may have influenced their belief that the continents were 'floating on an ocean of water': "But God remembered Noah and all the wild animals and the livestock that were with him in the ark, and he sent a wind over the earth, and the waters receded. Now the springs of the deep and the floodgates of the heavens had been closed, and the rain had stopped falling from the sky" (Genesis 8.1-2).[3]

The ancient Egyptians, like the early Hebrews, also believed this blue was an enormous body of water: "On First Dynasty engravings, the sun-god is shown travelling across the sky in a boat. Presumably the

---

[1] Bible, *New International Version*, page 1
[2] Bible, *New International Version*, page 1043
[3] Bible, *New International Version*, page 11

pharaoh and the souls buried with him would use their boats to accompany him".[1]

---

[1] *The History of the Ancient World*, Susan Wise Bauer, page 64

Chapter 4

The Flood story has an addendum

One of the next stories in the Bible tells of a great Flood. This story of Noah may have been written, at least in part, to teach people that God might well be expected to destroy anyone involved in a moral breakdown of society. The Hebrews who wrote their interpretation of this ancient story believed that their best chance of survival was to adhere to high moral values and to be loyal to this God who was above all other gods.

Many people in ancient times believed in a literal interpretation of the biblical Flood story. They believed that the vast amount of water that supposedly rained down for forty days and forty nights came primarily from that vast ocean of water above the vault or dome. Most biblical historians today are quick to discount the Flood story as myth since we now know that the earth is not flat and the blue of the sky is the earth's atmosphere, not a vast ocean of water suspended above the earth enclosing the entire universe, nor are all of the continents floating on an ocean of water.

If all the ice in the glaciers throughout the world and all the ice in the Arctic and Antarctic were to melt, the ocean levels would rise significantly. One recent estimate is 216 feet. That is certainly not enough water to submerge all of the mountains: "The waters rose and increased greatly on the earth, and the ark floated on the surface of the water. They rose greatly on the earth, and all the high mountains under the entire heavens were covered. The waters rose and covered the mountains to a depth of more than fifteen cubits [fifteen cubits equals twenty-two and one-half feet]" (Genesis 7.18-20).[1] Mount Everest is more than 29,000 feet above sea level.

Within the first few chapters of the Flood story God instructs Noah to bring a pair of each living creature onto the ark: "*You are to bring into the ark two of all living creatures, male and female, to keep them alive with you. Two of every kind of bird, of every kind of animal and of every kind of creature that moves along the ground will come to you to be kept alive. You are to take every kind of food that is to be eaten and store it away as food for you and for them.* Noah did everything just as God commanded him" (Genesis 6.19-22).[2]

According to the Flood story, God saved Noah and his family and thereby saved the human race from extinction. Everyone else in the entire world was supposedly destroyed because of their 'serious immorality': "Every living thing on the face of the earth was wiped out; people and animals and the creatures that move along the ground and the birds were wiped from the earth. Only Noah was left, and those with him in the ark" (Genesis 7.23).[3]

The Bible states that God destroyed the people in the Flood because they were all living evil lives. One might ask – were all the children and new-born infants who died in the Flood also immoral and living evil lives?

---

[1] Bible, *New International Version*, page 11
[2] Bible, *New International Version*, page 10
[3] Bible, *New International Version*, page 11

Several thousand years ago, the mightiest man-made weapon was the bow. Scriptures states that after the Flood, God placed his mighty bow in the sky. Even today we commonly refer to this mythical bow as a rainbow. This rainbow was supposed to remind people, following every rainstorm thereafter, that God would protect them from another flood of such magnitude: "And God said, *This is the sign of the covenant I am making between me and you and every living creature with you, a covenant for all generations to come: I have set my rainbow in the clouds, and it will be the sign of the covenant between me and the earth. Whenever I bring clouds over the earth and the rainbow appears in the clouds, I will remember my covenant between me and you and all living creatures of every kind. Never again will the waters become a flood to destroy all life*" (Genesis 9.12-15).[1]

The Flood story can be seen as myth for several reasons. There are millions of species of creatures scattered throughout the world – in the dense forests of South America, in the Arctic and Antarctic regions, on the islands of Madagascar and Galapagos, on the shores of the Nile and the Amazon rivers, in the Rocky Mountains of North America and in all of the areas between.

According to recent research by John Nobel Wilford, and others, the world is home to approximately 5,400 species of placental mammals (mammals that develop in uteruses with placentas). This includes 148 species of large mammals. There are also more than 10,000 species of birds and a multitude of reptiles and insects living all across the world.

---

[1] Bible, *New International Version*, page 13

27

The Pacific Ocean covers approximately one-third of the earth's surface and has an estimated 25,000 islands. Many of these islands each have their own unique variety of plants and animals.

Research recorded at the Botanical Gardens in Niagara Falls, Ontario, Canada states that there are approximately 20,000 species of butterflies in the world, with approximately one-half of these found in their natural habitat only in the Amazon rainforest. The most recent count of insect species just in Brazil's Amazon rainforest is approximately 2,500,000. It is estimated that 17,000 species of plants and animals were pushed into extinction in the Amazon rainforest in 2008.

The world's many species of creatures all live in unique ecosystems with their own nutritional needs. Noah would have had to collect food for all of the creatures he loaded into the Ark: *"You are to take every kind of food that is to be eaten and store it away as food for you and for them"* (Genesis 6.21).[1] Noah would have had to find, identify, gather, transport, store and preserve this huge volume of food to sustain himself, his family and an untold number of creatures for approximately seven months $(40 + 150 + 7 + 7 + 7 = 211$ days).

"For forty days the flood kept coming on the earth, and as the waters increased they lifted the ark high above the earth. The waters rose and increased greatly on the earth, and the ark floated on the surface of the water. They rose greatly on the earth, and all the high mountains under the entire heavens were covered. The waters rose and covered the mountains to a depth of more than fifteen cubits. Every living thing that moved on land perished – birds, livestock, wild animals, all the creatures

---

[1] Bible, *New International Version*, page 10

that swarm over the earth, and all mankind. Everything on dry land that had the breath of life in its nostrils died. Every living thing on the face of the earth was wiped out; people and animals and the creatures that move along the ground and the birds were wiped from the earth. Only Noah was left, and those with him in the ark. The waters flooded the earth for a hundred and fifty days" (Genesis 7.17-24).[1]

"After forty days Noah opened a window he had made in the ark and sent out a raven, and it kept flying back and forth until the water had dried up from the earth. Then he sent out a dove to see if the water had receded from the surface of the ground. But the dove could find nowhere to perch because there was water over all the surface of the earth; so it returned to Noah in the ark. He reached out his hand and took the dove and brought it back to himself in the ark. He waited seven more days and again sent out the dove from the ark. When the dove returned to him in the evening, there in its beak was a freshly plucked olive leaf! Then Noah knew that the water had receded from the earth. He waited seven more days and sent the dove out again, but this time it did not return to him" (Genesis 8.6-12).[2] Then, after the water receded, Noah ostensibly returned these tens-of-millions of creatures to all corners of the world, with no apparent means of transportation over sea or land to ecosystems that, after having been submerged under water for more than seven months, would no longer have existed.

The number seven is a very symbolic number throughout the Bible. This can be seen in the second version of the Flood story: "Take with

---

[1] Bible, *New International Version*, page 11
[2] Bible, *New International Version*, pages 11-12

you seven pairs of every kind of clean animal, a male and its mate, and one pair of every kind of unclean animal, a male and its mate, and also seven pairs of every kind of bird, male and female, to keep their various kinds alive throughout the earth" (Genesis 7.2-3).[1]

This Jewish addendum to the Flood story supposedly allowed for the killing of some of the animals as offerings to God by Noah after the Flood without the elimination of those species: "Then Noah built an altar to the LORD and, taking some of all the clean animals and clean birds, he sacrificed burnt offerings on it" (Genesis 8.20).[2] Saving seven pair, not just one pair, of the 'ritually clean' mammals and birds would have increased considerably the number of animals that Noah would have had to find, capture, transport and feed.

There have been three major Ice Ages during the past 2.5 million years. The Ice Age that began approximately 80,000 years ago lowered the ocean level approximately three hundred feet below what it is today. As this ocean water evaporated, much of it fell as snow. As a result, much of the northern hemisphere was covered with ice thousands of feet deep. Then, between 15,000 and 10,000 years ago, most of that ice melted. This raised the sea level again, close to what it is today.

The melting ice raised the water level in most lakes. However, in some areas this major snowmelt formed new lakes. One example of this is glacial Lake Missoula. This was an Ice Age lake located in the Pacific Northwest.

---

[1] Bible, *New International Version*, page 10
[2] Bible, *New International Version*, page 12

As the snow and ice melted in northwestern Montana and southern Canada, the water flowed down the Clark Fork River. However, this flow was temporarily blocked by a glacier that filled a narrow valley near today's Clark Fork, a small town in northern Idaho. This 2,000 foot deep ice dam caused the water to back up approximately two hundred miles, filling the valley with a volume of water equal to Lake Erie and Lake Ontario combined. This was the largest glacial lake in the world.

Horizontal erosion marks on the hillsides more than 140 miles upstream, near Missoula, Montana indicate the lake level there reached a depth of 1,000 feet. Eventually, the rising water created too much pressure on the ice dam and it broke through, or it filled so much that it began flowing over or under the ice. Then, the glacial ice dam washed out and drained the entire lake in two or three days. The volume of flow for the first one or two days is estimated to have been ten times the combined flow of all the rivers in the world today.

Then the weather gradually cooled again, creating another glacial ice dam which also washed out. This happened approximately forty times during the past several Ice Ages. However, the lake did not always fill to the same level before washing out again. Each time Lake Missoula drained, the water flooded a vast area on its way to the Pacific Ocean, more than 400 miles away. There were similar floods in other countries as well during this era.

Tsunamis and hurricanes/typhoons/cyclones have always been a threat to people living in the coastal areas of the world and have taken many lives over the millennia. There surely would have been flood stories that developed following these tragic events. Floods resulting

31

from major weather and geologic events even in modern times have caused the death of many thousands of people. According to records from ancient times to the present, at least 500,000 people have died in the wake of tsunamis.

At least a few of the stories that were first told by those who witnessed any of these Ice Age floods, or any major flood, would have been passed down through many generations. With the lack of scientific knowledge about weather on a global scale, the mythical description of events would have prevailed.

It was more common for a smaller community to embrace or adopt a story from a larger community, not the other way around. The Gilgamesh Flood story, *The Epic of Gilgamesh,* appears to be much older than the Bible Flood story. Thus, many scholars today believe that the Flood story in the Bible is a Jewish adaption of the Mesopotamian Flood story.

There are many possible scenarios from which the Mesopotamian Flood myth may have originated. It may be that a tribal leader saved his family and a few others from the devastation of lowland flooding. He and his family and friends may have been forced to move all of their livestock and personal belongings to higher ground and develop new farmland or they may have given up their agricultural way of life and become nomadic shepherds. It is impossible to know the origins of these stories with any certainty.

There are many similarities between the story of Gilgamesh and the story of Noah. The boats were of similar design and in both stories the water level rose higher than the highest mountains. As the water receded the boats in both stories came to rest on a mountain somewhere in the Ararat mountain range (the Ararat Mountains are the source of the headwaters of the Tigris and Euphrates rivers). In both stories a bird was used to check when it was safe for the people to get off of their boats. Also, both groups sacrificed animals immediately after getting off of their boats.

Most of the events in the two stories occurred in the same sequence. However, the underlying theme is the major difference in the two Flood stories. In the Gilgamesh story the Flood was planned, for whatever reason, by the gods Anu, Enlil, Ninurta, Ennugi and Ea. Then the god Ea violated the pact with the other gods when he instructed Utnapishtim, a human, to build boats to avoid disaster. This caused a rift between Ea and the other gods, but saved the lives of Utnapishtim and his family.

There was another difference in the two stories. In Noah's story, it was Noah and his immediate family who were saved. In the Gilgamesh story it was not only Utnapishtim and his family but also their friends who were saved from drowning in the Flood.

Noah and Utnapishtim were only two heroes among many that can be found in the Middle Eastern and Greek deluge tales. Other flood heroes include Atrahasis, Zuisudra, Deucalion and Pyrrha.

In the Noah story, God was not pleased with the low morals of most of the people of the world but decided to give humans, through Noah and his family, a second chance. For many people, Noah has become a symbolic figure, a person who saved the human race from extinction. The Jewish people trace their covenant with God and the tradition of sacrificing animals back to the story of this mythical event.

For those Jewish and Christian people with doubts that there was enough water for the ocean levels to rise higher than the highest mountains, this story was acceptable, and still is. For them, this story was/is not so much about water or mountains or animals, but about a God who punishes immoral people and protects those who place their trust in him.

There are other stories in the Bible that are also not rational, but continue to be considered acceptable for a variety of reasons.

For the Jewish people, their Flood story was much more than a few people having averted a devastating disaster. Through their mythical form of writing they expressed a re-enactment of their interpretation of God's original creation. They believed that with the devastation of the Flood, the earth had again become a place without life as it was on the 'first day' of creation. The absence of life, except in Noah's ark, was expressed in the Flood story: "Everything on dry land that had the breath of life in its nostrils died. Every living thing on the face of the earth was wiped out; people and animals and the creatures that move along the ground and the birds were wiped from the earth. Only Noah was left, and those with him in the ark" (Genesis 7.22-23).[1] Then, supposedly, it was from this barren land that life was again brought forth.

The Hebrew people taught that the Flood survivors, Noah, his family and all of their descendants, were given another chance to prove their loyalty to God and a chance to avoid a fall from grace as Adam and Eve and so many others had done before. There are other stories in the

---

[1] Bible, *New International Version*, page 11

34

Bible that repeat this theme of 'Chosen People', of sin and punishment, of failure and new beginning.

Ceremonial washing – ritual immersion, baptism – was required of the Jewish people on a regular basis for spiritual purification and for the forgiveness of sins. Ceremonial washing for the Essenes (a Jewish religious sect of the Second Temple Period) included bathing every day.

The 'new beginning' described in the Flood story is re-enacted daily in many cultures through ceremonial washing. Traditionally, Catholics bless themselves upon entering a church by making the Sign of the Cross with holy water which is in part a symbolic way of re-enacting their own baptism. Catholic priests and other Christian clergy routinely bless others by sprinkling holy water on congregations and individuals on various occasions, including Holy Day celebrations, weddings, funerals, etc. as a sign of God's forgiveness. Baptism continues to be used as a sign of official acceptance into church membership.

Chapter 5

The first Hebrews came from Ur

The Bible states that Abraham came from Ur. There was a rather large city by that name located in today's Iraq on the banks of the Euphrates River, near the Persian Gulf. However, there are many Jewish people today who believe that this Ur was not the original homeland of Abraham.

There was another city by the same name located a short distance north of the Assyrian border, in southeastern Turkey. This city was much closer to Canaan and was very likely the birth place of Abraham. Canaan was the country where Abraham eventually settled.

Flavius Josephus, a first century Jewish historian, wrote that Abram (Abraham) was forced to leave Ur and thus lost what would have been his land handed down from his father: "And indeed Abraham, the forefather of our race, was led out of his land, because he had offended his brother in the division of their territories; and whereby he sinned, even thereby he received also his punishment. And again for his obedience He [God] gave him the promised land".[1] Also: "He does not wish to tell the Gentiles [in Canaan] that it was a quarrel between

---

[1] *Josephus, The Jewish War, Volume IV, Appendix,* Thackeray, page 444

Abraham and his brother Haran [Aran] which drove him out of the country".[1]

Josephus wrote: "Now Abraham, having no legitimate son, adopted Lot, his brother Aran's son and the brother of his wife Sarra [Sarai/Sarah/Sara]; and at the age of seventy-five he left Chaldaea, God having bidden him to remove to Canaan, and there he settled, and left the country to his descendants. He was a man of ready intelligence on all matters, persuasive with his hearers, and not mistaken in his inferences. Hence he began to have more lofty conceptions of virtue than the rest of mankind, and determined to reform and change the ideas universally current concerning God. He was thus the first boldly to declare that God, the creator of the universe, is one, and that, if any other being contributed aught to man's welfare, each did so by His command and not in virtue of its own inherent power".[2]

Abraham lived sometime between 2,000 B.C.E. and 1,600 B.C.E. The Bible does not contain a reliable time-line for that era. The years, and even the century, when Abraham lived have long been debated by many scholars. Adding to the uncertainty is that it appears that there is no historical record, outside of the Bible, of any individual with that name who lived any time within those 400 years.

Portions of Canaan were well suited for agriculture. Most farmers and sheepherders in Canaan depended on rainfall to produce grass and grain for their livestock. However, because of the geographical location, the amount of precipitation varied considerably from year to year.

---

[1] *Josephus, The Jewish War, Volume IV, Appendix*, Thackeray, page 444
[2] *Josephus, Jewish Antiquities, Volume V, Book I*, Thackeray, page 77

Periods of drought were not uncommon. Those droughts sometimes caused food shortages and occasionally, very severe shortages. It was during these times that many Canaanites purchased grain from Egyptian farmers.

Long before the time of Abraham, the Egyptian farmers had developed irrigation systems on the banks of the lower Nile that utilized the river water to irrigate their fields. They built diversion dams in the Nile River. These dams extended away from the river bank and a short distance upstream to channel river water into canals. These canals carried the river water onto their many acres of relatively flat farm land. This allowed the Egyptians to be much less dependent on annual precipitation to produce their grain and other crops.

During the drought years, some people in Canaan moved their families to Egypt to avoid starvation. Some of these families returned to Canaan when the drought ended, others remained in Egypt. Eventually, there developed a large population of Hebrews/Israelites in Egypt, especially in the towns and villages bordering the northern shores of the Nile River.

The story of Joseph, the son of Jacob (Genesis 41.35-36), speaks of the Egyptians setting aside some of their grain in the years when there was a higher yield to help them through the years when there was less yield. The people in Canaan, in all probability, did the same. However, sometimes a drought lasted longer than their grain reserves.

Not long after Abram/Abraham moved from Ur to Canaan there was a famine. During this famine, Abram/Abraham and his wife (his brother's daughter, thus Abram/Abraham's niece) moved to Egypt:

"Now there was a famine in the land, and Abram went down to Egypt to live there for a while because the famine was severe. As he was about to enter Egypt, he said to his wife Sarai, *I know what a beautiful woman you are. When the Egyptians see you, they will say, 'This is his wife.' Then they will kill me but will let you live. Say you are my sister, so that I will be treated well for your sake and my life will be spared because of you.* When Abram came to Egypt, the Egyptians saw that Sarai was a very beautiful woman. And when Pharaoh's officials saw her, they praised her to Pharaoh, and she was taken into his palace. He treated Abram well for her sake, and Abram acquired sheep and cattle, male and female donkeys, male and female servants, and camels. But the LORD inflicted serious diseases on Pharaoh and his household because of Abram's wife Sarai. So Pharaoh summoned Abram. *What have you done to me?* he said. *Why didn't you tell me she was your wife? Why did you say, 'She is my sister,' so that I took her to be my wife? Now then, here is your wife. Take her and go!* Then Pharaoh gave orders about Abram to his men, and they sent him on his way, with his wife and everything he had" (Genesis 12.10-20).[1]

A close reading of this story reveals a very unreliable time-line. According to this story, the king of Egypt gave Abram/Abraham camels and other animals. However, camels were not domesticated until at least four centuries later, about 1200 B.C.E.

Ten years after Abram/Abraham and Sarai returned to Canaan, Sarai still had not borne Abram/Abraham a son. Sarai then gave her slave-woman Hagar to Abram/Abraham as a concubine so he could father a

---

[1] Bible, *New International Version*, pages 18-19

child for them: "Now Sarai, Abram's wife, had borne him no children. But she had an Egyptian slave named Hagar; so she said to Abram, *The LORD has kept me from having children. Go, sleep with my slave; perhaps I can build a family through her*. Abram agreed to what Sarai said. So after Abram had been living in Canaan ten years, Sarai his wife took her Egyptian slave Hagar and gave her to her husband to be his wife. He slept with Hagar, and she conceived" (Genesis 16.1-4).[1] Ishmael (Ismail in Arabic) was born of that union. Even today, Abraham is held in high esteem by Muslims because they believe the Islamic religion came to them through Abraham and Ishmael/Ismail. Abraham had other children as well: "Abraham had taken another wife, whose name was Keturah. She bore him Zimran, Jokshan, Medan, Midian, Ishbak and Shuah" (Genesis 25.1-2).[2]

'Amah' is a Hebrew word meaning a young slave-woman or slave-wife: "When Sarah [Sarai] insists that Ishmael shall not inherit because he is the son of an *amah*, Gen. 21.10, or when Jotham speaks in the same manner of Abimelech, Judg. 9,18, one gets the impression that it was taken for granted that the *ben-ha'amah* [son of an amah] does not inherit. But, of course, amah here may mean the unmarried slave girl, not the slave-wife".[3] In either case, amah referred to a female slave. Hagar was Sarai's amah. Centuries later, the Hebrew word amah would take on a different meaning, at least for Christians.

---

[1] Bible, *New International Version*, page 22
[2] Bible, *New International Version*, page 39
[3] *Marriage Laws in the Bible and the Talmud*, Epstein, footnote, page 61

The mandate for Hebrew men not to marry or have children by non-Hebrew women was not always a high priority. Several of the patriarchs besides Abraham fathered children by non-Hebrew women. Not long after the birth of Ishmael, Abram's wife Sarai gave birth to a son: "Now the LORD was gracious to Sarah as he had said, and the LORD did for Sarah what he had promised. Sarah became pregnant and bore a son to Abraham in his old age, at the very time God had promised him. Abraham gave the name Isaac to the son Sarah bore him. When his son Isaac was eight days old, Abraham circumcised him, as God commanded him" (Genesis 21.1-4).[1]

The mandate to circumcise Hebrew/Jewish males was established at this time. From the beginning, this included all males in the home: "This is my covenant with you and your descendants after you, the covenant you are to keep: Every male among you shall be circumcised. You are to undergo circumcision, and it will be the sign of the covenant between me and you. For the generations to come every male among you who is eight days old must be circumcised, including those born in your household or bought with money from a foreigner" (Genesis 17.10-12).[2]

It was through this son Isaac that Abram, thereafter known as Abraham, would become the father of the Hebrew/Jewish nation: "When Abram was ninety-nine years old, the LORD appeared to him and said, *I am God Almighty; walk before me faithfully and be blameless. Then I will make my covenant between me and you and will greatly increase your numbers.* Abram fell facedown, and God said to him, *As for me, this*

---

[1] Bible, *New International Version*, page 31
[2] Bible, *New International Version*, page 24

41

is my covenant with you: You will be the father of many nations. No longer will you be called Abram; your name will be Abraham" (Genesis 17.1-5).[1] It was at this time that Sarai's name was changed to Sarah.

Even though Ishmael was Abraham's firstborn son, he was not destined to be heir to Abraham's fortunes because he was born of an amah – a slave-woman.

Abraham instructed his servant to choose a wife for Isaac from among relatives in Ur, not a woman from Canaan: "He said to the senior servant in his household, the one in charge of all that he had, *Put your hand under my thigh. I want you to swear by the* LORD, *the God of heaven and the God of earth, that you will not get a wife for my son from the daughters of the Canaanites, among whom I am living, but will go to my country and my own relatives and get a wife for my son Isaac"* (Genesis 24.2-4).[2]

Abraham's servant traveled to Ur, as Abraham had requested, to find a woman who would agree to marry Isaac. Within a few weeks after arriving in Ur Rebecca, the granddaughter of Abraham's brother Nahor, agreed to become Isaac's wife. They returned to Canaan. Very soon after Rebecca arrived in Canaan, Isaac and Rebecca were married. Isaac was Abraham's son and Bethuel was Nahor's son. Rebecca was Bethuel's daughter. Thus, Isaac married his first cousin's daughter.

Isaac and Rebecca had twin sons, Esau and Jacob. Shortly before Isaac's death Jacob, through deception, became heir to Isaac's wealth.

---

[1] Bible, *New International Version*, pages 23-24
[2] Bible, *New International Version*, page 35

He went on to marry first Leah and then Rachel, both granddaughters of Nahor.

It seems that not only was Esau, the older son, cheated out of his inheritance, but his children and his children's children were categorically despised by God through no fault of their own: *"And now, you priests, this warning is for you. If you do not listen, and if you do not resolve to honor my name,* says the LORD Almighty, *I will send a curse on you, and I will curse your blessings. Yes, I have already cursed them, because you have not resolved to honor me. Because of you I will rebuke your descendants"* (Malachi 2.1-3).[1]

Maintaining a pure bloodline was supposedly a mandate from God. According to Hebrew Scriptures, God's promises to Abraham were to be fulfilled only within this royal (Hebrew) family: "I will establish my covenant as an everlasting covenant between me and you and your descendants after you for the generations to come" (Genesis 17.7).[2]

However, Scriptures identifies quite a number of Hebrew men who married or had extramarital sexual relations with non-Hebrew women, presumably producing numerous children. According to later interpretation of Scriptures, the children from these various sexual encounters would not have been considered Hebrew.

Jacob, Abraham's grandson, fathered eight sons by two Hebrew wives and four sons by the female slaves of these wives, and probably at least a few daughters by these four sex partners of his: "Jacob had twelve sons: The sons of Leah: Reuben the firstborn of Jacob, Simeon, Levi,

---

[1] Bible, *New International Version*, page 1605
[2] Bible, *New International Version*, page 24

43

Judah, Issachar and Zebulun. The sons of Rachel: Joseph and Benjamin. The sons of Rachel's servant Bilhah: Dan and Naphtali. The sons of Leah's servant Zilpah: Gad and Asher" (Genesis 35.22-26).[1] However, it appears that the sons of the female slaves were later considered equal in status to their Hebrew siblings since all twelve of Jacob's sons became Jewish patriarchs.

Reuben, Jacob's oldest son, had sex with a concubine: "The sons of Reuben the firstborn of Israel (he was the firstborn, but when he defiled his father's marriage bed, his rights as firstborn were given to the sons of Joseph son of Israel; so he could not be listed in the genealogical record in accordance with his birthright, and though Judah was the strongest of his brothers and a ruler came from him, the rights of the firstborn belonged to Joseph)" (1 Chronicles 5.1-2).[2]

Judah, Jacob's fourth son, had several children by a non-Hebrew Canaanite woman: "At that time, Judah left his brother and went down to stay with a man of Adullam named Hirah. There Judah met the daughter of a Canaanite man named Shua. He married her and made love to her; she became pregnant and gave birth to a son, who was named Er. She conceived again and gave birth to a son and named him Onan. She gave birth to still another son and named him Shelah" (Genesis 38.1-5).[3]

Jacob's son Joseph had children by his Egyptian wife: "Before the years of famine came, two sons were born to Joseph by Asenath daughter of Potiphera, priest of On. Joseph named his firstborn Manasseh and

---

[1] Bible, *New International Version*, page 61
[2] Bible, *New International Version*, page 668
[3] Bible, *New International Version*, page 66

44

said, *It is because God has made me forget all my trouble and all my father's household.* The second son he named Ephraim and said, *It is because God has made me fruitful in the land of my suffering*" (Genesis 41.50-52).[1] Esau, Jacob's older brother, had two Hittite (non-Hebrew) wives.

Hebrew men were permitted, at least for a time, to have sexual relations with women who had been taken as prisoners of war: "When you go to war against your enemies and the LORD your God delivers them into your hands and you take captives, if you notice among the captives a beautiful woman and are attracted to her, you may take her as your wife. Bring her into your home and have her shave her head, trim her nails and put aside the clothes she was wearing when captured. After she has lived in your house and mourned her father and mother for a full month, then you may go to her and be her husband and she shall be your wife. If you are not pleased with her, let her go wherever she wishes. You must not sell her or treat her as a slave, since you have dishonored her" (Deuteronomy 21.10-14).[2]

Samson married Delilah, a Philistine girl: "Samson went down to Timnah and saw there a young Philistine woman. When he returned, he said to his father and mother, *I have seen a Philistine woman in Timnah; now get her for me as my wife*" (Judges 14.1-2).[3]

King David had quite a few wives before Bathsheba: "David had also married Ahinoam of Jezreel, and they both were his wives. But Saul

---

[1] Bible, *New International Version*, page 73
[2] Bible, *New International Version*, pages 328-329
[3] Bible, *New International Version*, page 425

had given his daughter Michal, David's wife, to Paltiel son of Laish" (1 Samuel 25.43-44).[1] Also: "Sons were born to David in Hebron: His firstborn was Amnon the son of Ahinoam of Jezreel; his second, Kileab the son of Abigail the widow of Nabal of Carmel; the third, Absalom the son of Maakah daughter of Talmai king of Geshur; the fourth, Adonijah the son of Haggith; the fifth, Shephatiah the son of Abital; and the sixth, Ithream the son of David's wife Eglah" (2 Samuel 3.2-5).[2] David also had sexual relations with many other women as well: "After he left Hebron, David took more concubines and wives in Jerusalem, and more sons and daughter were born to him" (2 Samuel 5.13).[3]

After moving from Hebron to Jerusalem, David took more concubines and wives, and had more sons and daughters: "The king [King David] set out, with his entire household following him; but he left ten concubines to take care of the palace" (2 Samuel 15.16).[4] Apparently, it was acceptable for David to have had quite a number of wives and even more concubines: "For David had done what was right in the eyes of the LORD and had not failed to keep any of the LORD's commands all the days of his life – except in the case of Uriah the Hittite" (1 Kings 15.5).[5]

The book *2 Samuel* (second book of Samuel) states that David had a son by Bathsheba. She was the wife of a Hittite man before David had

---

[1] Bible, New International Version, page 492
[2] Bible, New International Version, page 505
[3] Bible, New International Version, page 509
[4] Bible, New International Version, page 527
[5] Bible, *New International Version*, page 585

him killed: "One evening David got up from his bed and walked around on the roof of the palace. From the roof he saw a woman bathing. The woman was very beautiful, and David sent someone to find out about her. The man said, *She is Bathsheba, the daughter of Eliam and the wife of Uriah the Hittite.* Then David sent messengers to get her. She came to him, and he slept with her. (Now she was purifying herself from her monthly uncleanness.) Then she went back home. The woman conceived and sent word to David, saying, *I am pregnant*" (2 Samuel 11.2-5).[1]

David, upon realizing he had impregnated Bathsheba, tried to cover up this adulterous affair. He had Uriah recalled from the battlefront to spend the night with his wife Bathsheba. However, as was traditional in those days, Uriah chose not to sleep with her that night because he would be going into battle the next day. Instead, he slept outside with the other soldiers: "But Uriah slept at the entrance to the palace with all his master's servants and did not go down to his house" (2 Samuel 11.9).[2] David was apparently hoping that Uriah would violate a Hebrew purity law that night which reads: "But the priest answered David, *I don't have any ordinary bread on hand; however, there is some consecrated bread here – provided the men have kept themselves from women.* David replied, *Indeed women have been kept from us, as usual*" (1 Samuel 21.4-5).[3]

The next morning Uriah returned to battle as he was supposed to. Therefore, David could not credit Uriah with getting her pregnant.

---

[1] Bible, *New International Version*, page 517
[2] Bible, *New International Version*, page 517
[3] Bible, *New International Version*, page 484

When his first attempt to cover up this adulterous affair failed, David ordered his military commander to send Uriah into a forward position during the very next battle. Then, in the heat of battle he was to pull all of the other troops back so Uriah would be killed by the enemy. The commander followed David's orders and Uriah was indeed killed.

That child of David's died in infancy. David and Bathsheba went on to have other children, including Solomon.

The Bible's depiction of Solomon starts out on a positive note. In Jewish tradition Solomon was, and still is, revered by Jews for his wisdom during his early years of rule. However, his later years are seen as less than virtuous.

According to the Bible, Solomon had many wives and concubines from non-Hebrew tribes in Canaan and many others from neighboring countries. This was considered a major factor in his allowing the introduction of idolatry into Israel: "King Solomon, however, loved many foreign women besides Pharaoh's daughter – Moabites, Ammonites, Edomites, Sidonians and Hittites. They were from nations about which the LORD had told the Israelites, *You must not intermarry with them, because they will surely turn your hearts after their gods.* Nevertheless, Solomon held fast to them in love. He had seven hundred wives of royal birth and three hundred concubines, and his wives led him astray. As Solomon grew old, his wives turned his heart after other gods, and his heart was not fully devoted to the LORD his God" (1 Kings 11.1-4).[1]

---

[1] Bible, *New International Version*, page 576

Solomon angered the Hebrew people when he imposed high taxes for the construction of a new Temple and palace, and he required every Hebrew man to donate one month of labor to the project each year, for several years: "At the end of twenty years, during which Solomon built these two buildings – the temple of the LORD and the royal palace" (1 Kings 9.10).[1] He fueled their anger even more when he continued to demand the building tax long after the construction was completed. All of this, combined with his extravagant lifestyle and poor military decisions, were considered major factors in the subsequent downfall of the Hebrew nation.

Hebrews marrying non-Hebrews became more of an issue during this period. Some people advocated a prohibition of Hebrews marrying non-Hebrews. This prohibition included everyone with mixed blood. The prophet Ezra taught that documented genealogy was required for every Hebrew marriage: "In other words, mixing Hebrew blood with that of the heathen was to him [Ezra] synonymous with adulterating the ancestral faith".[2]

Verification of Hebrew parentage during several periods of Jewish history was required in order to establish an individual's Jewish and tribal identity, in spite of the less-than-virtuous choices of some of the early patriarchs. The oral history of the genealogy of Hebrew families developed as an essential part of their collective memory: "Of old, the Jews had maintained family records, preserved both in their home

---

[1] Bible, *New International Version*, page 572
[2] *Marriage Laws in the Bible and the Talmud*, Epstein, pages 162-163

country and in exile".[1] However, it was not until many centuries after Abraham's death that family and tribal genealogy records were maintained in written form.

In their efforts to maintain this 'pure' bloodline, the Hebrew patriarchs realized that the paternity of a child might sometimes be in question. But the child's mother could easily be verified by having the birth of the child witnessed by another person who was not a relative, usually a midwife. Thus, if the mother was Hebrew the child was also Hebrew. The paternity of the child determined the child's tribal identity.

Several centuries after the death of Moses, the prophet Nehemiah wrote: "I made them take an oath in God's name and said; *You are not to give your daughters in marriage to their sons, nor are you to take their daughters in marriage for your sons or for yourselves*" (Nehemiah 13.25).[2] However, even during the Second Temple Period (539 B.C.E. to 70 C.E.) this mandate was not always adhered to.

Ruth, the great-grandmother of King David, was not a Hebrew: "In the days when the judges ruled, there was a famine in the land. So a man from Bethlehem in Judah, together with his wife and two sons, went to live for a while in the country of Moab. The man's name was Elimelek, his wife's name was Naomi, and the names of his two sons were Mahlon and Kilion. They were Ephrathites from Bethlehem, Judah. And they went to Moab and lived there. Now Elimelek, Naomi's husband, died and she was left with her two sons. They married Moabite women, one

---

[1] *Marriage Laws in the Bible and the Talmud*, Epstein, page 163
[2] Bible, *New International Version*, page 825

named Orpah and the other Ruth" (Ruth 1.1-4).[1] As mentioned earlier, Solomon's mother Bathsheba also was not Hebrew.

The second-class people were those with mixed-blood and those who may have been from a 'pure' bloodline but did not have the necessary documentation to support their claim. The third-class people included the remainder of the population who were not slaves or foreigners. Slaves and foreigners were at the bottom of this social structure.

Throughout much of Jewish history, slaves could not legally marry. However, in some cases they were permitted to have monogamous relationships and raise their own children. The laws concerning Temple admittance and worship, property ownership, taxes, marriage, political position, priesthood and many other laws were written by and for the men of the ruling class with possibly minor input from the women.

The New Testament has several stories relating to the planting of seeds. Several of these can be found in the gospels (Matthew 13.4-8, Mark 4.19 and Luke 8.4-8). It was Hebrew/Jewish teaching that the 'male seed' provided the beginning of a new life and was the source of the new individual's body. The mother's womb was the 'field' in which this new life grew. The Hebrews believed that the male seed became a new individual when it first contained blood. Today's science shows this to be on the eighteenth day after conception.

The Hebrew people were not aware of the existence of the female ovum or its contribution to a new individual. It was incorrectly assumed that the mother's reproductive system only provided a 'fertile field' in

---

[1] Bible, *New International Version*, page 441

51

which the male seed would grow, that it was the mother's blood that would then flow into the veins of the embryo/fetus to give the new individual a resemblance to herself and sustain the child's life and growth throughout the pregnancy.

For the Hebrew people, blood was God's gift of life. It was the symbol of life and *the very essence of life*. They believed that human blood was being passed from mother to child down through the generations. This made human blood very sacred to the Hebrew/Jewish people and supported the importance they placed on women concerning genealogy issues.

The blood of animals was never to be consumed: "But you must not eat meat that has its lifeblood still in it" (Genesis 9.4).[1] "For the life of a creature is in the blood" (Leviticus 17.11).[2] "Do not eat any meat with the blood still in it" (Leviticus 19.26).[3]

The spilling of blood was taken very seriously. A woman was 'unclean' during menstruation: "When a woman has her regular flow of blood, the impurity of her monthly period will last seven days, and anyone who touches her will be unclean till evening" (Leviticus 15.19).[4] A woman was 'unclean' after the birth of a male child: "A woman who becomes pregnant and gives birth to a son will be ceremonially unclean for seven days, just as she is unclean during her monthly period. On the eighth day the boy is to be circumcised. Then the woman must wait

---

[1] Bible, *New International Version*, page 13
[2] Bible, *New International Version*, page 196
[3] Bible, *New International Version*, page 199
[4] Bible, *New International Version*, page 192

thirty-three days to be purified from her bleeding. She must not touch anything sacred or go to the sanctuary until the days of her purification are over" (Leviticus 12.2-4).[1] A woman was 'unclean' for a longer time after the birth of a female child: "If she gives birth to a daughter, for two weeks the woman will be unclean, as during her period. Then she must wait sixty-six days to be purified from her bleeding" (Leviticus 12.5).[2]

During menstruation, and the allotted time after childbirth, a woman was not allowed to prepare any food that was to be eaten by others. She was not allowed to have sexual intercourse or to sleep in the same bed with her husband or to even touch any man. Oftentimes, a woman was confined to her home for the entire time. Jewish law today states that menstrual 'impurity' lasts twelve days – an estimated seven days for her period plus the following five days.

Ancient Hebrew law stated that a priest who touched the body of a dead person or someone who was bleeding or who was having any discharge was to wash/cleanse himself as soon as possible and then wait ten days. Only then would he be allowed to enter the Temple or perform any sacred ritual.

No one, male or female, adult or child, was allowed to enter the Temple with an open sore or was bleeding or had a discharge of any kind because every such person was 'unclean'.

Many of these blood-related traditions and laws were unique to the Hebrews/Jews and were a source of contention in Judea during the last few decades of the Second Temple Period. Blood-related 'impurity'

---

[1] Bible, *New International Version*, page 183
[2] Bible, *New International Version*, page 183

violations by the Herods and others within the Temple were among the major reasons for the Jewish war against the Romans.

Knowledge about reproduction during biblical times was limited. If a woman was not able to conceive upon having sexual relations, it was presumed that her womb was 'barren' because it would not support the growth of a new child.

A law, which was sometimes enforced, required a man to 'set aside' his wife if she was barren for the first ten years of their marriage. Abiding by this law was more often required of the Jewish priests than the general population. The man was then to marry another woman so that he might fulfill the first command in Jewish Scriptures which required a man to have children. This command in Jewish Bibles does not specify that a man have more than one child.

Abraham's wife Sarah was supposedly barren for 'many years'. However, she was very likely still in her late thirties or early forties when she conceived Isaac 'late in life' when many other women were becoming grandmothers.

Ancient understanding of reproduction changed very little until years after the invention of the microscope in the seventeenth century. It was then discovered that the female ovum and the male sperm contributed equally to conception as well as to the genetic makeup of a child. Many in society, especially the leaders of the Catholic Church, were slow to accept this new science which contradicted biblical teaching and long-standing Church doctrine.

Chapter 6

The Exodus story has conflicting information

The *Exodus* story begins 400 years before the time of Moses when Joseph, the great-grandson of Abraham, was sold into slavery in Egypt. A few years later, there was a severe drought in the Middle East and northern Egypt: "There was no food, however, in the whole region because the famine was severe; both Egypt and Canaan wasted away because of the famine" (Genesis 47.13).[1] "When Jacob learned that there was grain in Egypt, he said to his sons, *Why do you just keep looking at each other? He continued, I have heard that there is grain in Egypt. Go down there and buy some for us, so that we may live and not die*" (Genesis 42.1-2).[2]

Then, many years after Joseph was sold into slavery, Moses led the Israelites out of Egypt: "Now the length of time the Israelite people lived in Egypt was 430 years. At the end of the 430 years, to the very day, all the LORD'S divisions left Egypt" (Exodus 12.40-41).[3] This exodus supposedly began sometime between 1,300 B.C.E. and 1,200 B.C.E. It is very doubtful that the Israelites remembered the <u>exact day</u> of the year that they entered Egypt and the <u>exact day</u> of the year that they left Egypt, yet failed to record either date in the *Exodus* story.

---

[1] Bible, *New International Version*, page 84
[2] Bible, *New International Version*, page 74
[3] Bible, *New International Version*, page 111

The *Exodus* story describes how Moses and more than a million other people fled Egypt and walked across the desert to the Promised Land: "The Israelites journeyed from Rameses to Sukkoth. There were about six hundred thousand men on foot, besides women and children. Many other people went up with them, and also large droves of livestock, both flocks and herds" (Exodus 12.37-38).[1] Chapter one in the fourth book of the Bible, the *Book of Numbers*, gives the total number of Hebrew men twenty years old and older and fit for service to be 603,550. This journey would have required these million-plus men, women and children to walk hundreds of miles with their livestock and supplies across a very inhospitable land.

The number 'forty' is one of several re-occurring numbers in the Bible. In the Flood story it supposedly rained for forty days and forty nights. In the *Exodus* story the Hebrews/Israelites supposedly lived in the desert for forty years.

Recently, one well-known Jewish leader questioned the number of people Moses was supposed to have led across the desert: "Ben-Gurion soon emerged as a leader of the socialist Labor party, which dominated Israeli politics from well before the state's declaration of Menachem Begin's electoral victory in 1977. Though personally not religiously observant, [David] Ben-Gurion was deeply influenced by the Bible, particularly by the writings of the prophets. During his years as prime minister, he actively participated in Bible study sessions, which met at his home. He once caused a governmental crisis by publicly questioning

---

[1] Bible, *New International Version*, page 111

the accuracy of the verse in Exodus that claimed that 600,000 adult Jewish males accompanied Moses on his departure from Egypt: Ben-Gurion insisted that the number of Jews who wandered in the desert must have been much smaller. Members of the Israeli religious party Mizrachi, which formed part of Ben-Gurion's coalition, threatened to bolt from the government if he did not cease attacking the Bible's credibility".[1]

There is no archaeological evidence of a mass migration of a million-plus people, as described in the *Exodus* story, traveling from Egypt to Canaan: "One may argue that a relatively small band of wandering Israelites cannot be expected to leave material remains behind. But modern archaeological techniques are quite capable of tracing even the very meager remains of hunter-gatherers and pastoral nomads all over the world. Indeed, the archaeological record from the Sinai Peninsula discloses evidence for pastoral activity in such eras as the third millennium BCE and the Hellenistic and Byzantine periods. There is simply no such evidence at the supposed time of the Exodus in the thirteenth century BCE. The conclusion – that the Exodus did not happen at the time and in the manner described in the Bible – seems irrefutable when we examine the evidence at specific sites where the children of Israel were said to have camped for extended periods during their wandering in the desert (Numbers 33) and where some archaeological indication – if present – would almost certainly be found. According to the biblical narrative, the children of Israel camped at Kadesh-barnea for thirty eight of the forty years of the wanderings. The general location of this place is clear from the description of the southern

---

[1] *Jewish Literacy*, Rabbi Joseph Telushkin, page 298

border of the land of Israel in Numbers 34. It has been identified by archaeologists with the large and well-watered oasis of Ein el-Qudeirat in eastern Sinai, on the border between modern Israel and Egypt".[1]

The Egyptian writer Manetho of the third century B.C.E. recorded a very different version of the *Exodus*. According to him, and other Egyptian writers, the Hebrew people did not ask to leave but were forced out of Egypt: "This author, having promised to translate the history of Egypt from the sacred books, begins by stating that our ancestors entered Egypt in their myriads and subdued the inhabitants, and goes on to admit that they were afterwards driven out of the country".[2] Manetho described the *Exodus* as follows: "Amenophis [the Egyptian king] subsequently advanced from Ethiopia with a large army, his son Rampses at the head of another, and that the two attacked and defeated the shepherds and their polluted allies, killing many of them and pursuing the remainder to the frontiers of Syria".[3]

Manetho identified Moses, the leader of the exodus: "It is said that the priest who gave them a constitution and code of laws was a native of Heliopolis, named Osarsiph, after the Heliopolitan god Osiris, and that

---

[1] *The Bible Unearthed*, Israel Finkelstein and Neil Asher Silberman
    page 63
[2] *Josephus, The Life Against Apion, Volume I, Book I*, Thackeray
    page 255
[3] *Josephus, The Life Against Apion, Volume I, Book I*, Thackeray
    page 265

when he went over to this people he changed his name and was called Moses".[1]

The *Exodus* story, as with the Flood story, was written in the mythical style of writing. The Scripture writers wrote the *Exodus* story in such a way as to recapture the drama of the Creation and Flood stories, those times when God had given his Chosen Ones a new beginning.

Sea of Reeds in the ancient Jewish Bible was changed in the Greek LXX translation of the Bible to Red Sea. Sea of Reeds was very likely not synonymous with Red Sea.

The African Rift, which divides two tectonic plates, extends from southern Africa northward, the full length and beneath the center of the Red Sea. It continues northward through Jordan, Israel and into Syria. The Red Sea at its deepest point is approximately 7,254 feet below sea level and at its widest point is 221 miles across: "By the blast of your nostrils the waters piled up. The surging waters stood up like a wall; the deep waters congealed in the heart of the sea" (Exodus 15.8).[2]

Many areas in the bottom of the Red Sea have steep cliffs, rocky hills and rugged valleys. However, according to the *Book of Psalms* the Israelites were said to have tread through mud, not on 'solid ground' at the bottom of the sea: "Rescue me from the mire, do not let me sink" (Psalms 69.14).[3] Some of the deepest areas of the rift are home to hot

---

[1] *Josephus, The Life Against Apion, Volume I, Book I,* Thackeray page 265

[2] Bible, *New International Version,* page 116

[3] Bible, *New International Version,* page 968

hydrothermal brines that are approximately 140 degrees Fahrenheit (60 degrees Celsius).

The *Exodus* story contains a great deal of myth. It also contains a considerable amount of insight into the history of the Israelite people and their struggles as a society. Most importantly for the Hebrew people, *Exodus* depicted the ritualistic cleansing of the Chosen People as they passed through the water of the 'Red Sea'. The *Exodus* story, like the biblical Flood story, was written in a figurative style of writing, not a literal presentation of historical events.

The Pharaoh may have been reluctant to have the Israelites leave Egypt because he needed their slave labor. Or, he may have wanted them to leave his country because of a food shortage. In either case, the Israelites left Egypt.

Did the Israelites' journey out of Egypt take <u>forty years,</u> across an arid desert? Or did they follow the well-established trade-route north along the Nile River or the Red Sea which could easily have taken approximately <u>forty days</u>? Did Moses lead all of the Israelites out of Egypt? Did the Israelites all leave at the same time? Or did they leave in smaller groups over a period of forty years? Was Moses the first of several, and thus the most famous of their leaders? There is very little, if any, record of the Israelites' exodus outside of the Bible, especially the route or number of Israelites that supposedly left Egypt during that period of history.

Regardless of how the events portrayed in *Exodus* played out, the most comprehensive 'code of ethics' ever established came primarily from this period in history through the efforts of the Israelite people.

However, their concept of God, in lieu of the instructions that God supposedly gave to the Israelites, is considered by many to be quite problematic. This will become apparent within the biblical quotations within the next few paragraphs.

It was not uncommon for biblical writers to attribute many heroic events and teachings to a single individual for a variety of reasons: "The Pentateuch now presents a large number of laws as having been given to Moses at Sinai (e.g., the Ten Commandments and the Covenant Code {Exodus 20-23}; the Holiness Code {Leviticus 17-26}), but it is very difficult to say how much, if any, of this formed part of the original Sinai experience. All of the laws, deriving mostly from later periods in Israel's history, can easily be grouped under the heading of either right worship of God or of correct social behavior. These are all only further specifications of the basic covenant obligations. As later generations of Israel retold and renewed their basic covenant story, they included new laws and regulations which made their covenant real for them in the new situations of their lives. All of these developments were attributed to Moses at Sinai because this was where their covenant began".[1] "While Isaiah lived in the eighth century B.C.E., most Bible scholars assume that chapters 40-66 (or at least 40-55) were written some two centuries later, after the destruction of the Temple in 586 B.C.E. The author of these later chapters is commonly referred to by Bible scholars as the Second Isaiah".[2] "Ecclesiastes is, indeed, one of three books attributed by Jewish tradition to the tenth-century-B.C.E. king Solomon. The rabbis believed

---

[1] *The Anchor Bible Dictionary*, Mosaic Covenant, volume 4, page 907
[2] *Jewish Literacy*, Rabbi Joseph Telushkin, page 84

he wrote the exuberantly romantic Song of Songs as a young man, the wise and reflective Proverbs in his middle years, and the gloomy Ecclesiastes in his old age. Today, few scholars accept the attribution of the book's authorship to Solomon. For one thing, Ecclesiastes uses words that were unknown in Solomon's time. For example, *pardes* (see 2:5), a Persian word meaning both 'grove' and 'paradise', first became known to the Jews probably no earlier than the sixth century B.C.E. Finding it included in a work supposedly written four centuries earlier is as jarring as it would be to find the word 'Oldsmobile' in a sonnet attributed to Shakespeare".[1]

The fifth book of the Bible, which is also the last book of the Torah, is *Deuteronomy*. This book is organized as a series of addresses given by Moses to the Israelites near the end of their forty-year exodus from Egypt. Many of the chapters in *Deuteronomy* detail the laws the Hebrew people were to observe as the Chosen People.

The Hebrews believed that they were God's 'Chosen People' and that Canaan was their 'Promised Land'. However, Moses was not going to be the one to lead the Israelites the final few miles into Canaan. That responsibility was given to Joshua since God had told Moses that he and Aaron would not enter Canaan because they had not followed God's instructions at Meribah. Moses then assigned Joshua to be their new leader.

God instructed Joshua to invade and conquer Canaan: "After the death of Moses the servant of the LORD, the LORD said to Joshua son of Nun, Moses' aide; *Moses my servant is dead. Now then, you and all*

---

[1] *Jewish Literacy*, Rabbi Joseph Telushkin, page 99

these people, get ready to cross the Jordan River into the land I am about to give to them – to the Israelites. I will give you every place where you set your foot, as I promised Moses. Your territory will extend from the desert to Lebanon, and from the great river, the Euphrates – all the Hittite country – to the Mediterranean Sea in the west" (Joshua 1.1-4).[1]

Joshua and his men were to destroy all of the people in Canaan who did not flee – the men, women and children in the entire country: "When the LORD your God brings you into the land you are entering to possess and drives out before you many nations – the Hittites, Girgashites, Amorites, Canaanites, Perizzites, Hivites and Jebusites, seven nations larger and stronger than you – and when the LORD your God has delivered them over to you and you have defeated them, then you must destroy them totally. Make no treaty with them, and show them no mercy. Do not intermarry with them. Do not give your daughters to their sons or take their daughters for your sons, for they will turn your children away from following me to serve other gods, and the LORD's anger will burn against you and will quickly destroy you" (Deuteronomy 7.1-4).[2] "However, in the cities of the nations the LORD your God is giving you as an inheritance, do not leave alive anything that breathes. Completely destroy them" (Deuteronomy 20.16-17).[3]

Joshua is the sixth book in the Bible. It tells of all the cities that the Israelites conquered. Jericho was the first of many cities that Joshua and his men are said to have invaded: "Now the gates of Jericho were

---

[1] Bible, *New International Version*, page 357
[2] Bible, *New International Version*, page 306
[3] Bible, *New International Version*, page 327

securely barred because of the Israelites. No one went out and no one came in. Then the LORD said to Joshua, *See, I have delivered Jericho into your hands, along with its king and its fighting men. March around the city once with all the armed men. Do this for six days. Have seven priests carry trumpets of rams' horns in front of the ark. On the seventh day, march around the city seven times, with the priests blowing the trumpets. When you hear them sound a long blast on the trumpets, have the whole army give a loud shout; then the wall of the city will collapse and the army will go up, everyone straight in*" (Joshua 6.1-5).[1] "When the trumpets sounded, the army shouted, and at the sound of the trumpet, when the men gave a loud shout, the wall collapsed; so everyone charged straight in, and they took the city. They devoted the city to the LORD and destroyed with the sword every living thing in it – men and women, young and old, cattle, sheep and donkeys. Joshua said to the two men who had spied out the land, *Go into the prostitute's house and bring her out and all who belong to her, in accordance with your oath to her.* So the young men who had done the spying went in and brought out Rahab, her father and mother, her brothers and sisters and all who belonged to her. They brought out her entire family and put them in a place outside the camp of Israel" (Joshua 6.20-23).[2]

Damascus is very likely the oldest continuously occupied city in the western portion of the Middle East. Jericho may have been an earlier community, though it appears that it was not always occupied. Jericho was one of those communities that struggled with weather-related issues,

---

[1] Bible, *New International Version*, page 363
[2] Bible, *New International Version*, page 364

especially a lack of rain for their crops. It was abandoned at least a couple of times prior to and during the biblical era.

There is evidence that the 'walls of Jericho' had crumbled and were then rebuilt several times over the course of several thousand years. According to recent archeological findings, the 'walls of Jericho' had fallen into disrepair and the city was nearly abandoned during the time period that the Bible has Joshua conquering the city.

The book of *Joshua* tells of many other conquests. The Israelites supposedly killed tens-of-thousands of men, women and children: "When Israel had finished killing all the men of Ai in the fields and in the wilderness where they had chased them, and when every one of them had been put to the sword, all the Israelites returned to Ai and killed those who were in it. Twelve thousand men and women fell that day – all the people of Ai" (Joshua 8.24-25).[1]

The killing continued: "That day Joshua took Makkedah. He put the city and its king to the sword and totally destroyed everyone in it. He left no survivors. And he did to the king of Makkedah as he had done to the king of Jericho. Then Joshua and all Israel with him moved on from Makkedah to Libnah and attacked it. The LORD also gave that city and its king into Israel's hand. The city and everyone in it Joshua put to the sword. He left no survivors there. And he did to its king as he had done to the king of Jericho. Then Joshua and all Israel with him moved on from Libnah to Lachish; he took up positions against it and attacked it. The LORD gave Lachish into Israel's hands, and Joshua took it on the second day. The city and everyone in it he put to the sword, just as he

---

[1] Bible, *New International Version*, page 368

had done to Libnah. Meanwhile, Horam king of Gezer had come up to help Lachish, but Joshua defeated him and his army – until no survivors were left. Then Joshua and all Israel with him moved on from Lachish to Eglon; they took up positions against it and attacked it. They captured it that same day and put it to the sword and totally destroyed everyone in it, just as they had done to Lachish. Then Joshua and all Israel with him went up from Eglon to Hebron and attacked it. They took the city and put it to the sword, together with its king, its villages and everyone in it. They left no survivors. Just as at Eglon, they totally destroyed it and everyone in it. Then Joshua and all Israel with him turned around and attacked Debir. They took the city, its king and its villages, and put them to the sword. Everyone in it they totally destroyed. They left no survivors. They did to Debir and its king as they had done to Libnah and its king and to Hebron. So Joshua subdued the whole region, including the hill country, the Negev, the western foothills and the mountain slopes, together with all their kings. He left no survivors. He totally destroyed all who breathed, just as the LORD, the God of Israel, had commanded" (Joshua 10.28-40).[1]

The Bible identifies approximately 300 cities in Canaan where Joshua and his men supposedly annihilated the entire population, and all of the people in many of the towns and villages around these cities. If the stories in *Exodus* and *Joshua* are interpreted literally, this was a horrendous genocide, not just sanctioned by God, but commanded by God. However, it would be difficult, if not impossible, to find any record in history outside of the Bible of any such invasion, war or mass killing.

---

[1] Bible, *New International Version*, pages 373-374

This story and the Flood story are similar in several ways. Both stories have God's Chosen People 'saved' and given a chance at a new beginning. In both stories God commanded the death of a multitude of men, women, children and even infants. In *Joshua*, all of the Canaanites who died, and were not among the Chosen People, died because they were evil. However, it is not reasonable to presume that all of the Canaanite men who died defending their families and homes were evil and that their families, the women, the children and even the infants died because all of them were evil.

Could it be that in 1977 when David Ben-Gurion made the statement questioning the historical accuracy of the *Exodus* events, he did so in an effort to simultaneously discredit the genocide supposedly carried out by his ancestors, as recorded in the book of *Joshua*?

Chapter 7

The ten northern Hebrew tribes
lost their tribal identity

At some point, Canaan was divided among the descendants of the sons of Jacob. The southern portion was more suited for grazing livestock. This territory was divided between the descendants of Judah and Benjamin. It became known as Judea. The northern region continued to be called Israel with a large percentage of the area being well suited for raising field crops. This portion of Canaan was divided among the descendants of Reuben, Simeon, Gad, Issachar, Zebulun, Ephraim, Manasseh, Dan, Asher and Naphtali. The portion that would have been assigned to Joseph was divided between his sons Ephraim and Manasseh (the sons of Joseph and his Egyptian wife).

Members of the twelfth tribe, the descendants of Levi, were not assigned any land: "The ancestral tribe of the Levites, however, was not counted among with the others. The LORD had said to Moses: *You must not count the tribe of Levi or include them in the census of the other Israelites. Instead, appoint the Levites to be in charge of the tabernacle of the covenant law – over all its furnishings and everything belonging to it*" (Numbers 1.47-50).[1]

---

[1] Bible, *New International Version*, pages 220

The Levites were assigned 48 cities and were to be the priests and guardians of the sacred Hebrew literature and folklore. They were also responsible for the preservation and additions to the genealogy records and were given the responsibility of collecting the annual tithing (taxes) for their own living expenses and for the operation of the government.

From that time on, at least for many years, the Hebrews (Israelites) had control of Israel and Judea. The Hebrews and the non-Hebrews alike were required to follow many of the Hebrew laws. Moses had re-enforced Abraham's stipulation that Hebrew men were to marry only women from among Abraham's descendants. Also, no one was allowed to publicly worship any god but the Hebrew God, all in accordance with the laws in Scriptures: "But you must keep my decrees and my laws. The native-born and the foreigners residing among you must not do any of these detestable things, for all these things were done by the people who lived in the land before you, and the land became defiled. And if you defile the land, it will vomit you out as it vomited out the nations that were before you" (Leviticus 18.26-28).[1]

Judea/Israel became a country ruled by a succession of kings. The biblical stories that tell of the conquests of these kings contain a great deal of myth. There is controversy among scholars even today as to the authenticity of the size and grandeur of King Solomon's temple as it is described in Scriptures, as well as to the expanse of territory that those early Hebrews supposedly conquered.

Rabbi Joseph Telushkin addressed this issue in his recently published book *Jewish Literacy*: "The kingdom of Israel, composed of

---

[1] Bible, *New International Version*, pages 197-198

the ten northernmost tribes, was established in 931 B.C.E. after the death of King Solomon. It lasted for 209 very turbulent years, marked by numerous royal assassinations, repeated successions of new dynasties, and frequent reversions to idolatry. Although Israel had periods of considerable military strength (e.g., during King Ahab's reign), it often fell under foreign domination. In the late eighth century B.C.E., Assyria [later referred to as Syria] ruled over Israel. But upon the death of Assyria's King, Tiglath-Pileser, in 727 [B.C.E.], Hoshea, the king of Israel, rebelled. The Assyrians responded with a siege of Israel that culminated with the kingdom's fall and the deportation of many of her inhabitants in 722".[1] "Ever since Assyria dispersed Israel, the fate of the Ten Tribes has remained a mystery. Clearly, not all of the people assimilated into foreign nations and religions. Some fled to the still-surviving Jewish kingdom of Judah, and remained part of the Jewish people. However, the majority apparently did assimilate into the societies to which they were exiled".[2]

Susan Wise Bauer, in her book *The History of the Ancient World*, states that Assyria conquered Israel, and she explains the fate of the lost ten tribes: "Sargon's own inscriptions note that he removed 27,290 Israelites from their homeland, and settled them from Asia Minor all the way over to the territory of the Medes. These Israelites became known as the 'lost ten tribes,' not because the people themselves were lost, but because their identity as descendants of Abraham and worshippers of

---

[1] *Biblical Literacy*, Rabbi Joseph Telushkin, pages 266-267
[2] *Biblical Literacy*, Rabbi Joseph Telushkin, page 267

Yahweh was dissipated into the new wild areas where they were now forced to make their homes".[1]

---

[1] *The History of the Ancient World*, Susan Wise Bauer, page 375

Part Two

The early second Temple period

(539 B.C.E. to 4 B.C.E.)

Chapter 8

King Cyrus allowed the Chosen People
to return to the Promised Land

Persia conquered Babylon as well as most of the other Middle
Eastern countries and territories, all the way to the Mediterranean Sea:
"King Cyrus of Persia defeats Babylon [in 539 B.C.E.] and permits the
Judean exiles to return to, and rebuild, Israel".[1] Also: "Although most
elect to remain in Babylon (see *The Babylonian Exile*), about forty
thousand take up his offer and reestablish a Jewish state under Persian
rule".[2] Persia, prior to this major expansion, was within approximately
the same borders as today's Iran.

King Cyrus took this opportunity to establish new sources of trade
goods and to re-establish old trade routes into Egypt, Parthia and Assyria
(Syria). He formed an alliance with the Phoenicians who owned and
operated most of the merchant ships that sailed the Mediterranean Sea
and the northwestern coast of Africa. It was a time of wealth and
prosperity for the entire region, especially the newly expanded Persian
Empire.

King Cyrus placed delegates in his newly conquered countries to
manage their new governments and to keep him informed of their

---

[1] *Biblical Literacy*, Rabbi Joseph Telushkin, page 599
[2] *Jewish Literacy*, Rabbi Joseph Telushkin, page 106

loyalty. He also had these delegates collect, under pain of death, an annual Persian tax.

He used a different strategy than many other rulers of that era to control the people in his vassal states: "The newness of Cyrus's empire lay in his ability to think of it, not as a Persian nation in which the peoples must be made more Persian, but rather as a patchwork of nations under Persian rule. Unlike the Assyrians, he did not try to destroy national loyalties or identities. Instead, he portrayed himself as the benevolent guardian of those very identities".[1]

He went even further to assure the loyalty of the re-established Hebrew nation: "Cyrus also returned the valuables from the Temple of Solomon that he found in the treasury of Babylon, in another example of his using wealth (in this case, captured by others) to strengthen his own position. For this, he earned himself the title from the Jews 'Anointed of the Lord'".[2]

The Hebrews who returned from exile and their descendants remained a separate social group for many years. The small city of Jerusalem was then established as a Persian military outpost. King Cyrus ordered the rebuilding of the Jewish Temple as much for his own benefit as for the Jewish people.

King Cyrus issued the order to have the Temple rebuilt at his own expense with a written mandate: "In the first year of King Cyrus, the king issued a decree concerning the temple of God in Jerusalem: *Let the temple be rebuilt as a place to present sacrifices, and let its foundations*

---

[1] *The History of the Ancient World*, Susan Wise Bauer, page 468
[2] *The History of the Ancient World*, Susan Wise Bauer, pages 466-467

be laid. It is to be sixty cubits high and sixty cubits wide, with three courses of large stones and one of timbers. The costs are to be paid by the royal treasury" (Ezra 6.3-4).[1] He built this fortress as a defense against possible Egyptian invasion into his territory.

After their return to Judea, the prophet Ezra became one of the most influential figures within this Jewish community: "Jewish tradition regards Ezra as having saved the Jewish people from extinction. The Talmud declares: *Ezra would have been worthy of receiving the Torah for Israel had not Moses preceded him (Sanhedrin 21b)*. His public reading of the Torah [sometimes referred to as The Law] democratized the holy document, making it as much a possession of the commonest Jewish laborers as of the priests. As harsh as Ezra's measures against intermarriage were, had they not been carried out there might be no Jews today; they probably would simply have assimilated into the religions and lifestyles of their neighbors".[2]

The history of the Hebrew people, as written by the Jews, dates back to the days of the legendary patriarch Abraham: "He also said to him, *I am the LORD, who brought you out of Ur of the Chaldeans to give you this land to take possession of it*" (Genesis 15.7).[3]

It is very unlikely that the first five books of the Bible were written by Moses, except possibly a few small portions. Most of the writing was done much later: "c. 450-400 B.C.E. Ezra returns to Judah with the '*torah* of Moses,' and with Nehemiah begins reform of Judaism in the spirit of

---

[1] Bible, *New International Version*, page 787
[2] *Jewish Literacy*, Rabbi Joseph Telushkin, page 107
[3] Bible, *New International Version*, page 22

the Torah; Torah begins to gain recognition as Scripture".[1] It was during this time that the Torah, the first five books of the Bible, were brought together, edited, formalized and canonized (given the official stamp of approval). The scribes and priests compiled the ancient Hebrew legends and writings: "A more immediate legacy of the reading of the *Torah* was the establishment, with the full knowledge of the Persians, of a theocratic state in Judah".[2]

Israel Finkelstein & Neil Asher Silberman, in their recently published book *The Bible Unearthed*, wrote that it is much more likely that it was at this time that many of the Mosaic laws first came into being, not during the Israelites' journey across the desert: "In the last few decades scholarly opinions about the dates and authorship of these individual sources have varied wildly. While some scholars argue that the texts were composed and edited during the existence of the united monarchy and the kingdoms of Judah and Israel (c. 1000-586 BCE), others insist that they were late compositions, collected and edited by priests and scribes during the Babylonian exile and the restoration (in the sixth and fifth centuries), or even as late as the Hellenistic period (fourth-second centuries BCE). Yet all agree that the Pentateuch is not a single, seamless composition but a patchwork of different sources, each written under different historical circumstances to express different religious or political viewpoints".[3]

---

[1] *Essential Judaism*, George Robinson, page 542

[2] *Essential Judaism*, George Robinson, page 298

[3] *The Bible Unearthed*, Israel Finkelstein and Neil Asher Silberman
    page 13

It was not until the 'Dark Ages' that the books of the Bible were delineated by chapter. This was done by the Catholic Archbishop of Canterbury, England who lived from c. 1150 C.E. to 1228 C.E. Prior to this translation, the Bible was divided by book and verse.

The return of the Hebrews to Judea occurred over a long period of time: "No doubt these years had not been an entirely happy time for many Jews, as we can discern from the poignant words of Psalm 137, but life was perhaps not too harsh in Babylon since the return from exile took place in waves over the next hundred years. Many Jews had therefore been exposed to the alien religious ideas of both their erstwhile Babylonian captors and those taught by the sophisticated Zoroastrian religion, many of which were to be adopted and eventually to have a profound influence on Jewish religious thinking. This foreign influence is especially marked among members of the various Jewish sects that developed in later centuries down to the time of the Dead Sea Scrolls".[1]

Within the next few decades the Hebrew people incorporated some of the history collected from the descendants of the lost tribes into Scriptures. David Biale, author of *Cultures of the Jews*, suggested that it is likely that the Canaanites and the twelve tribes of Hebrews were one and the same people: "The Exodus story itself admits that the nation left Egypt as a 'mixed multitude' (Exodus 12.38), the very opposite of an ethnic or tribal group with a common lineage. Much later, the prophet Ezekiel would thunder: *By origin and birth you are from the land of the Canaanites – your father was an Amorite and you are a Hittite* (Ezekiel

---

[1] *The Dead Sea Scrolls Rediscovered*, Stephen Hodge, page 32

16.3)".[1] "So, to speak of the culture of ancient or biblical Israel immediately raises the question of whether we are talking about the *actual* culture of those Israelites described in the Bible, or, conversely, about how their culture was *imagined* by later generations".[2]

The city of Samaria, located in the northern region, was the capital of Israel until it was destroyed by the Assyrians in 722 B.C.E. From that time forward those people of the northern tribes who survived the Assyrian invasion and continued to follow the Hebrew/Jewish faith were referred to as Samaritans.

Within several decades after the Hebrews returned from slavery in Assyria and Babylon they were able to reclaim what had been their property in Judea and fully implement a functioning government. In 515 B.C.E.: "The Second Temple is completed".[3]

The Hebrew religion and government then became centralized. Israel and Judea became a unified country under the name *Judea*. The non-Jewish people were invited to join in religious celebrations. They were also invited, at least for a period of time, to convert to Judaism if they were willing to live by the Jewish laws, including the law that prohibited marriage to non-Jews or those who refused to live by the laws of Judaism.

The Jewish people, from that time forward were generally referred to collectively as *Jews*: "… the Jerusalem Temple had been rebuilt and

---

[1] *Cultures of the Jews*, David Biale, pages 3-4
[2] *Cultures of the Jews*, David Biale, page 4
[3] *Biblical Literacy*, Rabbi Joseph Telushkin, page 599

78

rededicated largely at Persian expense, ushering in the so-called Second Temple Period".[1]

However, many of the Jewish people in Judea distanced themselves from the Samaritans. They believed the northern Hebrew community that had come together, after the Assyrian invasion, was comprised of both Hebrews and non-Hebrews, and that some of the Hebrews had intermarried with non-Hebrews: "The Samaritans have insisted that they are direct descendants of the N Israelite tribes of Ephraim and Manasseh, who survived the destruction of the N kingdom of Israel by the Assyrians in 722 B.C.E. The inscription of Sargon II records the deportation of a relatively small proportion of the Israelites (27,290, according to the annals {ANET, 284-85}), so it is quite possible that a sizeable population remained that could identify themselves as Israelites, the term that the Samaritans prefer for themselves".[2]

The Samaritans built their own temple on Mount Gerizim in 388 B.C.E. The Judean Jews would have considered this an act of blasphemy. The Jewish king, King Hyrcanus, destroyed this temple in 128 B.C.E. However, there were other theological and cultural controversies between the Judean Jews and the Samaritans during this era that created hostility between them which lasted for centuries: "Any Israelite or any foreigner residing among them who offers a burnt offering or sacrifice

---

[1] *The Dead Sea Scrolls Rediscovered*, Stephen Hodge, pages 32 and 34
[2] *The Anchor Bible Dictionary*, Samaritans, volume 5, page 941

and does not bring it to the entrance to the tent of meeting to sacrifice to the LORD must be cut off from the people of Israel" (Leviticus 17.8-9).[1]

After the Jews returned from captivity in Assyria, many of them placed a high degree of importance on genealogy and often treated the Samaritans with disdain. The Samaritan community had been decimated by the Assyrians. This left them little opportunity to maintain a Hebrew community. They had not maintained family records and supposedly failed to marry only those who were Hebrew. Thus, from the Jewish perspective, they had forsaken their heritage.

From this bias against the Samaritans the attitude developed that no good could ever come from these 'second-class' people. In the New Testament (Luke 10.25-37) Jesus told the story of 'the good Samaritan' as a way of speaking out against the bias toward the Samaritans by the Sadducees, and very likely at least a few of the Pharisees.

The Persian rulers continued to demand the allegiance of the Jews: "[In 450 B.C.E.] Nehemiah, a Jewish official in Persia, is dispatched to Jerusalem to supervise the community. [In 428 B.C.E.] Ezra comes to Judea and is authorized by Persia to establish a theocracy in which the Jews are required to live according to Torah law".[2] In any case, the Jewish people were a group of people set apart by unique laws, customs and dress. During the centuries following the Jewish people's return from Babylonian captivity, they were seldom completely independent. Judea was a relatively small country and was controlled at various times

---

[1] Bible, *New International Version*, page 196
[2] *Biblical Literacy*, Rabbi Joseph Telushkin, page 599

by Egyptians, Persians, Macedonians, Parthians, Syrians, Greeks and Romans.

Chapter 9

The Greeks and Romans greatly influenced the formation of Jewish sects

Alexander the Great of Macedonia (northern Greece) conquered southern Greece, much of Europe, northern Egypt, much of western Asia, Israel and Judea in the fourth century B.C.E.

Soon after Alexander conquered Israel he gained the support of the Samaritans. They contributed 8,000 troops to his military campaign in Egypt. However, while Alexander was in Egypt many of the residents of Samaria revolted and killed their newly appointed governor Andromachus. In retaliation, Alexander put down the revolt and decimated the Samaritan community. He then established a resident garrison of 600 troops.

The Jewish leadership in Judea also underwent changes during this era: "Still nominally under Persian overlordship, the inhabitants of Judah were nevertheless allowed to organize themselves as a distinct religious and political community. Crucially for our story, the now hereditary office of High Priest was to become overwhelmingly important: all internal authority within Judah was concentrated in the hands of this figure, who was not only the supreme head of religious affairs but also the *de facto* head of state for life. This situation continued even when there was a change of masters after the Persian Empire fell to the armies of Alexander the Great".[1]

Following these conquests, and Alexander's subsequent death in 323 B.C.E., his generals divided their newly acquired empire into five major and several minor states, but only after an intense power struggle. The wars between the army generals in these territories continued for seventy-five years. By the end of these wars, the Wars of the Successors, Alexander's conquests were consolidated into three kingdoms ruled by the Greeks. The Greeks ruled the European territory from the city of Rome, Italy – the Near East from Antioch, Syria – and northern Africa from Alexandria, Egypt.

Control of Judea, a territory located between Antioch and Alexandria, was often violently disputed: "At first Judea was under the benign rule of Egypt, which allowed the Jews considerable religious freedom; but the aggressive campaigns of the eastern Seleucids eventually wrested Judea from Ptolemaic control, and the wheels of Jewish revolt were gradually set in motion".[2] "As a rule, [Jewish] relations with the Greek Ptolemies in Egypt were more cordial than those with the Seleucids at Antioch, the Ptolemies being more tolerant".[3] Seleucid is the Greek word for Syrian.

The Syrian culture, following the invasion of Alexander and his troops, became increasingly based on Greek religious laws and values. Many of the Jews of the area set aside some of the old Hebrew laws as

---

[1] *The Dead Sea Scrolls Rediscovered*, Stephen Hodge, page 34
[2] *The Dead Sea Scrolls Rediscovered*, Stephen Hodge, page 35
[3] *James, the Brother of Jesus*, Robert Eisenman, page 18

they became increasingly 'Hellenized'. Hellene is the Greek word for Greek.

During this era the Greeks coined the term 'barbarian'. They applied this term 'barbarian' to everyone who was not Greek, or at least not 'Hellenized'. Thus, polarization greatly increased in the entire Near East, especially within the Jewish population. Some of the Jews favored Hellenization while others resisted.

Aramaic was a widely used language in the area. However, in the business world Greek was usually the language of choice. Many people spoke at least two languages. However, the Jews preferred their Hebrew language for religious writing and services, and still do even today. Hebrew and Aramaic were very similar dialects within the same Middle Eastern language.

The next two hundred years were filled with civil wars and defensive wars against neighboring countries: "But throughout all this time, both the Ptolemies and the Seleucids vigorously fostered Alexander's vision of a Hellenic world. This process was so successful that by the time of the Maccabean Revolt, which began in 168 B.C.E., most of the Middle East had become thoroughly Hellenized, especially the nobility and aspiring middle class".[1]

Judea, from the establishment of Ezra's dictates in the fifth century B.C.E. to the destruction of the Temple in 70 C.E., was a very class-oriented society, in many ways closely resembling the serfdoms in Europe during the Middle Ages. The elite class within the Jewish

---

[1] *The Dead Sea Scrolls Rediscovered*, Stephen Hodge, page 35

communities included only those with 'official' documentation of Hebrew/Jewish genealogy.

The Jews had their sacred Scriptures to justify the re-establishment of a segregated society. This segregation was based on a caste system that drew very clear lines between the ruling class (those who had the 'God-given right' to rule the country), the working class (those who owned small businesses or farms, or were laborers) and the slaves (those who were classified as property). The people within the ruling class typically owned large businesses or farms. Women always ranked below men within their respective caste.

During the time of Moses, the attitude and laws of the Hebrew people concerning slavery was very likely quite similar to most cultures of the world at that time: "If you buy a Hebrew servant, he is to serve you for six years. But in the seventh year, he shall go free, without paying anything. If he comes alone, he is to go free alone; but if he has a wife when he comes, she is to go with him. If his master gives him a wife and she bears him sons or daughters, the woman and her children shall belong to her master, and only the man shall go free. But if the servant declares, *I love my master and my wife and children and do not want to go free*, then his master must take him before the judges. He shall take him to the door or the doorpost and pierce his ear with an awl. Then he will be his servant for life" (Exodus 21.1-6).[1]

Another story concerning the Jewish attitude toward slavery during this era can be found in *Joshua*. Representatives of the people of Gibeon dressed in ragged clothes and approached Joshua to ask for a treaty

---

[1] Bible, *New International Version*, page 126

85

stating that they were from a distant land. However, Joshua soon realized that they were less than truthful. He then declared a penalty for all of the people of that territory: "Then Joshua summoned the Gibeonites and said, *Why did you deceive us by saying, 'We live a long way from you', while actually you live near us? You are now under a curse: You will never be released from service as woodcutters and water carriers for the house of my God*" (Joshua 9.22-23).[1]

The self-imposed religious segregation of people has always presented a paradox, a contradiction. Most religions have as a basic precept the tolerance and acceptance of people outside of their own community. Yet, it is only by remaining a group apart from others that makes it possible for them to sustain their membership and pass on their own teachings.

The Temple was central to the Hebrew/Jewish faith for centuries. The Jews had very strict regulations that specifically stated Temple admittance requirements and restrictions. The high priest entered the Holy of Holies only once a year, on Yom Kippur, the Day of Atonement, to pray for the forgiveness of the sins of all Jewish people who had unknowingly violated a law and for their sins of omission.

Flavius Josephus gives a detailed physical description of Jerusalem and the Temple. The Holy of Holies was the innermost chamber within the Temple. Surrounding this were three stories of chambers that were all interconnected. Only those Jewish men who were 'thoroughly clean' were allowed entrance into these inner court chambers. Men who were

---

[1] Bible, *New International Version*, page 371

less than 'thoroughly clean', women, children and Gentiles were allowed only inside the outer courtyard, or holy place.

Jesus sent a man to the Temple officials after the man was cured so they could verify that he no longer had a health issue that prohibited him from entering the Temple's inner chambers: "If the raw flesh changes and turns white, they must go to the priest. The priest is to examine them, and if the sores have turned white, the priest shall pronounce the affected person clean; then they will be clean" (Leviticus 13.16-17).[1]

Women were allowed inside this outer courtyard: "... since in this quarter a special place of worship was walled off for the women".[2] The Temple was closed to women during their menstruation. Persons afflicted with gonorrhea or leprosy were banned not just from the Temple, but also from the entire city of Jerusalem.

The increase in commerce with other Asians, Europeans and Africans increased the Hellenistic influence on Jewish customs and beliefs. However, this also expanded financial opportunities for many of the Jews.

Many of the Jewish people met these new challenges and benefited from the financial upsurge even though this sometimes required them to make compromises with their religious beliefs: "Continued peace with the Parthians was important for Roman prosperity. It meant that the trade route to India and perhaps even farther to the east was now passable, rather than blocked by a solid wall of hostility".[3]

---

[1] Bible, *New International Version*, pages 184-185
[2] *Josephus, The Jewish War, Volume IV, Book V*, Thackeray, page 61
[3] *The History of the Ancient World*, Susan Wise Bauer, page 706

However, the course of Jewish history took a new direction, primarily due to the lack of compassion of one particular Syrian ruler, Antiochus Epiphanes IV. Antiochus attempted an invasion of Egyptian territories in 168 B.C.E.: "The spoiling of the temple was pure opportunism; Antiochus was broke and needed the sacred treasures. On his pass through Judea, he not only plundered the Temple treasury and butchered a great many citizens of Jerusalem, but also installed a garrison in Jerusalem to keep the Jews loyal".[1] "If it had not been for the crass insensitivity of the Seleucid ruler Antiochus Epiphanes IV, it is quite likely that Judaea would have completely lost its Jewish identity and world history would have traveled down a very different path".[2]

Antiochus struck at some of the most basic Jewish laws. He outlawed circumcision, Sabbath observance and even the possession of Scriptures. The Temple was transformed into a sanctuary of Zeus. He had pigs offered as sacrifice on the Temple altar. Those Jewish men who attempted a revolt against Antiochus were massacred. Many of the Jewish women and children were either killed or sold into slavery.

Antiochus committed many other atrocities against the Jewish people: "Antiochus's fanatical oppression happily sparked a successful revolt, led by Mattathias and the Maccabees. After that, Antiochus Epiphanes (or Anthony God-Manifest in modern English) faded from Jewish history. He died four years later, in 163 B.C.E.".[3]

---

[1] *The History of the Ancient World*, Susan Wise Bauer, page 645
[2] *The Dead Sea Scrolls Rediscovered*, Stephen Hodge, page 35
[3] *Jewish Literacy*, Rabbi Joseph Telushkin, pages 111-112

The Maccabean War of Independence began in 167 B.C.E. in the city of Modi'in, 17 miles northwest of Jerusalem: "Aided by his five sons, Mattathias undertook a guerrilla war against the Syrian troops".[1] "Within a year of launching the revolt Mattathias died. Although, he had left instructions that his third son, Judah, should assume the military command. Judah's fighting style was so aggressive that he was nicknamed Maccabeus, 'the Hammer'. The name was fitting. He 'hammered away' continuously at every Syrian outpost, and two years later the Syrians sued for peace".[2]

These men and their followers included many Sadducees, the descendants of the ancient patriarch Zaddok. This Jewish religious sect was composed primarily of wealthier landholders and their families. They took control of the country and imposed a theocratic form of government whereby their religious laws superseded any and all civil law. The Sadducees were most often in control, or at least very influential, in religious affairs throughout the Second Temple Period.

David Biale, in his recently published book *Cultures of the Jews*, gives his perspective of the influencing factors that led up to the Maccabean (Hasmonaean) War: "Those who remained committed to the more conservative way of life were called 'pious ones', or *Hassidim*".[3] "The awakening resistance to the Greeks may have thus created new forms of piety".[4] "The Hasmonaeans [Latin for *Hassidim*] were rural

---

[1] *Jewish Literacy*, Rabbi Joseph Telushkin, page 113
[2] *Jewish Literacy*, Rabbi Joseph Telushkin, page 113
[3] *Cultures of the Jews*, D. Biale, page 144
[4] *Cultures of the Jews*, D. Biale, page 144

priests, and their role in the revolt may have had something to do with their rejection of the more cosmopolitan urban priesthood of Jerusalem. The Hasmonaean Revolt was, in some measure, an uprising of the countryside against the city".[1]

The Hasmonaeans, immediately following their newly won independence, re-established the duties and powers of the priesthood and appointed Judas Maccabee as High Priest. Judas Maccabee was supposedly the last surviving member of the tribe of Levi, the original priestly family.

Traditionally, the high priest had not only a strong influence on religious matters but also considerable political power. The Hasmonaeans followed the dictates in Scriptures and promptly removed all idols from the Temple, including the statue of the Greek god Zeus. They purified the Temple, which had been polluted by idols and pagan sacrifices. The Temple was then rededicated and henceforth declared off limits to all non-Jews. Hanukkah, the Holy Day of Lights, is the annual remembrance of this rededication of the Temple. A more complete explanation of *Hanukkah, historical roots* can be found in *Essential Judaism* written by George Robinson.

The non-Jewish residents of Judea, as a result of these stricter laws, were no longer allowed to have any meaningful religion of their own. All of their public places of worship and prayer were destroyed. They could no longer publicly acknowledge any god but the Jewish God. They were required to observe many of the Jewish laws and conform to many of the Jewish customs.

---

[1]*Cultures of the Jews*, D. Biale, page 144

However, those who were not Jewish by blood, but were otherwise observant Jews, were still allowed to enter the outer areas of the Temple and synagogues. Only documented Jewish men were allowed to read Scriptures, or even have Scriptures in their possession. As one might have expected, the relations between the Jews and the non-Jews became a bit strained, to say the least.

Even though Judah (*Judas* in Greek) and his followers had won limited religious independence, they were faced with strong opposition from the Pharisees (Pharisee – Greek for *splinters away* or *those who separated from*).

The Pharisees' first act of defiance that set them apart from the Sadducees was to break with tradition and appoint a Jewish man to the high priesthood who was not a resident of Judea. This action was met with strong opposition from the Sadducees who interpreted Scriptures to dictate that the high priest was in essence the king of Judea and was therefore required to be a Jewish man who had been born and raised in Judea.

Diaspora is a Greek word meaning *to scatter* or *to sow* and generally refers to those Jews living outside of Judea/Israel. A majority of the Jews in the Diaspora during that era were Pharisees: "Distraught by the Maccabean victory, some of the local Jewish Hellenizers joined forces with Syrian soldiers and continued to harass Judah. In 160 [B.C.E.], the Syrians returned en masse, killed Judah, and defeated the Jews. Two years later, Judah's brother Jonathan emerged from a desert hiding place, and initiated another rebellion. He succeeded in winning a measure of Jewish autonomy, but after a few years, the Syrians returned again and murdered him. His brother Simon now took over the battle. In 142 [B.C.E.], the Maccabees (the followers of Judas Maccabee) finally achieved an enduring victory".[1] The Seleucid (Syrian) prohibitions against Judaism, including circumcision and other Jewish rituals, were finally removed.

Many of the ancient laws addressed by this new government dealt with marriage, sex and fornication issues. The laws against fornication, and there were many, were again strictly enforced, at least while the Hasmonaeans were in control of the country.

The Hasmonaeans declared that any and all residents of Judea would be punished for violating any Jewish law. They quoted Scriptures when they declared that marriage to certain foreigners was a form of fornication: "Do not intermarry with them. Do not give your daughters to their sons or take their daughters for your sons" (Deuteronomy 7.3).[2] Many of those Jews who were married to non-Jews, as well as their children, were executed by the new rulers, the Hasmonaeans: "They had grown so accustomed to fighting that they seemed incapable of working with anyone who disagreed with them about anything. Simon's grandson, King Alexander Yannai, executed eight hundred of his Pharisee opponents, after first forcing them to witness the murders of their wives and children. While the slaughter was going on, Yannai was present, hosting a Greek-style drinking party".[3] "The Maccabees' terrible moral and religious decline explains why there is almost no mention of

---

[1] *Jewish Literacy*, Rabbi Joseph Telushkin, pages 113-114
[2] Bible, *New International Version*, page 306
[3] *Jewish Literacy*, Rabbi Joseph Telushkin, page 114

them in the Talmud".[1] "The Talmud is a two-stage compilation of the laws of Synagogue Judaism. The first stage is the Mishna. It was compiled, primarily out of oral materials, about A.D. 175 [175 C.E.]".[2] "The second stage is known as Gemara. Mishna, the first stage, plus Gemara, the second, equal Talmud".[3]

In 125 B.C.E., contrary to Jewish law at that time, the Sadducees, under the rule of John Hyrcanus, introduced Jewish conversion: "The Hasmonaean kings enlarged the orbit of Jewish culture by forcibly converting inhabitants of the biblical lands of Ammon and Edom, east of the Jordan".[4] "In fact, the evolution of a strict procedure of conversion probably began at this time and was finally codified by the rabbis in the second century C.E.".[5]

[1] *Jewish Literacy*, Rabbi Joseph Telushkin, page 114
[2] *Judaism and Christian Beginnings*, Samuel Sandmel, page 103
[3] *Judaism and Christian Beginnings*, Samuel Sandmel, page 103
[4] *Cultures of the Jews*, D. Biale, page 146
[5] *Cultures of the Jews*, D. Biale, page 5

Chapter 10

Different interpretations of Scriptures created tension within the Jewish community

By the year 67 B.C.E., Judea was again engulfed in civil war. This time it was Hyrcanus II against Aristobulus II. Both were grandsons of Judas Maccabee. Both sought the support of the Roman military. The Roman General Pompey sent military troops into Judea and gave his support to Aristobulus because he believed him to be the stronger leader.

Antipas was a very influential Jewish leader in Edom (Idumaea, land of Esau) during this war. He and his family were among those who had Judaism forced upon them. Subsequently, many of them were Jews in name only and gave little support to the long-established Jewish communities that had continued to teach traditional Jewish values.

With mounting hostilities against them, Hyrcanus and Antipas pleaded with General Pompey to withdraw his support of Aristobulus and join them. Subsequently, Pompey changed his tactics and gave his support to Hyrcanus. However, in spite of overwhelming odds, Aristobulus held out against Hyrcanus and the Roman troops.

Aristobulus and his militia were eventually forced to retreat to the Temple in Jerusalem, their last stronghold. Finally, in 63 B.C.E., after a three-month siege, Hyrcanus, with his Idumaean and Roman troops, broke through the walls that encompassed the Temple grounds and stormed the Temple. They slaughtered more than 12,000 men, women and children, which was just a sample of what was to happen later, during the First Jewish War (66 C.E. to 70 C.E.) and the Second Jewish War (132 C.E. to 135 C.E.).

After the fall of Jerusalem, Judea became an occupied country, a Roman province with a constant military presence that was to remain for many centuries: "The Jews of the first century B.C.E. must have reflected often and sadly on the fact that this had all come about because *Jews* had called in Rome [the Roman military] to settle an internal Jewish dispute. As if to discourage excessive Jewish breast-beating over Hyrcanus and Aristobulus's self-destructive act, historian Menachem Stern suggests the following meager consolation: *Once Rome had decided to annex Syria, its intervention in Judah became inevitable. The fraternal war that broke out ... only accelerated the intervention*".[1]

Rome was undergoing an intense political struggle of its own during this time. Julius Caesar began his career as a common soldier and soon worked his way up to the rank of commander. Later, Julius Caesar, the Senate and the military generals, including Pompey, all competed for control of the military: "The Senate, disliking so much power concentrated in the hands of one man, objected; but the Assembly voted to approve Pompey's appointment. His success was drastic and enormous and made him increasingly popular. His family was rapidly rising to become one of the most powerful in Rome; in fact, Julius Caesar (who had returned to Rome after Sulla's death) asked to marry his

---

[1] *Jewish Literacy*, Rabbi Joseph Telushkin, page 117

daughter Pompeia. Pompey agreed to the wedding, and immediately set off again on campaign".[1] Sulla was also a Roman general.

Pompey and his troops marched against Egypt in 47 B.C.E. However, they soon found themselves outnumbered. Pompey asked Caesar for additional troops. Caesar, with the help of the Jewish commander Antipater, recruited troops from Judea. Caesar and his troops, along with Antipater's troops, marched into Egypt to help Pompey. Caesar arrived just as Pompey finished winning the battle. Even though Caesar and his troops hardly engaged the enemy at all, Rome still gave him credit for 'saving the day'. Pompey made it known that he did not appreciate Caesar stealing his glory.

Caesar was grateful for Antipater's support. When Caesar came to Syria later that year he named Hyrcanus ethnarch of the Jews over and above his position as high priest. He honored Antipater, the effective power behind Hyrcanus' throne, with Roman citizenship and freedom from Roman taxation. He also appointed him procurator/ruler of Judea. The ethnarch title carried with it a higher rank than tetrarch. A tetrarch was a procurator/ruler but not a high priest.

Antipater, the Roman-appointed ruler of Judea, was very wealthy and had the support of the largest army in the world. His wife Cypros came from a wealthy Egyptian family who was well connected in the spice, incense and balsamic oil business that reached as far east as Persia, northern India and possibly into western China.

Rome continued to support Antipater and the Herods as rulers of Judea for many years. This created a serious problem for most Jews

---

[1] *The History of the Ancient World*, Susan Wise Bauer, page 683

because it violated several Jewish laws. These requirements were spoken of in Scriptures: "be sure to appoint over you a king the LORD your God chooses. He must be from among your fellow Israelites. Do not place a foreigner over you, one who is not an Israelite. The king, moreover, must not acquire great numbers of horses for himself or make the people return to Egypt to get more of them" (Deuteronomy 17.15-16).[1]

Several centuries later, these requirements were clearly defined in the Talmud: "He should: Be a born Israelite [law 498]. Not acquire an unduly large number of horses [law 499]. Not settle Israelites in the land of Egypt [law 500]. Not take a large number of wives [law 501]. Not amass for himself great wealth [law 502]".[2]

However, at least a few of these ideals were not adhered to in ancient times. David had at least eighteen wives (many more, depending on which Bible is quoted) before he moved to Jerusalem: Michal, Ahinoam, Abigail, Carmel, Maacah, Haggith and Abital. He also had many concubines.

His grandson King Rehoboam also had multiple wives and concubines: "In all, he had eighteen wives and sixty concubines, twenty-eight sons and sixty daughters" (2 Chronicles 11.21).[3]

Antipater, the Roman governor of Syria, was assassinated (poisoned) in 41 B.C.E. His son Herod then ruled in his place. A Parthian attack came just months later, in 40 B.C.E.: "The Parthians swept down through Syria into Palestine, intending to kill the Roman governor

---

[1] Bible, *New International Version*, page 323
[2] *Biblical Literacy*, Rabbi Joseph Telushkin, page 574
[3] Bible, *New International Version*, page 734

Herod. He fled to Rome, so the Parthians instead dragged out Hyrcanus (who was the High Priest and Ethnarch of Judea, reporting to Herod) and cut both of his ears off. This kept him from serving as high priest any longer, as Jewish law dictated that the high priest be unmutilated".[1] "The Parthians, under Phraates IV, tried to defend the Syrian holdings, but Antony managed to drive them back out of Palestine. In 37 BC [B.C.E.], he installed Herod as a vassal king of Rome: a secular King of the Jews, doing away with a combined priesthood and kingship".[2] This Herod would later become known as Herod the Great.

Herod came from a wealthy family and did not belong to any Jewish sect. Herod and his many sons considered themselves to be above Jewish law. This attitude contributed considerably to an increase in riots and civil disobedience throughout Judea. Herod was a cruel and sometimes paranoid ruler. As time went on, he became increasingly cruel. He had many Jews murdered for minor offenses and complaints. Eventually, out of fear for his life, he fled to Rome.

---

[1] *The History of the Ancient World*, Susan Wise Bauer, page 702
[2] *The History of the Ancient World*, Susan Wise Bauer, page 702

Chapter 11

The Herods became powerful and corrupt

After Caesar was assassinated in 29 B.C.E., Mark Antony sent Herod back to Judea with sufficient troops to put down the Jewish revolt. Mark Antony helped Herod regain the Jewish crown. Herod then executed Aristobulus for his part in the revolt and murdered forty-five members of the Sanhedrin who had spoken out against him.

Herod's position as king violated many of the same Jewish laws that had been violated by his father, Antipater. Many of Herod's sons became Roman appointed governors.

Most Jews strongly resented the Herods for their support of Roman occupation and the high taxes they imposed. However, Herod's renovations to the Temple made it one of the most magnificent buildings of antiquity. But, at the same time, Herod imposed upon the Jews a loyalty oath to Caesar Augustus and executed a number of those who refused to comply.

Herod claimed to be a Hebrew, a descendant of Benjamin. However, his mother was a 'high-born' Arab who was without Jewish ancestry. According to the Sadducees' interpretation of Jewish law during this time period, a person was a Jew only if his/her mother was born a Jew: "For anyone whose mother was Jewish, the question is moot.

Your mother was a Jew? Then you're a Jew".[1] Herod was a Jew by Roman genealogy standards which generally followed paternal lineage.

It is questionable if Antipater, or any of his descendants, could trace their maternal or paternal ancestry back to any member of the tribe of Benjamin: "Ever since [Israel was defeated by Assyria in 722 B.C.E], no Jews have been able to trace their ancestry accurately to any tribe except for Judah and Levi".[2]

By this time, many of the Pharisees (the Conservative Jews) were beginning to accept converts as legitimate members of Judaism. The Conservative Jews *conserved* (adhered to) *the spirit of the law* more than *the letter of the law*. The Orthodox Jews strongly objected to Oral Law. They believed in a literal interpretation of Written Law, including the forgiveness of all loans to fellow Jews in the seventh year and the return of land to the owner of record every fiftieth year.

The issue of *Who is a Jew?* continues even today: "In fact, the continuing controversy has greater emotional than practical significance; few Reform or Conservative converts to Judaism make aliyah [journey or pilgrimage] to Israel: Their combined number is probably less than ten a year. The issue's emotional resonance, however, is great. Currently, an estimated 30 to 40 percent of American Jews intermarry. Most parents whose children intermarry hope that their son- or daughter-in-law will convert to Judaism. When conversions do occur – approximately five to ten thousand Gentiles convert in the United States annually – they are overwhelmingly performed by Reform or Conservative rabbis. Tens of

---

[1] *Essential Judaism*, George Robinson, page 179
[2] *Jewish Literacy*, Rabbi Joseph Telushkin, page 79

thousands of American Jews, therefore, understood that the 'Who is a Jew?' bill being considered by the Knesset [Israeli parliament] would be a formal denial of the Jewishness of their grandchildren, even when the child's mother had undergone a Reform or Conservative conversion. Hundreds of thousands of Reform and Conservative Jews were infuriated that the Knesset, composed largely of secular Jews, and non-Jews (as well as Orthodox Jews), was considering a law declaring non-Orthodox conversions to be invalid".[1]

"In 1983, Reform [a Jewish sect] altered the traditional definition of a Jew (a child born to a Jewish mother) to include anyone born of a Jewish father and a non-Jewish mother, as long as the child is raised with a Jewish identity. This decision has proved particularly controversial, since it means that Reform Judaism recognizes people as Jews whom Conservative and Orthodox Jews do not. As regards conversion, Reform has dropped the requirement of circumcision for males and immersion in a *mikveh* [ritual bath] for both female and male converts. In addition, Reform rabbis tend to be much more lenient regarding the rituals and Jewish laws they expect converts to observe subsequent to their conversion. In large measure, as a result of the more liberal standards of Reform Judaism, most conversions to Judaism in the United States are performed by Reform rabbis. The converts are most often non-Jews intending to marry Jews. Most converts are women".[2]

Herod further angered the Jewish people when he repeatedly ignored their marriage and sex laws. He married his sister-in-law and

---

[1] *Jewish Literacy*, Rabbi Joseph Telushkin, page 359
[2] *Jewish Literacy*, Rabbi Joseph Telushkin, page 428

various other relatives and had numerous children by his nine or ten wives. His sons became known collectively as *the Herods*.[1]

Apart from Judaism, the practice of rulers marrying their sisters, daughters and in-laws was not uncommon: "Ptolemy Ceraunus promptly claimed the Macedonian-Thracian throne for himself and married his sister Arsinoe. This was an Egyptian custom, not a Greek one".[2] "All of these people were related to each other anyway, in a big Faulknerian mess of marriages. Caesar's aunt was married to Marius. Caesar's first wife was Cinna's daughter, and his second wife was Sulla's granddaughter (Pompeia Sulla, whose mother was Sulla's daughter and whose father was a cousin of Pompey's). Pompey's second wife was Sulla's stepdaughter, and his fourth wife was Caesar's daughter, Julia. When Caesar broke Julia's engagement, Pompey offered the jilted fiancé *his* own daughter, even though she was already engaged to Sulla's son. Crassus married his own brother's widow and left it at that, although he was rumored to be carrying on an affair with one of the Vestal Virgins".[3]

"His [Caesar's] choice turned out to be less than objective. He was smitten with Cleopatra's beauty and ordered her brother deposed in her favor".[4] "Cleopatra [Cleopatra the seventh, 69-30 B.C.E.] was coronated

---

[1] *Biblical Literacy*, by Joseph Telushkin, gives an excellent overview of these laws. Many of them address marriage and sex issues. The Talmud states that intermarriage was prohibited, as is reflected in Scriptures (Deuteronomy 7.3).

[2] *The History of the Ancient World*, Susan Wise Bauer, page 623

[3] *The History of the Ancient World*, Susan Wise Bauer, footnotes page 686

[4] *The History of the Ancient World*, Susan Wise Bauer, page 693

[crowned] and ceremonially married to her younger brother, an Egyptian custom that the Ptolemys had been following for some time. Meanwhile Caesar carried on a furious affair with Cleopatra which kept him idle (politically, at least) in Alexandria for some months. When he was finally able to tear himself away, leaving her pregnant, he made a military tour around the edge of the Roman Republic".[1] After the death of Caesar, Cleopatra and Mark Antony entered into a romantic relationship. Several years later they both committed suicide.

Herod the Great had at least two Jewish wives, both daughters of high priests, both with the name Mariamme (Mariamne/Mary). One of his wives, Mariamme, carried in her veins the Maccabean bloodline of Levite priests. Jonathan, Mariamme's brother, celebrated his thirteenth birthday in 36 B.C.E. This was the age of majority, the age at which a Jewish boy became a man.

A few years later, Jonathan donned the vestments of the high priest during a celebration: "For Herod had not spared even this poor lad; he had bestowed upon him in his seventeenth year the office of high-priest, and then immediately after conferring this honour (honor) had put him to death, because, on the occasion of a festival, when the lad approached the altar, clad in the priestly vestments, the multitude with one accord burst into tears. He was, consequently, sent by night to Jericho, and there, in accordance with instructions, plunged into a swimming-bath by the Gauls and drowned".[2]

---

[1] *The History of the Ancient World*, Susan Wise Bauer, page 693
[2] *Josephus, The Jewish War, Volume II, Book I*, Thackeray, page 207

Herod even killed Mariamme, his 'favorite' wife, in 29 B.C.E. and his two adult sons by her, Alexander and Aristobulus. He also murdered five of his sons by other wives, one mother-in-law, a brother-in-law and the high priest.

Herod's fear of losing his kingship is reflected in the nativity story in the gospel of *Matthew* which states that Herod (more accurately a son of Herod the Great) killed all of the young male children in Bethlehem: "When Herod saw that he had been tricked by the wise men, he was infuriated, and he sent and killed all the children in and around Bethlehem who were two years old or under, according to the time that he had learned from the wise men" (Matthew 2.16).[1] Other incidents of child-killing can be found in *Exodus* and in the story of Rachel (Jeremiah31.15). In the *Exodus* story, the pharaoh supposedly had many of the Hebrew children killed in an effort to control the rapidly increasing Hebrew population because he feared a Hebrew take-over of his country or, more likely, because of a severe drought that created a country-wide food shortage.

Herod was a very unpopular ruler who had reason to fear for his kingship and his life. Not only did he kill some of his own relatives, but he also killed many of those who spoke out against him. His paranoia is quite understandable since assassination was one of the leading causes of death for rulers during that era, at least in Rome and the Middle Eastern countries.

Herod did not agree with many of the Sanhedrin rulings nor was he receptive to their criticism. He ignored the law prohibiting foreigners

---

[1] *The Jewish Annotated New Testament*, Levine and Brettler, page 6

from offering sacrifices in the Temple. He invited the Romans to place their military standards (banners) within the city of Jerusalem even after he had promised the Jewish leaders that he wouldn't allow it. He took possession of the high priest vestments and appointed his own high priest. Generally, to control these vestments was to control the Temple, and much more.

Herod was despised by most Jews. However, out of fear for their lives, members of the Sanhedrin offered little resistance to his violation of Jewish laws and customs. The Zealots – those who were zealous for the law – were infuriated that the Herod-appointed high priests performed sacred Temple rituals. They believed that the Herods, and the high priests appointed by them, were the worst violators of the sacredness of the Temple.

In defiance of Herod, the Zealots elected their own High Priest, Phineas. This man was a stonecutter of the humblest origins. He was a leader in his community who had already been presiding over the Jewish religious services in his community.

Herod had numerous spies and never stopped taking vengeance on those who opposed him. He crucified more than 1,000 Sadducees during one uprising. However, those who supported him were showered with benefits of all kinds.

Concerning the speeches of the Jewish authorities, Josephus wrote of Herod: "The plaintiffs, being given permission to state their case, began by enumerating Herod's enormities. *It was not a king*, they said, *whom they had had to tolerate, but the most cruel tyrant that ever existed. Numerous had been his victims, but the survivors had suffered so much that they envied the fate of the dead. For he had tortured not only the persons of his subjects, but also their cities; and while he crippled the towns in his own dominion, he embellished those of other nations, lavishing the life-blood of Judea on foreign communities. In place of their ancient prosperity and ancestral laws, he had sunk the nation to poverty and the last degree of iniquity. In short, the miseries which Herod in the course of a few years had inflicted on the Jews surpassed all that their forefathers had suffered during all the time since they left Babylon to return to their country in the reign of Xerxes".*[1] King Xerxes of the fourth century B.C.E. was the grandson of Cyrus the Great.

---

[1] *Josephus, The Jewish War Volume II, Book II*, Thackeray, page 355

Chapter 12

The Sanhedrin was the Jewish Court of Law

The Sanhedrin was the official Jewish Court of Law. It was through this court system that the Jews maintained their authority over religious and most civil matters for many centuries.

There were three types of court. The local courts were comprised of three judges. The more serious crimes were addressed by a panel of twenty-three judges. The high priest and the king very likely had the option of whether or not to be voting members of this panel of judges for any given case. The most serious crimes were tried by the Great Sanhedrin (bet din). This court was composed of seventy members, the high priest and the king. Again, the high priest and the king very likely had the option of whether or not to be voting members on this panel of judges. Sometimes the high priest was also the king.

Members of the Sanhedrin were traditionally elected by the men in the various Jewish communities located throughout the Mediterranean area. Prerequisites for a person to be elected to the position of Sanhedrin Judge included that he be a well-respected member of the community and have extensive knowledge of Scriptures, especially the Torah (Hebrew word for Teaching). The Torah was, and still is, often referred to as the *Book of Laws*.

The Great Sanhedrin court was comprised of seventy members, very likely in memory of the patriarch Jacob: "These are the names of the sons of Israel who went to Egypt with Jacob, each with his family: Reuben, Simeon, Levi and Judah; Issachar, Zebulun and Benjamin; Dan and Naphtali; Gad and Asher. The descendants of Jacob numbered seventy in all; Joseph was already in Egypt" (Exodus 1.1-5).[1] The number 'seventy' is also mentioned in other writings: "Then the LORD said to Moses, *Come up to the LORD, you and Aaron, Nadab and Abihu, and seventy of the elders of Israel*" (Exodus 24.1).[2] "The LORD said to Moses: *Bring me seventy of Israel's elders who are known to you as leaders and officials among the people*" (Numbers 11.16).[3]

The judges typically convened in the Temple in the morning and remained in session until early afternoon most days of the year. On any given day there would be any number of judges present, from a few to all seventy members. They did not convene or hand down any criminal or non-criminal decision between sundown and sunrise or on the Sabbath or during Passover or on any holy day.

The three-judge court tried cases that involved small monetary issues and other minor crimes or disagreements. A guilty verdict required the vote of at least two of the three judges. This court convened in the Temple and in the various communities. The law generally required that to have a three-judge court a town had to have a population of at least 120 men. A person facing a trial who lived in a community with fewer than 120 men was required to appear in court in a larger community.

---

[1] Bible, *New International Version*, page 92
[2] Bible, *New International Version*, page 132
[3] Bible, *New International Version*, page 242

More serious cases required a panel of twenty-three judges. There are historians who believe that this panel of judges may have been comprised of thirty-seven judges. The panel of twenty-three judges had the option of appointing up to seven additional non-voting judges to collect and present evidence for the prosecution and an equal number of judges for the defense (23+7+7=37).

An affirmative vote by all twenty-three judges or negative vote by all twenty-three judges could decide an issue in a non-criminal case. The non-criminal cases that lacked a 100% vote for or against an issue could still be decided by a majority of at least two.

In those cases where an individual was on trial in a criminal case, a vote of guilty by at least a majority of two but not all twenty-three judges was required to convict. At least one judge had to give a <u>not guilty</u> vote or the case had to be set aside and be heard by a different panel of judges. As one Jewish writer stated, this was to avoid a person being 'railroaded' for a crime that he may not have committed.

Once a judge argued during the trial for an acquittal he could not reverse his position. The judges with the least seniority declared their vote first to prevent undue influence or intimidation by the more senior judges.

Upon the conclusion of a criminal trial, each judge submitted a written summary of the reasons for his decision – the laws he believed were or were not violated and any mitigating factors that influenced his decision. The court could not reverse a not guilty verdict.

A statement of not guilty could be given to the defendant on the same day the court decided on the verdict. Following a verdict of guilty the court was required to wait until the following day to inform the convicted person of the guilty verdict and of his or her punishment. However, this decision could not be handed down between sundown and sunrise or on the Sabbath or during Passover or on any other holy day.

The most serious cases came before the Great Sanhedrin. This seventy-judge court met in Jerusalem in the Chamber of Hewn Stone on the Temple Mount. For convicting a person or persons of a crime, the Great Sanhedrin court was bound by the same rules as the twenty-three judge court.

The Great Sanhedrin also interpreted law, heard cases such as the trial of a tribe, a person accused of being a false prophet, as well as accusations against a high priest or king. It also sent men into war and decided on additions or changes to the Temple.

The Sanhedrin, prior to the rule of Herod the Great, was considered by the general population to be a legitimate court system. However, pressure from the Herods and politically-appointed members would certainly have influenced the outcome of some of the trials. In spite of this, many if not most Jews continued to regard the Sanhedrin to be an acceptable court, a legal system that had become the envy of other countries.

The Torah identified several capital cases that required a panel of twenty-three (or thirty-seven) judges: "Whoever sheds human blood, by humans shall their blood be shed; for in the image of God has God made mankind" (Genesis 9.6).[1] "Anyone who strikes a person with a fatal blow is to be put to death. However, if it is not done intentionally, but God lets

---

[1] Bible, *New International Version*, page 13

110

it happen, they are to flee to a place I will designate. But if anyone schemes and kills someone deliberately, that person is to be taken from my altar and put to death" (Exodus 21.12-14).[1] Many older Bibles read 'You shall not kill'. Generally, newer Bibles read: "You shall not murder" (Exodus 20.13).[2] At first glance, this difference may seem trivial. However, killing another person in self-defense in most, if not all, countries is considered justified. Also, killing enemy soldiers in battle has always been not only acceptable but oftentimes absolutely necessary for soldiers in uniform.

Serious physical abuse of a parent was also a capital crime: "Anyone who attacks their father or mother is to be put to death" (Exodus 21.15).[3] Scriptures required a person to testify on behalf of another: "Do not go around spreading slander among your people, but also don't stand idly by when your neighbor's life is at stake" (Leviticus 19.16).[4]

The abuse of a pregnant woman also carried serious punishment: "If people are fighting and hit a pregnant woman and she gives birth prematurely but there is no serious injury, the offender must be fined whatever the woman's husband demands and the court allows. But if there is serious injury, you are to take life for life, eye for eye, tooth for

---

[1] Bible, *New International Version*, page 127
[2] Bible, *New International Version*, page 125
[3] Bible, *New International Version*, page 127
[4] *Complete Jewish Bible*, page 199

tooth, hand for hand, foot for foot, burn for burn, wound for wound, bruise for bruise" (Exodus 21.22-25).[1]

Injury caused by a person's animal was also addressed in a law: "If a bull gores a man or woman to death, the bull is to be stoned to death, and its meat must not be eaten. But the owner of the bull will not be held responsible. If, however, the bull has had the habit of goring and the owner has been warned but has not kept it penned up and it kills a man or woman, the bull is to be stoned and its owner also is to be put to death. However, if payment is demanded, the owner may redeem his life by the payment of whatever is demanded. This law also applies if the bull gores a son or daughter. If the bull gores a male or female slave, the owner must pay thirty shekels of silver to the master of the slave, and the bull is to be stoned to death" (Exodus 21.28-32).[2]

It was a crime to bear false witness in a murder case: "The judges must make a thorough investigation, and if the witness proves to be a liar, giving false testimony against a fellow Israelite, then do to the false witness as that witness intended to do to the other party" (Deuteronomy 19.18-19).[3] In this particular circumstance it was the Sadducees who maintained that the death penalty was not justified as punishment of a false witness, at least not unless the accused was actually executed as a result of the false testimony of the witness.

Following is an interesting situation addressed by a Jewish writer and historian: "Another dispute concerned responsibility for damage to a

---

[1] Bible, *New International Version*, page 127
[2] Bible, *New International Version*, pages 127-128
[3] Bible, *New International Version*, page 326

third party caused by a slave, with the Sadducees holding that the owner of the slave is liable, in contrast to the Pharisees who held that each individual, including slave, is personally accountable for any damages they caused (mYad. 4:7). Who is being less severe here? That depends on whose point of view you are looking at this from. As far as the injured party was concerned, the Sadducees were being more liberal. What chance would someone have of recovering from a slave who has nothing? By holding the owner liable, the Sadducees were making sure damages would be paid. This seemed logical and fair to them just as if any animal or property of a person caused damage to another. But the Pharisees believed that a slave, who is an intelligent human being after all, could not be compared to an animal. More-over, they were worried that if a slave was angry at his owner for any reason, he could cost him money by deliberately damaging someone else's property. So the Pharisees chose the view that is lenient towards the owner of a slave, but harsher on the slave and the third party. The point of these final ruminations is that I do not want to be unfair to the Sadducees. They had their opinions about how written Torah should be applied, they must have fought hard to implement them, and at least sometimes they would have had the more sensible or humane opinion, or ones just as defensible as the Pharisees had. We should not caricature the Sadducees as the brutal, unfeeling taskmasters of ancient Judaism. Some nuanced judgments about them are only fair. But having said all this, the Pharisees still appear to be the ones who were most flexible about written Torah and willing to be creative to achieve humility and kindness".[1]

---

[1] *The Ghost in the Gospels*, Leon Zitzer, page 47

Kidnapping was a capital crime: "Anyone who kidnaps someone is to be put to death" (Exodus 21.16).[1]

Adultery was a crime, but seldom resulted in the death penalty. The incident with King David and Bathsheba is one early example. Scriptures does not have a record of any charge of adultery against either David or Bathsheba. Not only was David guilty of having sex with another man's wife, but he had her husband sent into battle into a situation where Uriah was going to be killed. David had instructed the commander to pull back the other troops during the heat of the battle to make sure Bathsheba's husband was killed, which indeed he was.

Even though the Sanhedrin Court had not been established until many years after King David's time there still would have been serious repercussions for King David if the Hebrew authorities had been aware of his crime at that time. However, it is very likely that David's plot to have Uriah killed was not discovered until at least a few years after David died.

"The Bible's definition of adultery is not the same as that used in contemporary society. According to biblical law, whether or not adultery has occurred depends exclusively on the woman's marital status. A married woman who has sexual relations with anyone other than her husband is regarded as having committed adultery, as is her lover. But an unmarried woman who has sex with a married man has not committed adultery, nor has her lover. Sexist as it may sound, biblical law permits men to have more than one wife; thus, having sex with a woman other than one's wife is not viewed – at least legally – as a betrayal of one's

---

[1] Bible, *New International Version*, page 127

114

spouse. However, since a woman is forbidden to have more than one husband, sex with someone other than her spouse is always regarded as a betrayal. In the ancient world, in which the biblical definition of adultery was similar to that of other societies, adultery was generally considered to be a crime against the husband alone. He thus had the right to either insist upon punishment for the adulterous couple, or to forgive them. In the biblical view, adultery is also regarded as a crime against God; therefore, it is not within the province of the cuckolded spouse to forgive the betrayal".[1]

A woman or girl who was raped within a city or town's boundary and did not cry out loud enough to have someone come to her aid could be presumed a willing participant and tried for the crime of fornication or adultery: "If a man happens to meet in a town a virgin pledged to be married and he sleeps with her, you shall take both of them to the gate of that town and stone them to death – the young woman because she was in a town and did not scream for help, and the man because he violated another man's wife" (Deuteronomy 22.23-24).[2]

"After the Second Temple's destruction in 70 C.E., the Sanhedrin was reconvened in Yavneh. After the failure of the Bar-Kokhba revolt, it met in various Galilean cities. The Sanhedrin seems to have disbanded under Roman persecution about 425 C.E.".[3]

---

[1] *Biblical Literacy*, Rabbi Joseph Telushkin, pages 434-435
[2] Bible, *New International Version*, page 331
[3] *Jewish Literacy*, Rabbi Joseph Telushkin, page 121

Chapter 13

Herod's disregard for Jewish customs
increased social unrest

After the death of Herod the Great in 4 B.C.E. the Romans divided Judea into several provinces to be ruled by Herod's sons. One of his sons, Philip, was then the tetrarch/governor of Trachonitus and Iturea (Batanea) from 4 B.C.E. to 34 C.E. His half-brother Archelaus was the ethnarch of Judea and Idumaea from 4 B.C.E. to 6 C.E.: "But he [Archelaus], anxious apparently not to be taken for a bastard son of Herod, had ushered in his reign with the massacre of three thousand citizens; that was the grand total of the victims which he had offered to God on behalf of his throne, that was the number of corpses with which he had filled the Temple at a festival!".[1] This territory was strife-ridden all through his reign: "Such was the end to which they ultimately came; but at the period of which we are speaking, these men were making the whole of Judaea one scene of guerrilla warfare".[2]

Josephus, in his writing *The Jewish War*, gives a unique perspective of the history of the Jewish people and the Roman military in Judea from 170 B.C.E. through the First Jewish War which ended in 70 C.E. His

---

[1] *Josephus,* The *Jewish War Volume II, Book II*, Thackeray, pages 35 and 357

[2] *Josephus, The Jewish War Volume II, Book II*, Thackeray, page 347

116

writings have a wealth of information on the events that transpired during that era.

Archelaus was the ruler referred to in the nativity story in the gospel of *Matthew*: "Get up, take the child and his mother, and go to the land of Israel, for those who were seeking the child's life are dead. Then Joseph got up, took the child and his mother, and went to the land of Israel. But when he heard that Archelaus was ruling over Judea in place of his father Herod, he was afraid to go there. And after being warned in a dream, he went away to the district of Galilee" (Matthew 2.20-22).[1]

Archelaus was removed from power in 6 C.E. because he was unable to control Jewish uprisings: "His reign was cut short when a deputation of the aristocracy from Samaria and Judaea went to Rome and complained about his outrageous behavior and misrule. He was deposed and the Romans placed his territory under their direct rule as an annex of the province of Syria, though with its own governor, the prefectus or, as he was later known, the procurator".[2]

Quirinius (Cyrenius), a Roman general was assigned the governorship of Syria in 6 C.E. and the northern portion of Judea. He answered directly to the Roman Emperor and Senate.

About this same time, the Romans established a large garrison of troops in the huge Antonia Fort in Jerusalem. A few years earlier Herod the Great had built this fort next to the Temple in order to effectively police the pilgrims who came to Jerusalem for the Passover and other holy day celebrations.

---

[1] *The Jewish Annotated New Testament*, Levine and Brettler, page 6
[2] *The Dead Sea Scrolls Rediscovered*, Stephen Hodge, page 58

Antipas II, another son of Herod the Great, was the tetrarch of Galilee and Perea from 4 B.C.E. to 39 C.E. This area was also besieged with civil strife: "On receiving the dispatches from Sabinus and his [Roman] officers, Varus was alarmed for the whole legion and resolved to hasten to its relief. Accordingly, mobilizing the two remaining legions with the four regiments of horse [mounted soldiers] which were attached to them, he marched for Ptolemais".[1] "Varus at once sent a detachment of his army into the region of Galilee adjoining Ptolemais, under the command of his friend Gaius; the latter routed all who opposed him, captured and burnt the city of Sepphoris and reduced its inhabitants to slavery".[2] "The whole district became a scene of fire and blood, and nothing was safe against the ravages of the Arabs".[3]

The sons of Herod the Great followed their father's example. They often ignored Jewish law and basic morality and did not hesitate to murder for money, lust and power. Many of the Jews, especially the Zealots, were outspoken against the Herods because of their total disregard for the Jewish marriage laws.

Herod Agrippa, Herod of Chalcis, Herod Agrippa II, and Antipas II as well as the Roman procurator (governor) Pontius Pilate all followed the same oppressive policies against any and all who dared to stand against them. Many in the Herod family assassinated members of their own family.

---

[1] *Josephus, The Jewish War Volume II, Book II,* Thackeray, page 349
[2] *Josephus, The Jewish War Volume II, Book II,* Thackeray, page 349
[3] *Josephus, The Jewish War Volume II, Book II,* Thackeray, pages 349 and 351

Several of the Herods had multiple wives, which the Jews considered a crime of fornication. Some had married their own sisters, granddaughters and cousins. The Jews maintained that this was not only fornication, but that it violated basic Jewish laws against incest.

All Jews were required to pay tribute/taxes to the Herods even though many of them considered the Herods to be both foreigners and fornicators whose authority in Judea could never be acquiesced to. Most Jews never accepted any member of the Herod family as a legitimate ruler.

The headquarters of the Roman military was moved from Caesarea to Jerusalem. This added to the tension between the Jews and the Romans.

The Zealots remained determined to force the Romans out of Judea and rid themselves of the Herods, at any cost. The Herods remained in power only because of Roman support and protection.

In 40 C.E. Gaius Caligula, one of Rome's less adept emperors, mandated that his statue be erected in the Temple. Thousands of Jews petitioned him to rescind the order or they would be forced to resort to violence to prevent the desecration of their most sacred religious site.

The political, religious and financial turmoil throughout the country during this era spawned many riots and street killings. The Romans would not tolerate any public gathering of people who advocated political dissent or displayed any civil disobedience. Any person or group found disturbing the peace for any reason was quickly and harshly dealt with which usually meant being whipped (scourged or flogged), put to the sword or, more often, crucified as an example to anyone else who might consider such actions. This added to the tension during holy days and Passover celebrations, especially in Jerusalem.

All of the various factions within Judea during this era have very bloody histories. The anger directed at the Herods and Romans sometimes escalated into outright warfare. Many of the non-Jews, the middle class, the lower class and the slaves were drawn into these uprisings against the Herods and the Romans.

The writings of the Jewish author Josephus state that before the end of the year 70 C.E., the final year of the First Jewish War, the fighting against the Romans and the Herods cost both the Jews and non-Jews of Judea and Jews in neighboring countries more than a million lives as well as the destruction of the Temple. The Samaritans lost more than 80,000 men. Josephus included these Samaritans in his count of Jewish casualties.

The writer Julius Africanus lived from 170 C.E. to 245 C.E. According to him, the Zealots, prior to the First Jewish War, were sometimes referred to as Galileans. These Jews, as well as the Essenes, tried to gain a consensus on a strict adherence to Jewish traditions, laws and customs.

The Messianic Sadducees subscribed to the belief that a 'savior', a descendant of Abraham and Isaac, would come forward to purge Judea of the Roman military occupation and any other foreign power. According to them, the Torah itself prohibited tribute to or rule by any foreign power. Many of them refused to pay taxes to the Herods or the Romans, which often resulted in the confiscation of their property, which increased their efforts to force the Roman military out of Judea. The annual Roman tax was one denarius. This was equal to one day's wages for a laborer.

The Essenes were the most non-conforming of all of the Jews. There were many rites and rituals within the Temple that they did not acknowledge as legitimate. They even refused to go onto the Temple grounds. Many of the Essenes also despised the Greek and Roman cultural influence in Judea.

The Sadducees and the Pharisees each used different calendars. One group used a lunar calendar while the other group used a solar calendar. As a result, they disagreed on the interpretations of those portions of Scriptures that established the dates on which to observe various holy days. This led to each sect celebrating some of the feast days at different times of the year –sometimes a difference of only one or two days.

They also disagreed on the validity of various laws: "Clearly, the most important distinction between Sadducees and Pharisees was on the issue of the legitimacy of the oral law, espoused by the Pharisees and rejected by the Sadducees".[1] The Oral Laws were the later interpretation of the Written Laws contained in Scriptures.

Many of the Sadducees were Orthodox Jews. Orthodox Jews believed that the laws contained in Scriptures almost always had to be interpreted literally. The Pharisees did not agree with the Sadducees on this issue: "The Oral Law is a legal commentary on the Torah, explaining how its commandments are to be carried out. Common sense suggests that some sort of oral tradition was always needed to accompany the

---

[1] *Judaism and Christian Beginnings*, Samuel Sandmel, page 158

121

Written Law, because the Torah alone, even with its 613 commandments, is an insufficient guide to Jewish life".[1]

The Orthodox Jews were opposed to nearly all Oral Law. They expected a literal application of Written Law. The Conservative Jews, which included many of the Pharisees, believed that a more humane interpretation was required, one that was more in line with what they considered to be the intent of the Written Law. They seldom, if ever, sought the death penalty. They argued that financial restitution made by the criminal or a term of imprisonment or both fulfilled the requirements of the law.

The Essenes, Sadducees and Pharisees each developed different beliefs in an afterlife. The Pharisees believed: "Every soul, they maintain, is imperishable, but the soul of the good alone passes into another body, while the souls of the wicked suffer eternal punishment".[2]

As with the Hebrews of earlier times, the Sadducees did not believe in an afterlife: "As for the persistence of the soul after death, penalties in the underworld, and rewards, they will have none of them".[3] Their focus was on a quest for knowledge and the adherence to high moral standards.

The Essenes had yet another belief in the afterlife: "For it is a fixed belief of theirs that the body is corruptible and its constituent matter impermanent, but that the soul is immortal and imperishable. Emanating from the finest ether, these souls become entangled, as it were, in the

---

[1] *Jewish Literacy*, Rabbi Joseph Telushkin, page 148

[2] *Josephus, The Jewish War Volume II, Book II,* Thackeray, pages 385 and 387

[3] *Josephus, The Jewish War Volume II, Book II,* Thackeray, page 387

prison-house of the body, to which they are dragged down by a sort of natural spell; but when once they are released from the bonds of the flesh, then, as though liberated from a long servitude, they rejoice and are borne aloft. Sharing the belief of the sons of Greece, they maintain that for virtuous souls there is reserved an abode beyond the ocean, a place which is not oppressed by rain or snow or heat, but is refreshed by the ever gentle breath of the west wind coming in from the ocean; while they relegate base souls to a murky and tempestuous dungeon, big with never-ending punishments".[1]

Today many, if not most, people believe in an afterlife in some form or another. There are also people who do not believe in an afterlife, but that it has been the fear of death, the permanent loss of loved ones and the desire for punishment of those guilty of serious crimes that have over the millennia compelled humans to develop a logic that offers life, love and reward in an afterlife for some and punishment, or at least the absence of reward, for others.

There were many differences between the three major Jewish sects that developed during this period of history: "Many Jews think that the current division of their community into different denominations is a new phenomenon, that before modernity all Jews thought and acted alike. In actuality, the Jewish sects that existed during the Second Temple Period had differences as profound as those that separate Reform, Conservative, and Orthodox Judaism today.

---

[1] *Josephus, The Jewish War Volume II, Book II,* Thackeray, pages 381 and 383

Pharisees. The most important thing to know about the Pharisees is that they are the ancestors of all contemporary Jews. The other sects that existed contemporaneously with them died out shortly after the Second Temple's destruction. Once they disappeared, the Pharisees were no longer called by that name; their religious practices became normative Judaism. *Unfortunately*, at the very time all Jews were increasingly identifying as Pharisees, the word began to acquire a new, highly pejorative [uncomplimentary] meaning. The New Testament repeatedly depicted the Pharisees as small-minded religious hypocrites. Eventually, the word 'pharisee' came to be synonymous in English with 'hypocrite' – a distortion as obnoxious to Jews as the expression 'to jew,' meaning 'to bargain down or to cheat'. In actuality, the greatest teachers of talmudic Judaism, men like Hillel, Rabbi Yochanan ben Zakkai, and Rabbi Akiva, were Pharisees. The Pharisees' understanding of Judaism was characterized by their belief in the Oral Law. They believed that when God gave the Torah to Moses, He also gave him an oral tradition that specified precisely how its laws were to be carried out. For example, although the Torah demands 'an eye for an eye', the Pharisees maintained that God never intended that physical retribution be exacted. Rather, a person who blinded another was required to pay the victim the value of the lost eye. The Pharisees believed that the Oral Law also empowered them to introduce necessary changes into Jewish law, and to apply the law to unanticipated circumstances".[1] "In defiance of their

---

[1] *Jewish Literacy*, Rabbi Joseph Telushkin, pages 129-130

Sadducean opponents, the Pharisees also believed in an afterlife in which God rewards the righteous and punishes the wicked".[1]

"*Sadducees.* The Pharisees' opponents, the Sadducees, generally belonged to the wealthier classes. Many were priests who served at the Temple. While the Sadducees had some orally transmitted traditions of their own explaining how to carry out the Torah's law, they rejected the Oral Law of the Pharisees, and came close to being biblical literalists. For example, they interpreted literally 'an eye for an eye'. They rejected the notion of an afterlife because it did not appear in the Torah.

Their major religious focus apparently was the Temple rituals and sacrifices. The Pharisees complained about what they felt was the Sadducees' obsessive interest in these matters: the *(ritual) uncleanness of the knife [used in a murder at the Temple] was to them worse than the murder itself.* (*Tosefta Yoma* 1.10). Unfortunately, no Sadducean writings survive, so all that we know about them comes from their Pharisaic opponents. The Sadducees went out of existence after the destruction of the Temple in the year 70 [C.E.]. Their religious life was apparently so centered on the Temple that its destruction robbed them of their *raison d'etre*. Some scholars speculate that the religious practices of the medieval Karaites (a Jewish sect that also rejected the Oral Law) were based in part on Sadducean teachings.

Essenes. In drawing historical parallels it is sometimes hard not to be reductionist; nonetheless, the third sect, the Essenes, come across as an ascetic and disciplined group of ancient hippies. Believing that city life was corrupting, they moved to sparsely populated parts of Palestine,

---

[1] *Jewish Literacy*, Rabbi Joseph Telushkin, page 130

particularly to the desert near the Dead Sea. Most Essene communities were celibate; thus, their survival depended on constantly winning new converts. More than anything else, their celibacy is probably what accounted for the group's short life span.

Unlike the Sadducees, the Essenes wanted nothing to do with the Temple; they apparently felt it had been corrupted by the Sadducean priests. The Essene communities practiced very strict laws of purity and impurity; immersion in a ritual bath seems to have been one of their most important ceremonies".[1]

"*Dead Sea Sect*. Among the sects living in the desert was another that came to be known as the Dead Sea Sect. Its existence, and its writings, were unknown until 1947, when a Bedouin shepherd discovered scrolls they had left behind in the cave of Qumran. The scrolls of this sect suggest that they were an extremist offshoot of the Essenes".[2]

---

[1] *Jewish Literacy*, Rabbi Joseph Telushkin, page 130
[2] *Jewish Literacy*, Rabbi Joseph Telushkin, pages 131-132

Chapter 14

The tax collectors worked with the Romans

Gold bullion and coins made of gold, silver and copper were used as currency during that era. A few coins were made of lead. One common Jewish coin was the shekel. It was similar to an ancient Babylonian unit of currency. Between 200 B.C.E. and 70 C.E. the Jewish people minted some coins of their own. These coins were stamped with impressions of plants or symbols of religious significance. Some had no markings at all. Grain, livestock and other farm products, as well as homemade goods were used for barter.

There are several gospel stories that speak of 'silver coins'. Today it would be difficult to determine what the value of any particular silver coin was during that era since several countries each minted different sizes of silver coins, which would have had different values.

Because of the varying size and types of coins in use in that part of the world, money was often weighed during a business transaction. Some people, especially the Romans, stamped markings on their coins that identified the weight or relative value of those coins. Without these markings, the common method of determining the value of a coin was to weigh it on a balancing scale.

This scale had a tray on each side of a pivot point. The tax collector or other businessman would place his pre-weighed coin or stone on one side of the tray and the taxpayer's or customer's coin on the other side of the scale to determine its value. The gospels indicate that at least a few tax collectors, moneychangers and merchants were less than honest in some of their business transactions.

All Jews were required to contribute annual tithing to the Temple, as mandated in Scriptures. A portion of this money was used to assist the poor, a cornerstone of Jewish social responsibility: "When you have finished setting aside a tenth of all your produce in the third year, the year of the tithe, you shall give it to the Levite, the foreigner, the fatherless and the widow" (Deuteronomy 26.12).[1]

There were many other expenses for the Jewish people besides Temple tithing and annual taxes. They were expected to make sin-offerings, first-born offerings and to take care of their extended families. They were also expected to donate to their local synagogue and to the Temple on holy days. As mentioned above, the taxes they hated the most were the taxes to support Rome, the Roman-appointed governors and the Roman military.

Many of the merchants who traded in Judea were from neighboring countries, countries that minted their own coins. Quite often these coins had the impression of a person, animal or a god stamped into them. Many of the Roman coins were stamped with the image of a Roman god or goddess, Caesar, or other Roman dignitary. The Torah forbade the Hebrew/Jewish people from making or using sculptures and images of people as objects of worship. It was considered by many to be blasphemous to use such coins for tithing or Temple offerings or to even carry these idolatrous coins onto the Temple grounds.

---

[1] Bible, *New International Version*, page 336

Most of the Jewish population during the time of Jesus lived outside of Judea. Many of them regularly made pilgrimage to the Temple even though such journeys had become increasingly expensive and dangerous. Every adult Jewish man was expected, barring a very serious reason, to make at least one pilgrimage to the Temple sometime during his adult life.

The coins these pilgrims brought with them were quite often not acceptable as Temple offerings or for tithing. This made it necessary for the Temple authorities to allow the moneychangers to set up shop just outside the Temple gates. These moneychangers would, generally for a fee, exchange the undesirable coins for coins that were acceptable for use within the Temple.

The laws related to this issue came from the commandment that forbade idolatry: "You shall have no other gods before me" (Exodus 20.3).[1] The Herods often ignored these laws and brought these 'undesirable coins' into the Temple courtyard. This created yet another source of tension, especially among the Zealots.

Herod's building tax was used to finance a variety of building projects: "Herod and his sons created work for the down-and-out by building new cities".[2] Tithing, Herod's tax, Rome's tax, the tax collectors' arbitrary commission and other community costs continually increased and reached as high as 50% of a Jewish family's annual income.

---

[1] Bible, *New International Version*, page 124
[2] *The Anchor Bible Dictionary*, Jesus Christ, volume 3, page 777

The tax collectors were responsible for collecting various taxes. They were accompanied by Roman soldiers for their own protection, for good reason. Sometimes the tax collectors served as interpreters for the soldiers who did not speak Aramaic, Hebrew or Greek. However, following the days of Alexander the Great, the use of the Greek language in Judea had gradually increased.

It was the tax collectors' responsibility to also collect past-due taxes. In lieu of payment by those who were unable or unwilling to pay, the tax collectors sometimes confiscated grain, sheep, etc. or even the land itself. Many of the tax collectors became very wealthy in the process, which added to the civil unrest. The Herods maintained a register of delinquent taxes in the newly-built Antonia Fort/Palace.

All Jews who came to the Temple in Jerusalem, whether they lived within Judea or in another country, were required to pay a half-shekel per year specifically for the Herods' massive building projects and to support the Herods' lavish lifestyle. Most Jews resented having to pay this tax. Their anger increased when, for a time, the tax collectors and the moneychangers were allowed to set up shop inside the Temple courtyard. Many Jews would certainly have considered this a desecration of the Temple not only because of business being conducted in 'the House of God', but also because it would likely have been inevitable that at least some 'idolatrous' coins would be brought into the sacred Temple area for exchange, donations or purchases.

The ever-increasing unrest in Judea required the Romans to also increase the number of troops to maintain order, which required more taxes to pay for their military expenses, which also added to the civil unrest.

Herod had as many Roman soldiers as necessary at his disposal to protect his tax collectors during the collection of these very arbitrary amounts of goods and coins. Occasionally, the Romans would confiscate land for unpaid taxes, for the widening and straightening of roadways and as punishment for disregarding military orders. Most Jews had little recourse to any excessive or disproportionate tax. The lower classes of people had no recourse other than protests and violence.

Contrary to Jewish law, the Roman governors granted 800 soldiers who had completed their tour of duty acreages of Judean farm land that had previously been confiscated. Land was also given or sold to retired officers and immigrating Roman farmers. At the same time, a high percentage of Jewish farmers were forced into poverty. Many of them moved into the cities, increasing the social unrest even more.

Many parts of Judea were plagued with riots during the rule of Archelaus (4 B.C.E. to 6 C.E): "This unrest reached such a point that Archelaus ordered his cavalry to put a stop to it; they killed some 3000 Jews in the Temple precinct during Passover".[1]

Archelaus was subsequently removed from power for several reasons: "Many of Archelaus' troubles were inherited from Herod, although he himself had offended Jewish tradition in a number of ways. First, he had deposed the high priest Joazar (because he had supported Jewish malcontents) and he had appointed Eleazar, Joazar's brother, to take his place (cf. Jos. *Ant* 18.93 on priestly vestments). Second, he had

---

[1] *The Anchor Bible Dictionary*, Archelaus, volume 1, page 367

married Glaphyra, daughter of Archelaus I of Cappadocia, a union which offended Jewish tradition because Glaphyra had already borne a son to Archelaus' brother, Alexander, her first husband. In fact, Archelaus was Glaphyra's third husband, since she had married King Juba II of Mauretania after Alexander's death".[1]

Shortly after the onset of the First Jewish War, many of the Jews who had delinquent taxes joined other angry Jews in the burning of Herod's palace. They wanted the Antonia Fort/Palace and all of its contents burned in order to destroy the tax records, especially the records of delinquent taxes. Others wanted it destroyed because it was a Roman military stronghold. Also, many Jews despised Herod for building his palace in such a position that from his balcony he could see over the Temple walls directly into the sacred areas of the Temple.

The Romans built a network of roadways in many countries, including Judea, primarily for the rapid movement of troops and easier transport of commerce. Many of the old roadways were straightened and made wide enough for troops to march five abreast.

The length of a marching Roman soldier's pace – right foot forward and left foot forward – multiplied by 1,000 was a Roman unit of measure. Using this unit of measure, the distance between towns was measured and marked. Recently, archeologists found a portion of roadway in southern Italy that still has these ancient Roman road markers that are spaced approximately 5,200 feet apart. Centuries later, the British and French, whose soldiers were slightly taller, and their stride

---

[1] *The Anchor Bible Dictionary*, Archelaus, volume 1, page 368

longer, extended this unit of measure to 5,280 feet. This unit of measure became known as a mile (*milion* or *mille*).

For many years prior to the Roman takeover of Judea the country had a theocratic form of government in which there was no separation of Church and State. The old aristocracy was comprised of the families who were documented Jews. Their ancient customs and laws depended on maintaining their class structured society. This class structure included the property owners with their slaves, the common workers and the foreign merchants. However, many aspects of their traditional way of life were no longer possible during the years of Roman occupation primarily due to the flagrant abuse of power perpetrated by the Roman-appointed governors.

The Roman occupation was perceived by many Jews to be God's punishment brought down on them because so many of them no longer followed the traditional Jewish laws and customs. Some members of the various sects turned increasingly to prayer, others to violence, still others preached on the streets and along the roadways between towns. Many of the Sadducees were willing to die for their country and their beliefs, which most of them did, rather than yield to any foreign power.

During the two centuries prior to and during the First Jewish War, many of the Judean Jews of all of the various sects and many of the Gentiles (the non-Jewish residents) lost their lives fighting against the Herods and the Romans. Flavius Josephus in his book *The Jewish War* gives a detailed account of the hundreds of thousands of lives lost during the riots and wars against the Herods and the Romans.

Chapter 15

Unemployment in Judea added to the social unrest

The increase in unemployment added to the number of people who were desperate to survive: "The administrative record of the Roman provincial governors of Judea varied from mediocre to atrocious. The heaviest burden on the Jews, however, was not inept or corrupt administration, but economic hardship and instability. Given a glaring inequality in the distribution of goods and a lack of agricultural land proportionate to a population of half a million, the combination of natural catastrophes (drought, earthquake, epidemic, famine – e.g., the great famine of A.D. 46-47) and oppressive taxation under competing tax systems, secular (Roman) and sacred (Jewish), were ruinous for the class of small landholders who constituted society's center of gravity, the marginal middle class. From this came periodic surges in the number of new poor, emigrants [immigrants], revolutionaries, bandits and beggars".[1]

During this same period, 46 C.E. through 70 C.E., many of the roadways became unsafe for travel, except in large groups, due to the increase in the number and boldness of road bandits. Some of the commercial routes became so plagued with these bandits that many caravans had to be accompanied by Roman military escorts. The Chinese

---

[1] *The Anchor Bible Dictionary*, Jesus Christ, volume 3, page 777

provided their own military protection for merchant caravans that traveled on the Silk Road. This road crossed central Asia westward into Roman-held territories.

Roman technology and innovation increased food production with less manpower. This was accomplished primarily through the increased use of animals, especially the horse, new and improved farm tools and implements as well as the consolidation of farms. Typically, upwards of 50% of the work-force was employed in agriculture. Thus, any substantial change in that part of the economy had a dramatic impact on the entire society.

The horse had become a very useful animal in much of the world. The horse was used for several purposes – to pull trailers and other agricultural implements, to herd cattle and sheep, to ride as transportation and to haul merchandise to market. Because the horse could also be used effectively in combat, especially against foot soldiers, the Romans confiscated all Jewish-owned horses in Judea during times of extreme political tension. The Jews were then forced to utilize the slower animals – the oxen and donkey – or increase the number of employees, which again added to their expenses.

Some areas of Judea had excellent climate and soil for the production of olives. This made olive orchards very valuable since there was a high demand for olives and olive oil throughout the Roman world. As a result, some property and business owners became very wealthy, while at the same time many more people became unemployed and destitute.

The Sadducees were the primary landholders in Judea and were generally the wealthier Jews. This gave them considerable financial influence, especially in Jerusalem. However, the balance of political power among the Jewish people, especially within the city of Jerusalem, shifted during the holy days because most of the pilgrims were Pharisees from neighboring countries. This increase in the number of Conservative Jews in Jerusalem also increased tensions, even within the Temple itself.

The holy days became a time of increased tension and conflict – the Orthodox against the Conservatives, the poor against the rich, the countryside against the urban and the non-Jews against the Jews. But, more than anything else, it was the Jews against the Herods and the Romans.

With the balance of power continually in flux, the number and frequency of riots in Jerusalem progressively increased. Uprisings, primarily against the Herods and the Romans, became such a problem during the major holy days that the Roman military commanders were forced to assign a full legion of soldiers to the city of Jerusalem to control the crowds: "The legion = about 6120 men [including officers]. If the *alae* [squadrons of cavalry] are reckoned at 500 men each, the total is 55,720; if at 1000 men, it amounts to 58,720".[1] Plus the servants: "Thus the total strength of the forces, horse and foot, including the contingents of the kings, amounted to sixty thousand, without counting the servants who followed in vast numbers".[2]

---

[1] *Josephus, The Jewish War Volume III, Book III,* Thackeray, page 25
[2] *Josephus, The Jewish War Volume III, Book III,* Thackeray, page 25

Many of the Roman soldiers lived in the homes of local residents, with or without the consent of the owners. The Romans posted guards at various locations within the city of Jerusalem and on the walls that encompassed the Temple grounds to watch for anyone causing a disturbance. During the years of Jesus' ministry, there was at least one Roman legion assigned to Jerusalem and another legion dispersed throughout the remainder of the country with additional troops available in Syria if and when they were needed.

The Romans and Herods quickly put down any sign of a riot to avoid an escalation that might develop into a costly war. Anyone who disturbed the peace was immediately arrested and harshly dealt with.

The Roman military often took pre-emptive measures to avoid riots and uprisings. Caesar and the other Roman rulers had no plans to leave Judea and had little or no concern for any clash of cultures. They were not about to let a few riots or insurrections in this relatively small country change that.

The Roman commander Crassus and his troops put down a major gladiator/slave revolt in 71 B.C.E. during the Third Servile War. This revolt took place on the Appian Way (road) near Capua, Italy and was led by the famous gladiator Spartacus. Spartacus was killed during the last minutes of the battle after his fleeing comrades left his side.

During this revolt, the Romans crucified 6,000 of the slaves and gladiators who were building this road that crossed Italy from Rome southeast toward Brindisi (a city on the west shoreline of the Adriatic Sea).

The crosses on which the slaves were crucified lined the roadside for more than a hundred miles. The Romans routinely captured and executed rebellious leaders and teachers from among all the various groups of Jews and non-Jews and quite often their followers and families as well. It was usually suicidal to claim any knowledge or relationship to any person sentenced to crucifixion, before or after his death. This would explain why the apostle Peter denied even knowing Jesus while Jesus was in Roman custody on 'Good Friday'.

The Romans often executed entire families and anyone else remotely associated with any rebel as well as individuals who were overly outspoken against Roman occupation. Crucifixion was the typical Roman and Herod punishment for those even suspected of revolutionary or subversive behavior, especially the people of low social status.

The Romans had little tolerance for resistance or civil unrest. Even prior to the First Jewish War, which began in 66 C.E., the Romans put thousands to the sword and the cross. Crucifixions were common, especially during the holy days when large crowds gathered and became riotous. The Romans were quick with their punishment of anyone or any group who instigated a disturbance or took a stand against them.

Those who were sentenced to crucifixion were stripped naked before being hung on a tree or a cross. They generally died a slow and painful death. Sometimes, if the condemned did not die before sundown, a soldier would finish killing the individual with his sword or spear. The Roman commanders sometimes demanded that a corpse be left hanging on the tree or cross until the scavengers (dogs, cats, birds, insects and worms) ate the flesh from the bones, leaving what was left of the corpse to fall to the ground. What remained of the corpse was often buried where it fell, in a shallow grave. Sometimes corpses were sprinkled with lime to discourage dogs from digging up the remains and to accelerate decomposition.

The Romans perceived death differently than the Jewish people. The Romans generally believed a person's physical life ended when the heart stopped beating and the person stopped breathing.

The Jewish people had a very different perception of death which for them added to the sanctity of a person's grave. They believed a person's spirit remained in the corpse until all of the flesh, which contained sacred blood, had decomposed and only the bones remained. Then, the tomb would be opened and the bones collected and placed in an urn or other small container and buried in a cemetery designated for the permanent burial of these remains. In this way, the first (large) tomb could be used again and again.

The Jews believed that a person's spirit left the body as soon as all of that person's blood left the body, even if it was immediately after the injury occurred.

It is not surprising that many of the Jewish people became very angry with Pilate when he confiscated money from the Temple treasury and used it to build an aqueduct through a cemetery into the city of Jerusalem: "After reporting the incident associated with the military standards, Josephus, in both of his works, goes on to report that Pilate used Jewish sacred funds to construct an aqueduct and that he encountered Jewish opposition which his troops put down bloodily".[1] "... it may be that the issue was not so much the use of sacred funds as a lack of concern for the water's ritual purity".[2] The Jews were angry with Pilate primarily because the water passed through this aqueduct on ground that contained 'sacred blood'.

The Roman presence in Judea served Rome in several ways. This was a strategic military outpost to protect trade routes to and from Egypt to the south, Syria and Parthia to the north, as well as Babylon, Persia, India and China to the east. It was also recruiting ground for additional soldiers.

Their recruits came from any and all territories under Roman control. During that era, the Roman soldiers were the best trained, armed and fed army in the world, usually at the expense of the conquered countries.

Some of the slaves of the Jewish landholders enlisted in the Roman army. This forced the landholders to purchase replacement slaves or hire others. Again, this often created additional financial hardship.

Some soldiers continued on after their term of enlistment, making the military their career. Slaves who served the prescribed four year term satisfactorily were discharged as free men. Some soldiers, upon finishing their term of enlistment, decided to become gladiators. This was a well paid and glorified occupation, though it included a much shorter life expectancy.

---

[1] *The Anchor Bible Dictionary*, Pontius Pilate, volume 5, page 399
[2] *The Anchor Bible Dictionary*, Pontius Pilate, volume 5, page 399

Many countries outside of Rome, including Judea, relied primarily on a militia for national defense. As a result, many of the non-Jews and slaves were regularly caught up in the violence and suffered the same fate as their employers, owners and recruiters. These militia men usually received minimal training and usually had inferior weapons. Typically, during a time of war, enlistment into the local militia was mandatory. However, it was not uncommon for the wealthy to pay others to take their place.

The Greeks and the Romans brought many changes to Judea. Some of these changes caused friction between themselves and the Jews. The Romans and Herods had taken away the Jewish people's political and financial independence.

In spite of Jewish pleading, the Romans brought their military and political banners and memorabilia into Jerusalem. They violated the sacredness of the Temple with their trespass. They stole money and other valuables from the Temple treasury. Even more blasphemous was their practice of offering pigs as sacrifice to their gods.

Pigs and cattle have cloven hooves. Cattle chew a cud. However, pigs do not chew a cud. Because of this (also probably because they are meat-eaters) pigs were considered 'unclean' and were generally not included in the Jewish diet and never as Temple sacrifice: "Normally, a Jew is permitted to eat pig if his life is at stake, but in a time of persecution – when an attempt is being made to destroy Judaism – every

Jew is commanded to sacrifice his life for even the most minor commandment".[1]

Many of the Jews disagreed among themselves on very basic Jewish teachings and cultural issues. However, the lack of central authority within the Jewish community prevented them from coming to a consensus on the interpretation and enforcement of many Jewish laws. This added to the ever-increasing tension throughout the country. The differences in interpretation of Scriptures, the degree of importance placed on sex and marriage laws, Temple admittance laws, high taxes, a disproportionate distribution of wealth, high unemployment, Roman occupation and Roman taxes were all critical issues in a collective social anger.

These issues were at the root of the nearly constant civil unrest that often led to riots and open warfare against the Romans and the Herods. For many, these issues were worth fighting to the death for, which many of them did.

The people of Judea lost their political independence when the Romans took control of the country. They also lacked a unified leadership, which made their situation more difficult. They had become a fractured society, a country in turmoil.

Judas the Galilean was an Orthodox Jew from Gaulonitis, today's Golan area. He was generally regarded by other Jews of his time as a person of high moral values. Judas led a rebellion against Roman occupation in 6 C.E. and thus became one of the first leaders of the Messianic Movement. Many Jewish people of this era believed that a

---

[1] *Jewish Literacy*, Rabbi Joseph Telushkin, page 116

messiah, a savior, would come forward, someone who would lead their countrymen in a war that would force all foreign power out of Judea.

Many of the Zealots were members of the Messianic Sadducee sect. Some of these Zealots were very radical in their beliefs and actions. The most radical of these men were referred to as <u>sicarii</u>. These men were responsible for the assassination of many Romans and liberal Jews.

Sicarii referred to the shape of the dagger these revolutionaries carried hidden under their clothing: "But while the country was thus cleared of these pests, a new species of banditti was springing up in Jerusalem, the so-called *sicarii*, who committed murders in broad daylight in the heart of the city. The festivals were their special seasons, when they would mingle with the crowd, carrying short daggers concealed under their clothing, with which they stabbed their enemies. Then, when they fell, the murderers joined in the cries of indignation and, through this plausible behaviour [behavior], were never discovered".[1] The sicarii might well have been described, using today's terminology, either as freedom fighters or terrorists, depending on one's political or religious persuasion.

The Greek (Hellenistic) and Roman influence in Judea added to the political and religious division among the Jewish people. During the decades preceding the First Jewish War the Jews realized that the Roman presence in Judea was not about to go away. Some of them decided that concessions would be necessary in order to co-exist. However, the majority of the Jewish population remained loyal to their faith and always opposed Roman domination and non-Jewish cultural influence.

---

[1] *Josephus, The Jewish War, Volume II, Book II*, Thackeray, page 423

Part Three

The life and death of Jesus

(4 B.C.E. to 33 C.E.)

Chapter 16

Matthew's nativity story speaks of terror, murder and flight

There is a considerable amount of information that has been recently excavated at Qumran (a village on the western shore of the Dead Sea) that was written by members of the Dead Sea Sect. The members of this religious sect were probably the most reclusive group of Jewish people in Judea during that era. Even though they chose to have minimal interaction with other Jews, it is evident by their writings that they were well aware of the political and religious turmoil in Judea. However, these writings do not speak of Jesus.

There is information about many of the influential Jews and Romans of that era which can be found in the writings of Flavius Josephus, Johanan ben Zacchai, Hillel, Gamaliel and other notable authors of that time. Except for the stories in the New Testament, there is very little information about Jesus in any historical document that was written during Jesus' lifetime or within the first few decades following his death.

The New Testament contains a wealth of information on the life of Jesus. However, these writings do not identify the year – much less the month or day of the month – that Jesus was born.

The gospels contain two nativity stories. A time-line drawn from the gospels and events recorded in Roman and Jewish history indicates that Jesus was born sometime between 4 B.C.E. and 7 C.E.

Neither of these nativity stories was written to record historical events. They were written to teach the writer's religious beliefs and to prophesy future events in Jesus' life. However, at least a few of the 'prophesies' in the nativity stories were written in retrospect. It appears that the general consensus among Jewish scholars is that the meaning of the word 'prophesy' was not the prediction of a future event, but rather a warning of consequences if people did not change their course of actions.

The nativity stories were among the last of the writings included in the gospels of *Matthew* and *Luke*. They were written approximately 100 years after the birth of Jesus and were written in a Jewish literary style to give a theological background to Jesus and his ministry. The *Matthew* nativity writer used a series of parallels and reverse-parallels to portray Jesus as the fulfillment of at least some of God's promises spoken of in Scriptures.

The writer did not have any firsthand knowledge of the circumstances of Jesus' birth nor of his early life, much less the very personal aspects of Mary or Joseph's sexual intimacies or any lack thereof. The nativity stories were written, at least in part, to show two different aspects of 'a new beginning'. They were not written to give the personal history of just this one family.

These two nativity stories were never meant to be taken literally. As with the Creation, Flood, *Exodus* and *Joshua* stories, they were written within a Hebrew mythical form of expression, not today's Western rationalism. Not surprisingly, they have irreconcilable differences.

Each story presents its readers with references to Hebrew patriarchs and biblical events and ties them to a political or religious situation in Judean history. Within these stories, the writer drew parallels between Esther, Moses, David and others of the Old Testament with Herod, the 'Three Wise Men' and others of the New Testament as a way of bringing Jesus, Mary and Joseph into the center of Jewish culture and ancient prophecies.

The gospel of *Matthew* has Joseph as the central figure and begins with Joseph's genealogy. It identifies Joseph as a direct descendant of Judah and King David: "... a virgin engaged to a man whose name was Joseph, of the house of David" (Luke 1.27).[1] The *Matthew* listing of Joseph's Hebrew/Jewish ancestors is irrelevant since the gospels state several times that Joseph was not the biological father of Jesus. There is no reason to doubt that Joseph was a Jew, though not necessarily 'of the House of David'. At the time of Jesus' birth the Davidic line of documented genealogy was, at best, very questionable.

Mary may have had direct Jewish ancestry. However, this is doubtful since nowhere in the New Testament is there any mention of Mary's parents or grandparents. The gospel of *Luke* indirectly suggests that Mary was a descendant of Levi: "And now, your relative Elizabeth in her old age has also conceived a son" (Luke 1.36).[2] And: "In the days of King Herod of Judea, there was a priest named Zechariah, who

---

[1] *The Jewish Annotated New Testament*, Levine and Brettler, page 99
[2] *The Jewish Annotated New Testament*, Levine and Brettler, page 99

belonged to the priestly order of Abijah. His wife was a descendant of Aaron, and her name was Elizabeth" (Luke 1.5).[1] Jewish officials would not have recognized this as legal documentation of Mary's Jewish genealogy. To this day, they still do not. The accuracy of the genealogy records of the tribe of Levi at the time of Jesus' birth is very questionable.

The *Matthew* nativity story places Joseph and Mary as residents of Bethlehem at the time of Jesus' birth. Shortly after the birth of Jesus they moved from Bethlehem to Egypt. Then, they moved from Egypt to Nazareth.

According to this story, the 'Three Kings of the Orient' came to see Jesus soon after his birth: "In the time of King Herod, after Jesus was born in Bethlehem of Judea, wise men from the East came to Jerusalem, asking, *Where is the child who has been born king of the Jews?*" (Matthew 2.1-2).[2]

After this meeting with Herod in Jerusalem, the 'Three Wise Men' continued to look for Jesus: "Then he sent them to Bethlehem, saying, *Go and search diligently for the child; and when you have found him, bring me word so that I may also go and pay him homage*" (Matthew 2.8).[3] They found the new-born Jesus in a house: "On entering the house, they saw the child with Mary his mother" (Matthew 2.11).[4]

---

[1] *The Jewish Annotated New Testament*, Levine and Brettler, page 97
[2] *The Jewish Annotated New Testament*, Levine and Brettler, page 5
[3] *The Jewish Annotated New Testament*, Levine and Brettler, page 5
[4] *The Jewish Annotated New Testament*, Levine and Brettler, page 5

Then, the angel warned Joseph: "Now after they had left, an angel of the Lord appeared to Joseph in a dream and said, *Get up, take the child and his mother, and flee to Egypt*" (Matthew 2.13).[1] "Then Joseph got up, took the child and his mother by night, and went to Egypt, and remained there until the death of Herod" (Matthew 2.14-15).[2]

Later, the gospel does not say how much later, the angel instructed Joseph to return to Israel: "Get up, take the child and his mother, and go to the land of Israel for those who were seeking the child's life are dead" (Matthew 2.20).[3] "But when he heard that Archelaus was ruling over Judea in place of his father Herod, he was afraid to go there. And after being warned in a dream, he went away to the district of Galilee. There he made his home in a town called Nazareth" (Matthew 2.22-23).[4]

This portion of the nativity story draws a parallel with the story of the *Exodus*. According to Jewish teachings however, the salvation of the Israelites was fulfilled through *Exodus* when they left Egypt and entered the Promised Land.

The nativity story also includes, with the story of Esther, a reverse-parallel. Esther lived in Mesopotamia a few decades after many of the Jews had returned to Judea in the fourth century B.C.E. Xerxes was the king of Mesopotamia at that time.

According to the story in the Old Testament, the book of *Esther*, Xerxes organized a very lavish party for officials from the neighboring

---

[1] *The Jewish Annotated New Testament*, Levine and Brettler, page 5
[2] *The Jewish Annotated New Testament*, Levine and Brettler, page 5
[3] *The Jewish Annotated New Testament*, Levine and Brettler, page 6
[4] *The Jewish Annotated New Testament*, Levine and Brettler, page 6

countries. His wife did the same for the women who would be coming to the party.

During the celebration, the king sent for his wife. He wanted her to join him. For whatever reason, she chose not to join him. He was offended and decided to replace her with a new wife. His servants selected several beautiful young women for him to choose from. He selected Esther, not realizing that she was a Jew.

Earlier, Xerxes had appointed Esther's step-father Mordecai to an administrative position within his royal palace. At some point, after Xerxes had selected Esther to be his wife, Mordecai refused to bow to the king, stating that he was a Jew and would bow only to God. Following this offence, the king's prime minster convinced the king to issue an order to have all Jews in all of the Middle Eastern countries killed because of this blatant disrespect by a prominent Jew.

When the king realized that his new wife was Mordecai's step-daughter he regretted issuing the order. However, he said that he could not rescind that order. So, he issued a new order stating that all Jews were authorized to kill anyone who attempted to kill any Jew. As a result, no Jews were killed.

King Xerxes found out that his prime minister had earlier plotted to kill him. For this, the king had the prime minister and his co-conspirators executed.

The 'Three Wise Men' came to Herod in their search for 'a new king'. The 'stars' had led them to Jerusalem. Herod believed that his family's position of power was threatened by this 'new king'. In an effort to eliminate this threat, Herod ordered that all of the children in

Bethlehem two years old and younger <u>were to be killed</u>. Conversely, Xerxes had issued an order <u>that saved the lives</u> of the Jews in the Middle Eastern countries, including the young children in Bethlehem, hence the reverse-parallel, <u>written within a Jewish literary style.</u>

Following is another quote that is quite often taken out of context in the gospel of *Matthew*: "And you, Bethlehem, in the land of Judah, are by no means least among the rulers of Judah; for from you shall come a ruler who is to shepherd my people Israel" (Matthew 2.6).[1] That prophecy was fulfilled many centuries earlier through King David. David was born in Bethlehem and went on, in spite of committing adultery and murder, to become one of the most famous kings of the Israelite nation.

According to the Jewish interpretation of Scriptures, God's promises were made to the Chosen People, the descendants of Abraham and Isaac. For many centuries Temple access, marriage regulations, property rights and religious obligations were defined by a person's genealogy.

The Sadducees placed a high degree of importance on a person's Jewish ancestry. They maintained that for a child to be legally recognized as a Jew the mother had to have documented Jewish parentage.

However, several decades before the birth of Jesus, the Sadducees had lost much of their control in the Jewish hierarchy and were forced to make compromises with the Pharisees.

The Pharisees placed much less importance on genealogy. As one of the compromises, the Sadducees reluctantly accepted converts into

---

[1] *The Jewish Annotated New Testament*, Levine and Brettler, page 5

Judaism and the children of converts. They also accepted those who may have had Jewish ancestry even though they had no official documentation to support it, as long as they embraced all aspects of the Jewish faith.

According to the gospels, Jesus was born and raised in a Jewish home and would have become familiar with much of Scriptures since everyone living in a Jewish home was required to live according to basic Jewish law.

The gospel of *Matthew* states that Joseph was not married to Mary when she became pregnant: "Now the birth of Jesus the Messiah took place in this way. When his mother Mary had been engaged to Joseph, but before they lived together, she was found to be with child" (Matthew 1.18).[1] "When Joseph awoke from sleep, he did as the angel of the Lord commanded him; he took her as his wife, but had no marital relations with her until she had borne a son, and he named him Jesus" (Matthew 1.24-25).[2]

According to Catholic interpretation of the New Testament, Jesus was not conceived by way of a traditional husband and wife sexual relationship. It is very doubtful that they were ever husband and wife or that Joseph was the biological father of Jesus.

The Catholic Church also teaches that Joseph and Mary never had a sexual relationship with each other or anyone else. However, according to Jewish law, as with the laws in probably all cultures during that era, and as is generally the case even today, a couple was/is not legally

---

[1] *The Jewish Annotated New Testament*, Levine and Brettler, page 4
[2] *The Jewish Annotated New Testament*, Levine and Brettler, page 5

married until they have consummated their commitment to marriage with sexual intercourse.

The Jews interpreted the *Genesis* command 'increase and multiply' to apply to all Jewish men. Thus, the first command in Scripture required Joseph to marry and produce at least one biological child of his own. This contradiction complicates Catholic doctrine: "Her husband Joseph, being a righteous man and unwilling to expose her to public disgrace, planned to dismiss her quietly" (Matthew 1.19).[1]

According to Jewish tradition, sexual relations between a husband and wife were/are not only sacred, but expected on a regular basis. Within traditional Jewish culture, virginity has never been viewed as a positive choice. Close study of women in the Bible, and Mary in particular, exposes as flawed and ill-founded the severe constraints that have been placed on women due to centuries of misreading the New Testament stories about Mary and Joseph.

---

[1] *The Jewish Annotated New Testament*, Levine and Brettler, page 4

Chapter 17

Luke's nativity story speaks of a manger, shepherds and the Temple

The writer of the *Luke* nativity story, who was very likely also the author of the *Matthew* nativity story, wrote about the 'virgin' Mary's unexpected pregnancy: "Mary said to the angel, *How can this be, since I am a virgin?*" (Luke 1.34).[1]

The *Luke* nativity story is written with Mary as the central figure. It places Joseph and Mary as residents of Nazareth at the time of Jesus' birth. It states that Joseph and Mary lived in Nazareth and traveled to Bethlehem where Jesus was born in a stable, not in a house: "Joseph also went from the town of Nazareth in Galilee to Judea, to the city of Nazareth in Galilee to Judea, to the city of David called Bethlehem, because he was descended from the house and family of David. He went to be registered with Mary, to whom he was engaged and who was expecting a child. While they were there, the time came for her to deliver her child" (Luke 2.4-6).[2] The shepherds, not the 'Three Wise Men', went to see Jesus: "So they went with haste and found Mary and Joseph, and

---

[1] *The Jewish Annotated New Testament*, Levine and Brettler, page 99
[2] *The Jewish Annotated New Testament*, Levine and Brettler, page 101

the child lying in the manger" (Luke 2.16).[1] The 'shepherds' is very likely making reference to King David who was a shepherd in his youth.

After their visit to the Temple in Jerusalem, they returned to Joseph's home in Nazareth: "When they had finished everything required by the law of the Lord, they returned to Galilee, to their own town of Nazareth" (Luke 2.39).[2] If read literally, this story contradicts nearly the entire *Matthew* nativity story.

Mary would not have been allowed in the Temple within the first few weeks after the birth of Jesus, as Catholic tradition teaches: "A woman who becomes pregnant and gives birth to a son will be ceremonially unclean for seven days, just as she is unclean during her monthly period. On the eighth day the boy is to be circumcised. Then the woman must wait thirty-three days to be purified from her bleeding. She must not touch anything sacred or go to the sanctuary until the days of her purification are over" (Leviticus 12.2-4).[3]

Caesar Augustus replaced the Jewish ethnarch Archelaus with Quirinius in 6 C.E. Quirinius was the Roman governor of northern Judea and Syria for less than two years. The gospel of *Luke* places the birth of Jesus during this census that was ordered by Quirinius.

The stories of Noah and Moses portray a 'new beginning' and salvation through these patriarchs. Early Christians chose the same theme when they selected the day of the year to celebrate the birth of Jesus. They selected winter solstice, December 25th, the beginning of a new

---

[1] *The Jewish Annotated New Testament*, Levine and Brettler, page 102
[2] *The Jewish Annotated New Testament*, Levine and Brettler, page 103
[3] Bible, *New International Version*, page 183

year. However, astronomers have more accurately calculated winter solstice to be on December 21st.

This gospel states that Joseph was required to 'register' in Bethlehem: "In those days a decree went out from Emperor Augustus that all the world should be registered. This was the first registration and was taken while Quirinius was governor of Syria. All went to their own towns to be registered. Joseph also went from the town of Nazareth in Galilee to Judea, to the city of David called Bethlehem, because he was descended from the house and family of David"(Luke 2.1-4).[1]

Joseph and Mary did not go to Bethlehem to 'register'. Joseph would have been extremely uncaring if he had taken his nearly nine-month pregnant 'betrothed' on a journey that would have taken approximately three days, walking or riding on a donkey. Such a journey would have exposed Mary to unnecessary hardships, including possible childbirth on the roadside, and both of them to the risk of becoming victims of road bandits, which was a common problem of the day.

Quirinius had been one of the most powerful men in Rome and would have been well aware of the friction between the Herods and much of the Jewish population. He therefore did not rely on the accuracy of the tax information recorded by Archelaus. Archelaus was a member of the Herod family. Quirinius ordered his own census of northern Judea, which included the small town of Nazareth.

The census takers traveled to the homes and businesses of the residents to inventory their property to establish a basis for each person's taxes. Slaves were always counted as property. Neither of the nativity

---

[1] *The Jewish Annotated New Testament*, Levine and Brettler, page 101

stories is clear as to which social class Mary would have been included in. Family members may have been counted, but they would not have had a bearing on the listing of taxable property or business assets. The Roman authorities would have had little reason to learn the tribal identity of any of the Jewish people. However, they would certainly have made themselves aware of the political and business affiliations of influential people.

There is additional information about the census in *The Anchor Bible Dictionary*: "These are:

1. There is no evidence for an empire-wide census in the reign of Augustus.

2. In a Roman census Joseph would not have been required to travel to Bethlehem, and he would not have been required to bring Mary with him.

3. A Roman census could not have been carried out in Herod's kingdom while Herod was alive. [Herod was the Roman-appointed governor of southern Judea which included the cities of Bethlehem and Jerusalem].

4. Josephus refers to the census of Quirinius in A.D. 6/7 [6 C.E.-7 C.E.] as something that was without precedent in the region".[1]

Many marriages during this era were arranged by the parents to make sure the two people were both within the same social class. Moses reinforced Abraham's stipulation that Hebrew men were to marry only women from among Abraham's descendants: "Do not intermarry with them. Do not give your daughters to their sons or take their daughters for

---

[1] *The Anchor Bible Dictionary*, Quirinius, volume 5, page 588

your sons" (Deuteronomy 7.3).[1] However, the gospels do not identify Joseph or Mary's social class.

A documented Jew was supposed to marry another documented Jew and a commoner was to marry only a commoner or a person of mixed Jewish blood. The joining of slaves was generally not recognized as marriage: "... a slave is incapable of marriage".[2]

The gospel of *Luke* states that Joseph was incorrectly assumed to be the father of Jesus: "Jesus was about thirty years old when he began his work. He was the son (as was thought) of Joseph son of Heli" (Luke 3.23).[3] However, this reference to the genealogy of Joseph is not relevant to Jesus genealogy since Joseph clearly was not the father of Jesus.

The New Testament speaks of the brothers and sisters of Jesus. According to the gospels, Mary's male children included James (Justus), Simon (Simeon/Peter), Jesus (Joshua), Joseph and Judas (Judah/Theadus). Mary's female children included Salome and at least two others that the gospels do not identify by name.

These are a few of the quotations identifying Jesus' brothers and sisters:

"Is not this the carpenter, the son of Mary and brother of James and Joses (Jose/Joseph) and Judas and Simon, and are not his sisters here with us?" (Mark 6.3).[4]

---

[1] Bible, *New International Version*, page 306
[2] *Marriage Laws in the Bible and the Talmud*, Epstein, page 64
[3] *The Jewish Annotated New Testament*, Levine and Brettler, page 105
[4] *The Jewish Annotated New Testament*, Levine and Brettler, page 71

"Is not his mother called Mary? And are not his brothers James and Joseph and Simon and Judas? And are not all his sisters with us?" (Matthew 13.55-56).[1]

"A crowd was sitting around him; and they said to him, *Your mother and your brothers and sisters are outside, asking for you*" (Mark 3.32).[2]

"While he was still speaking to the crowds, his mother and his brothers were standing outside, wanting to speak to him" (Matthew 12.46).[3]

"And he was told, *Your mother and your brothers are standing outside, wanting to see you*" (Luke 8.20).[4]

"There were also women looking on from a distance; among them were Mary Magdalene, and Mary the mother of James the younger and of Joses (Jose/Joseph), and Salome" (Mark 15.40).[5]

"After this he went down to Capernaum with his mother, his brothers, and his disciples" (John 2.12).[6]

"But after his brothers had gone to the festival, then he also went, not publicly but as it were in secret" (John 7.10).[7]

"All these were constantly devoting themselves to prayer, together with certain women, including Mary the mother of Jesus, as well as his brothers" (Acts 1.14).[1]

---

[1] *The Jewish Annotated New Testament*, Levine and Brettler, page 27
[2] *The Jewish Annotated New Testament*, Levine and Brettler, page 67
[3] *The Jewish Annotated New Testament*, Levine and Brettler, page 24
[4] *The Jewish Annotated New Testament*, Levine and Brettler, page 117
[5] *The Jewish Annotated New Testament*, Levine and Brettler, page 94
[6] *The Jewish Annotated New Testament*, Levine and Brettler, page 161
[7] *The Jewish Annotated New Testament*, Levine and Brettler, page 172

"Do we not have the right to be accompanied by a believing wife, as do the other apostles and the brothers of the Lord and Cephas [the 'rock']?" (1 Corinthians 9.5).[2]

"I [Paul] did not see any other apostle except James the Lord's brother" (Galatians 1.19).[3]

During this period in Jewish history there was considerable emphasis placed on monogamous marriages. Traditionally, Jewish laws and customs did not recognize any union between a Jewish man and a slave-woman as marriage: "C. H. 128 [the Code of Hammurabi]. By this law we understand that it is possible for an illegitimate wife to have a contract, but it is impossible for a legitimate wife to have no contract. If there is no contract, therefore, the marriage is of inferior order. It also stands to reason that no contract is possible for a freed captive or slave, except an instrument of liberation and elevation; but not a marriage contract".[4]

The New Testament has many references to slaves and slavery: "The community was classified by Ezra in three groups, those of pure blood, those of doubtful blood, and those of definitely foreign descent. The children of mixed marriages could not marry within the first class, and probably could not marry with those of the second class".[5] It is more likely that Mary was Joseph's servant/slave/handmaid and that Mary and

---

[1] *The Jewish Annotated New Testament*, Levine and Brettler, page 200
[2] *The Jewish Annotated New Testament*, Levine and Brettler, page 301
[3] *The Jewish Annotated New Testament*, Levine and Brettler, page 335
[4] *Marriage Laws in the Bible and the Talmud*, Epstein, footnote, page 41
[5] *Marriage Laws in the Bible and the Talmud*, Epstein, page 185

Jesus were both slaves at birth. Slavery was acceptable in the Middle East and Europe during this era and for many centuries after the birth of Jesus.

Joseph would not have had a sexual relationship with any servant/slave before or while he was married to another woman. During this era, sexual relations between a Jewish person and a non-Jewish slave were considered by many to be the equivalent of prostitution and an insult to Jewish heritage. Some Orthodox Jews believed they had the right to put such a person to death, without a trial.

Jewish parents could present their child to the Temple priest for a blessing: "Guided by the Spirit, Simeon came into the temple; and when the parents brought in the child Jesus, to do for him what was customary under the law, Simeon took him in his arms and praised God" (Luke 2.27-28).[1] The *parents* in this story refer to Joseph and Mary.

However, Joseph would have been lying to the priest if he stated, or even implied, that he was the father of Jesus since he clearly was not the biological parent of Jesus. This would have been a very serious offense against the law, which again, goes against the traditional view that 'Joseph was a man who always did what was right'.

This nativity story is a cultural adaptation by the writer who certainly was not an Orthodox Jew since the story does not fit the Jewish laws or customs at the time of Jesus' birth. Also, it is very likely that at least some changes were made to the nativity stories by the Christian Church authorities several decades or even centuries later **to create new theological teachings**. The identity of the biological father of Jesus and

[1] *The Jewish Annotated New Testament*, Levine and Brettler, page 102

any brothers or sisters Jesus may have had will probably always be a subject of debate and contention among Christians and non-Christians.

Centuries earlier, the Greek language had become a commonly used language for many of the Jewish people. To meet this change, the Jewish leadership had the majority of the Hebrew Scriptures – the Old Testament – translated from Hebrew into Greek in Alexandria, Egypt circa (approximately) 250 B.C.E. This Greek version of Scriptures became known as the Septuagint (Greek for the number seventy). Seventy Jewish priests, all fluent in the Hebrew and Greek languages, completed the first portion of the translation.

These writers had to make many compromises in the wordage in the Bible stories because of the differences between the Hebrew and Greek languages. Some Greek words took on new meaning when they were used within the context of the Bible stories. Even then, the scribes were forced to coin at least a few new Greek words in an effort to express the meanings of the Hebrew words and phrases within the biblical stories.

However, one of the words that did not translate well was the Hebrew word *amah* (amah / ha'almah / almah). The scribes translated *amah* to the Greek word *parthenos*.

Over the course of the following 100 years there were other sacred Hebrew/Jewish writings that were translated into Greek. The Jewish court in Jerusalem considered these later writings sacred. However, they did not allow some, or possibly any, of these later books to be included within their canonized (formally approved) Scriptures.

Amah is a Hebrew word meaning a young slave-woman or slave-wife: "When Sarah insists that Ishmael shall not inherit because he is the son of an *amah*, Gen. 21.10, or when Jotham speaks in the same manner of Abimelech, Judg. 9,18, one gets the impression that it was taken for granted that the *ben-ha'amah* [son of an amah] does not inherit. But, of course, amah here may mean the unmarried slave girl, not the slave-wife".[1] In either case, amah referred to a female slave. Hagar was Sarah's slave-woman and Abraham's concubine.

Early Christian biblical writers translated the Greek word *parthenos* as *a virgin*. This discrepancy in the translation was a major reason the Jewish people eventually discontinued the use of the Septuagint: "The use of the Septuagint among Christians, and their basing their claims and theological doctrines on it, sometimes on passages where the Septuagint is markedly different from the Hebrew, led the Rabbis to a virtual disowning of the Septuagint".[2] "The best known instance is Isa. 7.14. The Septuagint reads *virgin* and the verse is cited in Mt. 1.23 to prove the virgin birth of Jesus. The Hebrew word is '*alma*, which ordinarily means 'young woman'".[3]

The Jewish Bible *Complete Jewish Bible/New International Version* also explains the meaning of amah/almah/ha'amah: "The Hebrew word '*almah* in Isaiah 7.14 means 'a young woman'".[4] However, a more accurate translation is 'unmarried slave-girl' as can be seen in the story of Abraham having sex with Hagar, Sarah's female slave.

---

[1] *Marriage Laws in the Bible and the Talmud*, Epstein, page 61
[2] *Judaism and Christian Beginnings*, Samuel Sandmel, page 261
[3] *Judaism and Christian Beginnings*, Samuel Sandmel, page 462
[4] *Complete Jewish Bible*, page xxxiv, footnote 69

At least a couple of older Catholic Bibles translate the Hebrew word *amah* in the book of *Isaiah* (Isaiah 7.14) as a *young woman*. The Hebrew translation of *amah* is a young slave-woman or slave-wife: "the [amah] young [slave] woman will become pregnant" (Isaiah 7.14).[1]

It is very doubtful that the author of the nativity story in the gospel of *Matthew* even considered the less-than-accurate interpretation of *parthenos* to mean *a virgin* when he wrote of Mary: "Look, the [amah/parthenos] virgin shall conceive and bear a son, and they shall name him Emmanuel" (Matthew 1.23).[2]

It was not until after 200 C.E. that the Greek word *parthenos* was translated in *Matthew* 1.23 as *a virgin* instead of the correct translation which is *a young slave-woman*. This change allowed the Christian theologians to declare that Mary was a *virgin* even after she became pregnant with Jesus, and that Mary had become pregnant only by the action of God, not through normal sexual intercourse. With this interpretation, they concluded that Jesus was the Son of God from the moment of conception. It was only after this intentional incorrect translation of *parthenos* that Christians began teaching the theology of the virgin birth.

---

[1] Bible, *New International Version*, page 1154
[2] *The Jewish Annotated New Testament*, Levine and Brettler, page 5

Chapter 18

John the Baptist's criticism of Herod
cost him his life

The gospel of *Luke* begins with the story of John's parents and the birth of John: "In the days of King Herod of Judea, there was a priest named Zechariah, who belonged to the priestly order of Abijah. His wife was a descendant of Aaron, and her name was Elizabeth. Both of them were righteous before God, living blamelessly according to all the commandments and regulations of the Lord. But they had no children, because Elizabeth was barren, and both were getting on in years" (Luke 1.5-7).[1]

According to Jewish law at that time, a man who had been married for ten years without having children was allowed to divorce his wife and marry another woman. However, the Jewish community seriously discouraged couples from divorcing.

If a husband divorced his wife because of her 'barrenness' he was allowed to have her continue to live in his home. However, he would not have been allowed to continue a sexual relationship with her. Although, because of her 'barrenness' it would have been difficult for her to find a new husband, especially a man who had never been married or a man who did not already have at least one child from a previous marriage.

----

[1] *The Jewish Annotated New Testament*, Levine and Brettler, page 97

165

The Torah portrays several situations in which a husband could request or demand a divorce from his wife. There were more constraints on the wife if she was the one seeking the divorce. If the wife was the one seeking a divorce, it usually remained the husband's choice whether to allow her to divorce him or not: "While the Bible puts the right of divorce exclusively in the hands of the husband, documents found in the Jewish settlement of Elephantine, Egypt (fifth century BCE) indicate that the wife had the right to divorce her husband. This practice can be attributed to foreign influence. According to the Talmud, 'the altar sheds tears for the man who divorces his first wife' (*San.* 22a) and in the talmudic period, the law of divorce underwent a number of significant changes. Prominent among these was the establishment of a number of circumstances under which the court could compel a husband to grant his wife a divorce. These included: (1) if a wife remained barren after a period of ten years of marriage; (2) if a husband contracted a loathsome disease; (3) if a husband refused to support his wife or was in a position in which he could not support her; (4) if a husband denied his wife her conjugal rights; (5) if a husband continued to beat his wife, despite having been warned by the court to refrain".[1]

According to the nativity story, Zechariah did not 'set her aside' – no longer have a sexual relationship with her and/or divorce her – since Elizabeth did eventually become pregnant. Thus, Zechariah's obligation to have at least one child was fulfilled when his son John was born.

The gospel of *Matthew* begins with the story of John the Baptist as an adult, living in the desert. A few verses into this story, Jesus comes to

---

[1] *The Encyclopedia of Judaism*, page 210

John and is baptized by him. From there, John and Jesus each continue their teaching ministries. As mentioned above, Jesus is Greek for Joshua.

Herod, another grandson of Herod the Great, was the tetrarch of northern Judea during John the Baptist's ministry. As with most, if not all the Herod rulers, the Jews considered him a person of low morals.

John publicly spoke out against him because of his disregard for Jewish marriage and sex laws. He publicly and repeatedly admonished Herod for his ill-gotten riches and because of his marriage to Herodias: "But Herod the ruler, who had been rebuked by him because of Herodias, his [half] brother's wife, and because of the evil things that Herod had done, added to them all by shutting up John in prison" (Luke 3.19-20).[1] "For Herod had arrested John, bound him, and put him in prison on account of Herodias, his brother Philip's wife, because John had been telling him, *It is not lawful for you to have her*. Though Herod wanted to put him to death, he feared the crowd, because they regarded him as a prophet" (Matthew 14.3-5).[2] John also spoke out against Herod for not following the laws that forbade sleeping in the same bed with a woman during her menstrual period: "When a woman has her regular flow of blood, the impurity of her monthly period will last seven days, and anyone who touches her will be unclean till evening" (Leviticus 15.19).[3] John also spoke out against Herod for divorcing more than one wife and for killing whoever displeased him, which included at least two of his wives.

---

[1] *The Jewish Annotated New Testament*, Levine and Brettler, page 105
[2] *The Jewish Annotated New Testament*, Levine and Brettler, page 27
[3] Bible, *New International Version*, page 192

The gospel of *Matthew* portrays Herod (Philip) as having been afraid of John the Baptist: "Though Herod wanted to put him to death, he feared the crowd, because they regarded him as a prophet" (Matthew 14.5).[1]

Herod supposedly deferred to Herodias' and Salome's wishes as an excuse to have John executed: "Herod, that is, Herod Antipas (4 BC – 39 CE), as distinct from his father Herod the 'Great' (Herod *the Terrible* would be more appropriate), feared the influence John had over the Jewish mob, which, according to Josephus, was prepared to do anything John might suggest, a further indication of the *popularity* of these opposition leaders. Herod, consequently, feared that John would lead *an uprising* and decided to have him executed, lest later he would have cause to regret not having done so".[2] "The story of John we are more familiar with is, of course, the more romanticized one: the henpecked Herod deferring at his birthday celebration to the tantalizing dance of Herodias' daughter Salome (she is not named in the Gospels; we need Josephus for this), [asking for] John's head on a plate, Herod being loath [loathe] to execute John – all these the artistic embellishments of literary enhancement or creative writing, not to mention a certain amount of dissimulation".[3]

Baptism was a sacred ritual performed for the forgiveness of sins: "Then Jesus came from Galilee to John [the Baptist] at the Jordan, to be

---

[1] *The Jewish Annotated New Testament*, Levine and Brettler, page 27
[2] *James, the Brother of Jesus*, Robert Eisenman, page 62
[3] *James, the Brother of Jesus*, Robert Eisenman, page 62

baptized by him" (Matthew 3.13).[1] "In those days Jesus came from Nazareth of Galilee and was baptized by John in the Jordan" (Mark 1.9).[2] "Now when all the people were baptized, and when Jesus also had been baptized and was praying, the heaven was opened, and the Holy Spirit descended upon him in bodily form like a dove" (Luke 3.21-22).[3] "And people from the whole Judean countryside and all the people of Jerusalem were going out to him [John] and were baptized by him in the river Jordan, confessing their sins" (Mark 1.5).[4] This probably was not the first or the last time that Jesus was baptized since this was a religious ritual that the Jewish people participated in on a regular basis.

With this story of Jesus' baptism, the gospel writers proclaimed that Jesus was then publicly accepted as a member of the Chosen People: "And just as he was coming up out of the water, he saw the heavens torn apart and the Spirit descending like a dove on him. And a voice came from heaven, *You are my Son, the Beloved*" (Mark 1.10-11).[5] This story, with the dove, water and a 'new beginning', appears to present a parallel with the story of Noah and the Flood.

There is every indication that John the Baptist and Jesus shared the Conservative Jewish values: "His concern was for the 'shape' of his people's life. He [Jesus] did not seek to establish a new religion, but

---

[1] *The Jewish Annotated New Testament*, Levine and Brettler, page 7
[2] *The Jewish Annotated New Testament*, Levine and Brettler, page 58
[3] *The Jewish Annotated New Testament*, Levine and Brettler, page 105
[4] *The Jewish Annotated New Testament*, Levine and Brettler, page 58
[5] *The Jewish Annotated New Testament*, Levine and Brettler, page 58

spoke about and sought the renewal of Judaism".[1] "Jesus' voice is a Jewish voice, and what we shall call the alternative wisdom of Jesus is grounded in Judaism".[2]

John had also preached in southern Babylon where his teachings were accepted by many people. The Sabaeans of that area even today recall memories of John and live by many of the ancient laws that he taught. Some Iraqis continue to call their priests Nasuraiya (Nazoraeans). To be a nazir during the Second Temple Period was to live a conservative lifestyle. This included no consumption of alcohol, keeping one's hair relatively short and not touching any dead body, or at least completing a purification ritual after coming into physical contact with a corpse.

Herodias divorced Philip and married first one uncle then another which, according to Jewish law, was incestuous and illegal. Herodias and her daughter Salome may have been partly responsible for the beheading of John the Baptist, as indicated in the gospel. However, it was typical of the Herods to execute anyone who publicly spoke out against them on any issue. It was John's outspoken criticism of Herod that eventually cost him his life.

There were quite a number of situations in which the law required a person to be baptized – purified, cleansed, have their sins washed away. This ritualistic cleansing was required following the violation of a number of laws including any physical contact with a human corpse, the handling of swine or other 'unclean animal' and sexual purity violations.

---

[1] *The Anchor Bible Dictionary*, Teachings of Jesus, volume 3, page 806
[2] *The Anchor Bible Dictionary*, Teachings of Jesus, volume 3, page 806

A woman was not allowed to enter a synagogue or the Temple, prepare a meal to be shared by others or have sexual relations with her husband during or following menstruation or after childbirth until she washed herself and was baptized (ritually cleansed). This was because she had violated the sanctity of blood, even though it was unintentional and unavoidable.

Each Jewish sect placed varying degrees of importance on the need for ritualistic cleansing. The Essenes placed such great importance on this cleansing that they made bathing a daily requirement for all members.

Chapter 19

The Jewish marriage laws
had an impact on Mary Magdalene

The Talmud consists of 613 laws drawn from the commandments in Scriptures. Rabbi Joseph Telushkin's recently published book *Biblical Literacy* gives an overview of Jewish laws: "The Jewish teaching that the Torah enumerates 613 commandments does not in fact appear anywhere in the Bible. It is recorded in the Talmud: *Rabbi Simlai stated: 613 commandments (mitzvot) were told to Moses; 365 prohibitions corresponding to the number of days in the solar year, and 248 positive commandments corresponding to the number of organs and limbs in the human body* (Babylonian Talmud, *Makkot*, 23b). However, the Talmud never specifies exactly what the 613 *mitzvot* are".[1]

In accordance with ancient Hebrew laws, people were categorized – those with documented Hebrew/Jewish genealogy (including their tribal origin), those who had less than 100% Hebrew/Jewish blood, those who had no Hebrew/Jewish blood (but were citizens of the country), foreigners, slaves and criminals. These laws demanded a segregated society, not unlike many other societies of the time. The laws stated that only those from the tribe of Judah had the right to rule the country and

---

[1] *Biblical Literacy*, Rabbi Joseph Telushkin, page 513

only those from the tribe of Levi had rights and obligations to the priesthood.

Along with many other issues, these laws identified the distinction between individuals within the caste system and the laws that dealt with sex and marriage, such as first-wife and second-wife property rights, converts, slaves, concubinage, prostitution, incest, divorce, children from these various sexual unions and the caste system in general.

The gospels tell of many miracles. The first miracle that the gospel of *John* speaks of is the changing of water into wine at the wedding feast in Cana: "On the third day there was a wedding in Cana of Galilee, and the mother of Jesus was there. Jesus and his disciples had also been invited to the wedding" (John 2.1-2).[1] Cana is a small town approximately nine miles north of Nazareth. There is no mention of who the wedding couple was or what their connection was with Mary or Jesus, or why Joseph was apparently not invited. There certainly had to be much more to this story.

There are several women cited in the New Testament with the name Mary. The confusion between Mary of Bethany and Mary Magdalene may have originated from intentionally incorrect information given to the writer/writers, or information that had come from stories that had changed as they were passed down through many people.

It is almost certain that Mary of Bethany and Mary Magdalene were one and the same person: "Scholars continue to study the relationship between the Johannine narrative of Jesus' anointing by Mary of Bethany

---

[1] *The Jewish Annotated New Testament*, Levine and Brettler, page 161

and the Synoptic stories of the anointing of Jesus' head by an unnamed woman (Matt 26.6-13; Mark 14.3-9) and of the sinful woman forgiven by Jesus (Luke 7.36-50). The latter story was often later used as a link in the confusion between Mary Magdalene and Mary of Bethany, to which some Church Fathers (e.g., Augustine; Gregory the Great) and some gnostic texts (e.g., the *Secret Gospel of Mark*) attest".[1] The Mary that Jesus was most closely associated with, except for his mother, was born a Jew.

"From about the 6th century in the Western Church, but not in the Eastern, traditions developed that tended to identify Mary Magdalene with the sinful woman of Luke 7.36-50, and/or Mary [Magdalene] of Bethany (John 11.1-12:8; Luke 10.38-42)".[2] In ancient times <u>magdal</u> referred to a shepherd's lookout tower, vantage point or outpost.

It was common for the New Testament writers to use analogies and other literary forms that were not intended to be taken as a record of historical events but rather as a way of explaining the author's religious or political convictions: "In the Fourth Gospel, Martha and Mary, along with their brother Lazarus, are said to be loved by Jesus (John 11:5). In the canonical gospels [the gospels in the canonized version of the Bible – the gospels of *Matthew, Mark, Luke* and *John*], they are the only persons so described".[3] "Martha has been inserted into the narrative by the evangelist as a mouthpiece for his own theology".[4]

---

[1] *The Anchor Bible Dictionary*, Mary, volume 4, pages 581-582
[2] *The Anchor Bible Dictionary*, Mary, volume 4, page 580
[3] *The Anchor Bible Dictionary*, Martha, volume 4, page 574
[4] *The Anchor Bible Dictionary*, Martha, volume 4, page 574

Lazarus, a close friend of Jesus, had two sisters, Martha and Mary: "Now while Jesus was at Bethany in the house of Simon the leper, a woman came to him with an alabaster jar of very costly ointment, and she poured it on his head as he sat at the table. But when the disciples saw it, they were angry and said, *Why this waste? For this ointment could have been sold for a large sum, and the money given to the poor*" (Matthew 26.6-9).[1]

In the Jewish culture of that time the pouring of expensive oil by a woman onto a man's head was an expression of romantic affection. More than a hundred years later the writer of the gospel of *John*, or some writer even later, changed the story to meet a new theological agenda: "Mary took a pound of costly perfume made of pure nard, anointed Jesus' feet, and wiped them with her hair" (John 12.3).[2]

The writer of the gospel of *John* probably changed the story from she poured it on Jesus' head to she poured it on Jesus' feet to avoid any acknowledgement of a romantic relationship between Jesus and Mary Magdalene. However: "… in the Jewish world it was scandalous for a woman to let down her hair in the presence of a man who was not her husband".[3] "Of course, perfumes functioned as a cosmetic, providing pleasing fragrances as well as needed protection for the skin in the hot and dry climate of the ANE (Cant 1:3, 5:5). The more costly fragrances made them the rivals of gold (Matt 2:11) for the attention of the wealthy and a remarkable gift. The reaction of the disciples over the use of an

---

[1] *The Jewish Annotated New Testament*, Levine and Brettler, page 48
[2] *The Jewish Annotated New Testament*, Levine and Brettler, page 182
[3] *The Anchor Bible Dictionary*, Mary, volume 4, page 581

alabaster jar of nard [expensive perfume] to anoint Jesus' feet (Mark 14:3-5) is thus quite understandable. It was made even more expensive (300 denarii = worker's pay for half a year) by its costly container and the distance from which it had come (Nepal)".[1]

The gospels portray Mary Magdalene as being very close to Jesus on many occasions: "In the late–3d–century *Gospel of Philip*, Mary is called the companion of the Lord and described as one who always walked with him (*Gos. Phil.* 59, 63). She is portrayed as one whom Christ loved more than the other disciples and as one who was frequently kissed by Christ".[2]

It is very likely that the wedding feast at Cana was the celebration of the wedding of Mary Magdalene and Jesus: "On the third day there was a wedding in Cana of Galilee, and the mother of Jesus was there" (John 2.1).[3] Cana was generally considered 'a city of low morals', possibly because there was less emphasis on segregation in that small community many miles from Jerusalem.

Mary Magdalene and Jesus chose not to conform to the tradition of arranged marriages or submit to any requests or pressure from others for each of them to marry within their own caste. This was a marriage of two people celebrating their love for one another.

According to the gospel of *John*, Jesus preformed a miracle during this wedding feast by turning water into wine: "Jesus said to them, *Fill the jars with water.* And they filled them up to the brim. He said to them,

---

[1] *The Anchor Bible Dictionary*, Perfumes and Spices, volume 5, page 227
[2] *The Anchor Bible Dictionary*, Mary, volume 4, pages 580-581
[3] *The Jewish Annotated New Testament*, Levine and Brettler, page 161

Now draw some out, and take it to the chief steward. So they took it. When the steward tasted the water that had become wine, and did not know where it came from (though the servants who had drawn the water knew), the steward called the bridegroom and said to him, *Everyone serves the good wine first, and then the inferior wine"* (John 2.7-9).[1] Jesus was the bridegroom.

This was another instance of the writer drawing a reverse-parallel to a story in the book of *Isaiah*: "your choice wine is diluted with water" (Isaiah 1.22).[2] In this reverse-parallel Jesus represented the water changed to the good wine in that he was the one who had been a slave, but would now be able to preach Scriptures and go on to offer new hope to a struggling people: "I will restore your leaders as in days of old" (Isaiah 1.26).[3] Christians generally consider this quote to make reference to Jesus only. However, the quote speaks of leaders in the plural.

The Orthodox Jews would have strongly disapproved of the marriage of Mary Magdalene and Jesus. Because of their marriage, some Jewish people would have regarded both Mary Magdalene and Jesus as prostitutes since she was a woman of Jewish birth and Jesus was born a slave. The Conservative Jews (the Pharisees) did not place as great of an importance, or bias against, marriage between a person who was born Jewish and a person who was a convert.

Mary Magdalene was a woman of means who came to share Jesus' convictions. Whether they intended it or not their marriage would have

[1] *The Jewish Annotated New Testament*, Levine and Brettler, page 161
[2] Bible, *New International Version*, page 1144
[3] Bible, *New International Version*, page 1145

been a statement against segregation and racial discrimination – between the slave owners and the slaves, and between those with Jewish genealogy and those without. This marriage would have been welcomed by some and strongly disapproved of by others.

Following their marriage, Mary Magdalene's financial situation then gave Jesus, who was a servant/slave before she purchased his freedom, the opportunity to set aside his servitude and begin his ministry. Together they reached out to the less fortunate and used their now joint finances to travel, provide medical assistance to the infirm, feed the hungry and teach the basic moral principles set forth in Scriptures. Mary Magdalene very likely purchased the freedom of Jesus' mother, brothers and sisters as well, as a gift to Jesus.

Mary Magdalene's home was in Bethany. This was a small town two miles (approximately three kilometers) east of Jerusalem on the Mount of Olives. After their wedding, Jesus and Mary Magdalene lived in Bethany. Jesus went to and from Bethany quite a number times during his ministry. The following quote is but one example: "He left them, went out of the city to Bethany, and spent the night there" (Matthew 21.17).[1]

There is an easy solution to the confusion between Mary Magdalene and Mary of Bethany. Both names referred to the same person. Her name was Mary Magdalene and she lived in Bethany. Just as Jesus was referred to as Jesus of Nazareth, Mary Magdalene was referred to as Mary of Bethany.

---

[1] *The Jewish Annotated New Testament*, Levine and Brettler, page 38

Mary Magdalene's family very likely owned the olive orchard that included the Mount of Olives. There is no documentation for or against this scenario. However, it is made apparent in the synoptic gospels of *Matthew*, *Mark* and *Luke* that Jesus spent a considerable amount of time in Bethany and on the Mount of Olives during his final week of ministry: "Then he entered Jerusalem and went into the temple; and when he had looked around at everything, as it was already late, he went out to Bethany with the twelve" (Mark 11.11-12).[1] "Every day he was teaching in the temple, and at night he would go out and spend the night on the Mount of Olives, as it was called. And all the people would get up early in the morning to listen to him in the temple" (Luke 21.37-38).[2] "After he had said this, he went on ahead, going up to Jerusalem. When he had come near Bethphage and Bethany, at the place called the Mount of Olives, he sent two of the disciples, saying *Go into the village ahead of you, and as you enter it you will find tied there a colt that has never been ridden. Untie it and bring it here. If anyone asks you, 'Why are you untying it'? Just say this, 'The Lord needs it'*. So those who were sent departed and found it as he had told them" (Luke 19.28-32).[3]

"When they had come near Jerusalem and had reached Bethphage, at the Mount of Olives, Jesus sent two disciples, saying to them, *Go into the village ahead of you, and immediately you will find a donkey tied, and a colt with her; untie them and bring them to me. If anyone says*

---

[1] *The Jewish Annotated New Testament*, Levine and Brettler, page 83
[2] *The Jewish Annotated New Testament*, Levine and Brettler, page 144
[3] *The Jewish Annotated New Testament*, Levine and Brettler, page 140

anything to you, just say this, 'The Lord needs them'. And he will send them immediately" (Matthew 21.1-3).[1]

---

[1] *The Jewish Annotated New Testament*, Levine and Brettler, page 37

Chapter 20

Jesus taught the Conservative interpretation
of Jewish law

Alexander the Great and his fellow Greeks greatly influenced Jewish customs and beliefs after they conquered much of the Middle East. Centuries later, the Romans took control of Judea. This brought with it many more changes, especially during the several decades prior to and following the years of Jesus' ministry. These changes did not come easily to a people whose culture was more than a thousand years in the making.

During the century prior to the First Jewish War (66 C.E. – 70 C.E.) there was a substantial increase in the number of Conservative Jews and a decrease in the influence of the Orthodox Jews. This political power shift had far-reaching consequences within the Jewish culture. However, as with any country, these changes came about as a result of much debate by those in positions of power and the common people on the street.

Jesus' ministry took place during a time of national crisis, while the Jewish nation was fractured and under the control of an oppressive foreign military. During that period of history there were three major Jewish sects – the Pharisees, the Sadducees and the Essenes. The Dead Sea Sect, which is mentioned in several Jewish writings, appears to have been an ultra-Conservative offshoot of the Essene sect. There were also various other smaller groups. They each proclaimed their own set of political and religious beliefs and objectives. Jesus' teachings corresponded most closely to those of the Pharisees.

Reading Scriptures was restricted to Jewish men, after their *Bar Mitzvah*. Even today within the Jewish community it continues to be primarily the responsibility of the father to teach his sons the Scriptures: "The Mishnah says that boys are to begin the study of Torah at age five, Mishnah at age ten, and Talmud at fifteen".[1] During the medieval period, and in most Jewish communities well into the nineteenth century, girls were given no formal schooling. They were instructed in Judaism by their mothers. As one might expect, this is no longer the case today, even in the Orthodox communities.

Jewish children received their education primarily from their parents: "The educational system that Judaism offers to its young has its roots in the first century B.C.E., when Rabbi Simeon ben Shetakh established the first schools and ordered parents to send their [male] children to them. But it was in the first century C.E. that Rabbi Joseph ben Gamla, the High Priest of the Second Temple in Jerusalem until its destruction in 70 C.E., arranged for towns to have their own teachers with the result that education became a community function rather than a family one exclusively".[2] These were very likely the first community-sponsored schools in the world.

Jesus lived and taught the Jewish faith: "Is there a Jewish consensus on how *Jews* are to regard Jesus? Perhaps not, but in recent decades many Jewish scholars have tended to view him as one of several first-

---

[1] *Essential Judaism*, George Robinson, page 154
[2] *Essential Judaism*, George Robinson, page 155

and second-century Jews who claimed to be the Messiah, and who attempted to rid Judea of its Roman oppressors. However, almost no Jewish scholars believe that Jesus intended to start a new religion. Were Jesus to return today, most Jews believe, he undoubtedly would feel more at home in a synagogue than a church".[1]

The gospels indicate that the main focus of Jesus' ministry was to encourage his fellow Jews, as well as the marginalized Jews and non-Jews, to live their lives according to the moral principles contained within the Jewish Scriptures. However, some scholars today believe the gospels do not accurately portray the events and teachings credited to Jesus. Jesus' teachings were based on Scriptures: "Do not think that I have come to abolish the law or the prophets" (Matthew 5.17).[2]

Jesus was more 'Jewish' than is presented in many Christian writings. The disagreements he appears to have had with his fellow Jews can just as easily be seen as friendly bantering with other Pharisees, or more often with Orthodox Sadducees: "A Jesus at odds with his fellow Jews is a myth that has a deep hold on us".[3]

As can be seen in the gospels, Jesus was a Jewish man in his beliefs and his teachings. The Jewish elders supported his ministry: "He began to teach in their synagogues and was praised by everyone" (Luke 4.15).[4]

---

[1] *Jewish Literacy*, Rabbi Joseph Telushkin, pages 125-126
[2] *Jewish Annotated New Testament*, Levine and Brettler, page 10
[3] *The Ghost in the Gospels*, Leon Zitzer, page 3
[4] *The Jewish Annotated New Testament*, Levine and Brettler, page 106

"So he continued proclaiming the message in the synagogues of Judea" (Luke 4.44).[1]

There were officials in the Jewish community who respected Jesus: "Now when Jesus returned, the crowd welcomed him, for they were all waiting for him. Just then there came a man named Jairus, a leader of the synagogue. He fell at Jesus' feet and begged him to come to his house, for he had an only daughter, about twelve years old, who was dying" (Luke 8.40-42).[2]

Jesus also showed compassion for a Roman soldier: "When he entered Capernaum, a centurion came to him, appealing to him and saying, *Lord, my servant is lying at home paralyzed, in terrible distress.* And he said to him, *I will come and cure him.* The centurion answered, *Lord, I am not worthy to have you come under my roof; but only speak the word, and my servant will be healed*" (Matthew 8.5-7).[3]

The fifth book in the New Testament is *Acts* (Acts of the Apostles). Chapter 10 in *Acts* gives an example of Christian bias against the Jews. Peter was addressing a group of people sent by a Roman officer when he stated: "You yourselves know that it is unlawful for a Jew to associate with or to visit a Gentile" (Acts 10.28).[4] This apparently was not true since Gentiles were welcome within the Temple courtyard, at least those who lived by the basic tenets of the Jewish faith.

---

[1] *The Jewish Annotated New Testament,* Levine and Brettler, page 109
[2] *The Jewish Annotated New Testament,* Levine and Brettler, page 118
[3] *The Jewish Annotated New Testament,* Levine and Brettler, page 16
[4] *The Jewish Annotated New Testament,* Levine and Brettler, page 219

Jesus lived as a Jewish man all through his life. The apostles, even after the death of Jesus, remained very Jewish: "Day by day, as they spent much time together in the temple, they broke bread at home and ate their food with glad and generous hearts, praising God and having the goodwill of all the people" (Acts 2.46-47).[1]

Jesus lived in a flow of ongoing arguments and political debates. He took issue with the Sadducees, as did most Pharisees, on their literal interpretation of some of the Jewish laws. The gospels tell of situations where Jesus joined the Pharisees in challenging the Sadducees' position on topics such as donations to the Temple, equitable punishment for theft and blasphemy as well as loan repayment criteria.

The gospel of *Matthew* indicates that Jesus did not oppose divorce unconditionally: "It was also said, *Whoever divorces his wife, let him give her a certificate of divorce.* But I say to you that anyone who divorces his wife, except on the ground of unchastity, causes her to commit adultery; and whoever marries a divorced woman commits adultery" (Matthew 5.31-32).[2]

Jesus did not totally reject the Jewish dietary laws, as a closer reading of the gospels will show. He did reject the more stringent requirement that food be consumed in a ritually pure fashion. Also, he did not agree with the Sadducees that Jews be restricted from sharing meals with Gentiles.

The repayment of loans was another legal issue that the Sadducees and the Pharisees debated. The strict interpretation of Jewish law during

---

[1] *The Jewish Annotated New Testament*, Levine and Brettler, page 203
[2] *The Jewish Annotated New Testament*, Levine and Brettler, pages 11-12

that era required that every seventh year all fields be left idle and all personal loans between fellow Jews be forgiven: "At the end of every seven years you must cancel debts. This is how it is to be done: Every creditor shall cancel any loan they have made to a fellow Israelite" (Deuteronomy 15.1-2).[1] This law sometimes helped people who needed to borrow money or who had an outstanding loan that was going to be cancelled. Occasionally, however, it did just the opposite when a man who had money available chose not to extend a loan to a fellow Jew close to the seventh year since the prospective borrower might need more time to completely repay the loan.

As an alternative, the Pharisees pressured the Sadducee members of the court to allow a court-written contract whereby the person loaning the money became a business partner with the person borrowing the money. Then the person who borrowed the money would use the 'partner-income' to repay the loan. Thus, the contract was through the court, not just between the individuals. That way, the payments did not need to be completed or the debt be forgiven in the seventh year. This is an example of an Oral Law – a Written Law interpreted in such a way as to legitimately meet a social need.

Jewish law allowed for a loan to bear interest if the money was loaned to a non-Jew: "Do not charge a fellow Israelite interest, whether on money or food or anything else that may earn interest. You may charge a foreigner interest, but not a fellow Israelite" (Deuteronomy 23.19-20).[2]

---

[1] Bible, *New International Version*, page 319
[2] Bible, *New International Version*, page 332

It has always been a serious responsibility of Jewish parents to teach their children the Jewish faith by instruction and by example. Under Judea's theocratic form of government this was not only a religious obligation but also civil law. Every person in the household – relative, common worker or slave – was required to learn at least the basics of the Jewish faith and to strive to live by these tenets.

All non-Jews who were residents of Judea (Gentiles) were required to live by some of same laws as the Jews themselves. Cursing God, sexual immorality, robbery and idolatry were prohibited. They were also required to establish at least some form of court-of-law within their non-Jewish community.

For the Jews, forgiveness for offenses/sins was important for spiritual as well as legal reasons. A person who had been found guilty of theft or damage to property was required to make restitution to his victim. An individual who did not have the financial resources to pay restitution to the victim had at least a few alternatives. He could take out a loan or sell some of his property or work temporarily as an indentured servant. However, he could not sell himself as a slave nor could the Jewish authorities legally take all of his property and force him or his family to live in the street.

Jews were expected to study Scriptures daily, pray in the morning, at approximately three in the afternoon and in the evening, abide by all the dietary regulations, observe all holy days and adhere to many other Jewish laws and customs. Of the 613 laws identified in the Torah, fewer than 300 of these still apply today. This is primarily because the Jews discontinued animal sacrifice after the destruction of the Temple in 70 C.E.

The sacred writings of the Jewish people developed over a long period of time. The oldest of these is the Torah, the first five books of the Bible. The Torah contains the original Hebrew laws and is often referred to as the Written Law. The Oral Law is (written) commentary on the Written Law. The Mishnah is sixty-three tractates (categories) that systematically codify the Oral Law. The Talmud is comprised of the Mishna and later rabbinic discussions that were put into written form.

The writings of the New Testament developed over a long period of time. Many of the laws and moral guidelines taught by Jesus did not originate with him, as the gospels tend to imply. At least a few of these were already included within the Written Law and the Oral Law.

It is very likely that the 'Christian' community that produced the gospels credited Jesus, decades after his death, with setting down a wide range of moral guidelines. This not only gave them a single person as a role model and patriarch, but it also gave them a voice for their own teachings. As mentioned above, this was the case with Moses when he was given credit for many of the laws found in the Torah that had actually been developed by a whole community over many generations long after his death.

According to the gospel stories, Jesus taught the Jewish faith both to Jews and Gentiles, on the mountainside, along the roadway, beside the lake, in other public places and also in synagogues.

Recent estimates indicate that Jesus had between 120 and 200 followers at the time of his death. As you will see in the following chapters, it was not the number of his followers or his teachings that ultimately gained him such a significant place in history.

The *Letter of James* also indicates that Jesus taught Jewish beliefs and traditions: "You do well if you really fulfill the royal law according to the scripture, *You shall love your neighbor as yourself*" (James 2.8).[1]

This *Letter of James* does not contain anything derogatory about traditional Jewish law. Jesus taught one of the most basic moral laws in the Bible when he quoted *Leviticus*, the third book of the Old Testament: "Do not seek revenge or bear a grudge against anyone among your people, but love your neighbor as yourself" (Leviticus 19.18).[2]

The gospels indicate that Jesus held children in high regard: "People were bringing little children to him in order that he might touch them; and the disciples spoke sternly to them. But when Jesus saw this, he was indignant and said to them, *Let the little children come to me; do not stop them; for it is to such as these that the kingdom of God belongs. Truly I tell you, whoever does not receive the kingdom of God as a little child will never enter it.* And he took them up in his arms, laid his hands on them, and blessed them" (Mark 10.13-16).[3]

In the gospel of *Matthew* Jesus speaks about a man who received the same amount of pay for one hour's work as another man received for a full day's work. The man who was hired early in the morning agreed to work all day for one silver coin. Near the end of the day another man was hired. He agreed to work the last hour of the day also for one silver coin.

---

[1] *The Jewish Annotated New Testament*, Levine and Brettler, pages 431
[2] Bible, *New International Version*, page 199
[3] *The Jewish Annotated New Testament*, Levine and Brettler, pages 81

Then, at the end of the day each man was paid one silver coin. As one might expect, the man who worked all day grumbled about the unfairness of the pay. Jesus did not find fault with the owner of the field for this less than equitable wage. He simply stated that each man had agreed to this amount of work and pay when he was hired: "But he replied to one of them, *Friend, I am doing you no wrong; did you not agree with me for the usual daily wage? Take what belongs to you and go; I choose to give to this last the same as I give to you*" (Matthew 20.13-14).[1]

When interpreted literally, it appears that Jesus was condoning an unfair business practice. However, Jesus was not teaching a lesson on business contract. He was addressing a spiritual issue. 'Wages' was a commonly used metaphor that referred to a person's reward for making virtuous choices. He was telling people that those who choose to turn their life around and make better choices even late in life still had the opportunity to receive the same eternal reward as those who had been living their whole life righteously.

Jesus declared his belief in the laws contained in the Torah and in the Temple rituals when he instructed a man whom he had healed: "And he ordered him to tell no one. *Go*, he said, *and show yourself to the priest, and, as Moses commanded, make an offering for your cleansing, for a testimony to them*" (Luke 5.14).[2]

Some ailments were certainly not too difficult to heal for someone who had basic knowledge of 'home remedies' or had access to sufficient

---

[1] *The Jewish Annotated New Testament*, Levine and Brettler, pages 36
[2] *The Jewish Annotated New Testament*, Levine and Brettler, pages 110

finances to buy the more expensive medicines: "These are the regulations for any defiling skin disease, for a sore, for defiling molds in fabric or in a house, and for a swelling, a rash or a shiny spot, to determine when something is clean or unclean" (Leviticus 14.54-57).[1] "Fruit trees of all kinds will grow on both banks of the river. Their leaves will not wither, nor will their fruit fail. Every month they will bear fruit, because the water from the sanctuary flows to them. Their fruit will serve for food and their leaves for healing" (Ezekiel 47.12).[2]

A sinful habit was sometimes referred to as an illness. A person who had chosen an unconventional or less than righteous way of life was said to be 'possessed by a demon'.

Exorcism, at least sometimes, referred to spiritual renewal. Thus, when a preacher/teacher convinced an individual to change his/her way of life for the better he is said to have 'cast out the devil' or 'evil spirit'.

Epilepsy sometimes referred to uncontrolled behavior that was not always caused by a medical condition.

At least some of the 'miracles' performed by people over the centuries were home remedies: "*Saliva* was seen to have medicinal value".[3] "When he had said this, he spat on the ground and made mud with the saliva and spread the mud on the man's eyes, saying to him, *Go*,

---

[1] Bible, *New International Version*, page 190
[2] Bible, *New International Version*, page 1479
[3] *The Jewish Annotated New Testament*, Levine and Brettler, footnote, page 177

wash in the pool of Siloam (which means Sent). Then he went and washed and came back able to see" (John 9.6-7).[1]

There was a scaly skin condition that was sometimes referred to as leprosy which was not the same as the illness referred to today as leprosy. Sometimes a sinful habit was referred to as an 'illness'.

Jesus was not the only one who was said to have performed the miracle of 'casting out demons': "If I cast out demons by Beelzebul, by whom do your own exorcists cast them out?" (Matthew 12.27).[2]

---

[1] *The Jewish Annotated New Testament*, Levine and Brettler, page 177
[2] *The Jewish Annotated New Testament*, Levine and Brettler, page 23

Chapter 21

The Romans would not tolerate any disturbances within the Temple during the holy days

Many of the coins in circulation in Judea and the neighboring countries during the time of Jesus had the impression of a person or a god stamped into them. Such coins were not allowed as offerings within the Temple. Because of this, the pilgrims often needed to exchange their foreign coins for coins that were acceptable. Thus, the *moneychangers* were an essential component of the Temple proceedings.

According to the strict interpretation of Scriptures during the time of Jesus, these idolatrous coins were not supposed to be brought into the Temple courtyard, even for the purchase of sacrificial animals. Such coins were supposed to remain outside of the Temple gates. Some historians believe that this restriction was lifted for a short time during the last years of the Temple.

The *merchants* also provided a necessary service for the Temple proceedings. They provided the pilgrims and the local people who did not bring their own animals to be used as Temple offerings with the option of buying cattle, sheep, goats, pigeons and doves from them. And, as with most any business, the merchants set their own prices on their merchandise and services.

It appears that Jesus, and probably others, considered the prices charged by at least some of the *merchants* and *moneychangers* to be excessive and in violation of the sanctity of the Temple: "Do not have two differing weights in your bag – one heavy, one light" (Deuteronomy 25.13).[1]

Jesus went to Jerusalem to participate in the annual Passover celebration at least once. Christians celebrate his last journey to Jerusalem on Palm Sunday. However, the gospels do not have a consistent time-line for Jesus' arrival in Jerusalem in relation to his last meal with his apostles. The gospel of *Matthew* places his arrival two days before the Passover celebration was to begin: "When Jesus had finished saying all these things, he said to his disciples, *You know that after two days the Passover is coming, and the Son of Man will be handed over to be crucified*" (Matthew 26.1-2).[2]

The gospel of *Mark* has Jesus' arrival just hours before the Last Supper: "On the first day of Unleavened Bread, when the Passover lamb is sacrificed, his disciples said to him, *Where do you want us to go and make the preparations for you to eat the Passover?* So he sent two of his disciples, saying to them, *Go into the city, and a man carrying a jar of water will meet you; follow him, and wherever he enters, say to the owner of the house, 'The Teacher asks, 'Where is my guest room where I may eat the Passover with my disciples?'* He will show you a large room upstairs, furnished and ready. Make preparations for us there.* So the disciples set out and went to the city, and found everything as he had told them; and they prepared the Passover meal" (Mark 14.12-16).[3]

---

[1] Bible, *New International Version*, page 335
[2] *The Jewish Annotated New Testament*, Levine and Brettler, page 47
[3] *The Jewish Annotated New Testament*, Levine and Brettler, pages 89-90

The gospel of *Luke* has Jesus' arrival, not the day before the festival was to begin, but sometime during the celebration: "Then came the day of Unleavened Bread, on which the Passover lamb had to be sacrificed. So Jesus sent Peter and John, saying *Go and prepare the Passover meal for us that we may eat it.* They asked him, *Where do you want us to make preparations for it? Listen,* he said to them, *when you have entered the city, a man carrying a jar of water will meet you; follow him into the house he enters and say to the owner of the house, 'The teacher asks you', 'Where is the guest room, where I may eat the Passover with my disciples?' He will show you a large room upstairs, already furnished. Make preparations for us there.* So they went and found everything as he had told them; and they prepared the Passover meal" (Luke 22.7-12).[1]

The gospel of *John* has Jesus' arrival several days before the Passover celebration began: "Six days before the Passover Jesus came to Bethany" (John 12.1).[2] "The next day the great crowd that had come to the festival heard that Jesus was coming to Jerusalem. So they took branches of palm trees and went out to meet him" (John 12.12-13).[3]

The first Passover occurred in Egypt the night before the *Exodus* began: "Then Moses summoned all the elders of Israel and said to them, *Go at once and select the animals for your families and slaughter the Passover lamb*" (Exodus 12.21)[4]. And: "For seven days you shall dwell in booths; every citizen of Israel shall dwell in booths so that your

---

[1] *The Jewish Annotated New Testament*, Levine and Brettler, page 144
[2] *The Jewish Annotated New Testament*, Levine and Brettler, page 182
[3] *The Jewish Annotated New Testament*, Levine and Brettler, page 182
[4] Bible, *New International Version*, page 110

generations will know that I [God] made the children of Israel dwell in booths when I brought them out to the land of Egypt".[1]

Early in the week of Passover, while in the Temple courtyard, Jesus confronted the *merchants* and *moneychangers* and became very angry with them. He physically disrupted their business for violating the sacredness of the Temple. Jesus' anger was not directed toward them because they accommodated the Temple worshippers with what he surely recognized as necessary services. He was most likely objecting to their unfair prices or possibly because they conducted their business within the Temple courtyard, which led to the pilgrims bringing their 'idolatrous' coins into the Temple courtyard for the purchase of sacrificial animals or exchange for monetary Temple offerings: "Then they came to Jerusalem. And he entered the temple and began to drive out those who were selling and those who were buying in the temple, and he overturned the tables of the money changers and the seats of those who sold doves" (Mark 11.15).[2] "Then Jesus entered the temple and drove out all who were selling and buying in the temple, and he overturned the tables of the money changers and the seats of those who sold doves. He said to them, *It is written, 'My house shall be called a house of prayer'; but you are making it a den of robbers*" (Matthew 21.12-13).[3] "Then he entered the temple and began to drive out those who were selling things there; and he said, *It is written, 'My house shall be a house of prayer'; but you have made it a den of robbers*" (Luke

---

[1] *Essential Judaism*, George Robinson, page 101

[2] *The Jewish Annotated New Testament*, Levine and Brettler, page 83

[3] *The Jewish Annotated New Testament*, Levine and Brettler, page 38

19.45).[1] "Making a whip of cords, he drove all of them out of the temple, both the sheep and the cattle. He also poured out the coins of the money changers and overturned their tables. He told those who were selling the doves, *Take these things out of here! Stop making my Father's house a marketplace!*" (John 2.15-16).[2]

The gospels do not agree on the offense that set into motion the dramatic sequence of events that ended in the crucifixion of Jesus. However, it is apparent that the Romans dealt harshly with anyone who caused a disturbance within the Temple, or anywhere else in Judea, that required military intervention. The sequence of events and the people most involved during the days following this incident in the Temple are also not clear.

Barabbas had a pivotal role in the death of Jesus. The gospel of *Matthew* speaks of him. But, who was this man? Very shortly after Jesus caused the disturbance in the Temple, Barabbas was arrested: "At that time they had a notorious prisoner, called Jesus Barabbas. So after they had gathered, Pilate said to them, *Whom do you want me to release for you, Jesus Barabbas or Jesus who is called the Messiah?*" (Matthew 27.16-17).[3] "Jesus Barabbas was a real person who was arrested by mistake by the Roman soldiers when they were trying to find Jesus of Nazareth. You can see how the Romans might have been confused. They were looking for *Rabbi* Jesus of Nazareth and they came across a Jesus Bar-*rabbas* (it is actually Bar-Abba, Abba being a title like rabbi, but to

---

[1] *The Jewish Annotated New Testament*, Levine and Brettler, page 141
[2] *The Jewish Annotated New Testament*, Levine and Brettler, page 161
[3] *The Jewish Annotated New Testament*, Levine and Brettler, page 51

the Romans, it probably sounded like Barrabba). Pilate lets Jesus Barabbas go, when he is informed of the error, for good reason – *he was forced to do so under the circumstances*. Jesus Barabbas was innocent. He was the wrong man".[1]

But, what convinced the Romans that they had arrested the wrong man? How did they find out that it was Jesus of Nazareth who had caused the disturbance in the Temple?

It is very likely that it was within a day or two after the arrest of Jesus Barabbas that Jesus of Nazareth realized that Barabbas had been arrested for creating a disturbance in the Temple courtyard, **a disturbance which he himself was guilty of**.

Jesus then had to decide if he should turn himself in to the Roman authorities and admit that he, not Barabbas, had caused the disturbance in the Temple. Or, he could let Barabbas suffer Pilate's wrath for the disturbance in the Temple which he himself had caused.

This was quite a predicament he found himself in. If he let the Romans punish Barabbas, then he could continue his ministry as before. If he did not come forward and own up to what he had done, he would be a hypocrite of the worst kind – preach love your neighbor, but at the same time allow Barabbas to suffer, and possibly die, for something he himself had done. Jesus decided to turn himself over to the Roman authorities and face the consequences.

Shortly before his last Passover meal – the Last Supper – Jesus asked his younger brother Judas to meet with the Jewish authorities and ask for their help in obtaining the release of Barabbas and leniency for

---

[1] *The Ghost in the Gospels*, Leon Zitzer, page 115

Jesus. In exchange, Jesus agreed to turn himself over to Pilate. He surely was hoping that he would receive no more than a scourging/whipping for causing the disturbance in the Temple earlier in the week.

Jesus and his apostles met later that evening to celebrate the Passover meal (the Last Supper). After the meal Judas met with Annas, the retired High Priest. He asked Annas to go to Pilate to explain the situation and ask for leniency for Jesus. Annas' son-in-law Caiaphas was the High Priest at that time. Nearly two decades earlier, in 15 C.E., the Romans had forced Annas to give up his position as High Priest.

Annas and Caiaphas walked to the Roman headquarters to explain the situation to Pilate. It appears that Pilate agreed to release Jesus Barabbas if and when he had Jesus of Nazareth in custody. Judas then led the soldiers to the Garden of Gethsemane, the place where Jesus told Judas that he would be waiting for the Romans to come and arrest him.

However, the gospels give conflicting reasons why Jesus was arrested. These include his threat to destroy the Temple, for proclaiming that he was a Messiah, for stating that he was a king, for declaring that he was the 'Son of God' and for blasphemy: "Finally, in no Jewish sources of antiquity – biblical texts, Dead Sea Scrolls, Apocrypha Pseudepigrapha, Josephus, rabbinic writings – is the messianic figure ever either identified with God or worshipped".[1]

Many of the Jews, prior to the destruction of the Temple, were hoping for a savior, a messiah, someone who would unite their countrymen against foreign oppression, bring the Chosen People together

---

[1] *The Jewish Annotated New Testament*, Levine and Brettler, footnote, page 535

in spite of their sectarian differences, force the Romans out of Judea and give them at least the opportunity to once again become an independent country. But Jesus was not a revolutionary. There is no mention in any of the gospels of him advocating violence against the Romans.

The gospels do not agree as to who came to arrest Jesus. The gospel of *Mark* states that it was a crowd sent by Jewish officials: "Immediately, while he was still speaking, Judas, one of the twelve, arrived; and with him there was a crowd with swords and clubs, from the chief priests, the scribes, and the elders" (Mark 14.43).[1] However, the gospel of *John* states that it was Roman soldiers who arrested Jesus: "So Judas brought a detachment of soldiers together with police from the chief priests and the Pharisees" (John 18.3).[2]

Leon Zitzer, in his book *The Ghost in the Gospels*, stated the following: "I cannot stress enough what an unusual event it was for the time to see Roman soldiers and Jewish officials walking through the streets together. This never happened. All the Jewish witnesses to this, not just Jesus' followers, would have been shocked and appalled. This goes a long way towards explaining why Jewish leaders were eventually falsely accused of complicity in Jesus' execution. People reacted emotionally to the superficial sight of Jews and Romans together and did not stop to think that Jewish leaders requested permission to participate in order to try to save Jesus. The whole sequence of events had been so bizarre, so out of the ordinary: A wrong man, whose name and title was almost the same as another's, is arrested; the right man surrenders to save

---

[1] *The Jewish Annotated New Testament*, Levine and Brettler, page 91
[2] *The Jewish Annotated New Testament*, Levine and Brettler, page 190

the first man's life (how often did a Jew surrender to the Romans!?), sending an emissary, Judas, to arrange it; the priests are dragged into this to straighten out the confusion".[1] "It was this very noticeable part that made Jesus' followers angry. Most of the other things were behind the scenes. They probably did not think about the less visible features (Jesus deciding to surrender, priests requesting permission, etc.), or if any did, their opinions were drowned out by louder voices reacting emotionally to the sight of those Jews and Romans 'working together'".[2]

A closer look at the Jewish attitude toward the Romans during that time in history clearly defies any logic that any Jewish leader would turn over any fellow Jew for punishment by the Roman authorities, certainly not to be executed. The gospel writings that show the Jewish people a few hours later demanding that Jesus be crucified are equally implausible. It appears that there is no evidence in any Jewish writings, including those of Josephus, a famous writer of that era, indicating that any high priest or any other Jewish official was ever responsible for a fellow Jew being crucified by the Romans for violating any Jewish law.

Even before the time of Jesus, Jewish law forbade crucifixion as a form of punishment. Those Jews who came to Jerusalem to celebrate one of their most sacred holy days certainly would not have cried out for the crucifixion of Jesus, a fellow Jew who had just days earlier confronted the *merchants* and *moneychangers* for violating the sacredness of the Temple.

---

[1] *The Ghost in the Gospels*, Leon Zitzer, page 131
[2] *The Ghost in the Gospels*, Leon Zitzer, page 131

There is little doubt that Jesus considered the Temple to be sacred: "There is no evidence for Jesus/Joshua having a negative relationship to the Temple. *None whatsoever.* Scholars have constructed a fantasy world, a world of the most blatant staged readings, to produce a "Gospel" version of events that bears no resemblance to the real Gospels. Jesus/Joshua probably did utter a prophecy of the destruction of the Temple, but this is evidence of his love for the Temple. Scholars have completely missed what Jewish prophecy is about. A Jewish prophet does not predict catastrophes. He tries to *prevent catastrophes* by telling people that they will lose a beloved institution if they do not change their behavior".[1]

The Jews certainly would not have conspired against anyone who was willing to take a stand against the despised Herods and Romans. Then, Jesus was brought before Pilate who supposedly questioned him to find a reason to prosecute Jesus: "Pilate asked him, *Are you the King of the Jews?*" (Mark 15.2).[2] If Pilate had been concerned that Jesus was a revolutionary or an aspiring king, the soldiers that he sent to arrest Jesus would have also arrested the others who were with Jesus in the Garden of Gethsemane.

Jesus certainly is not the first or the only person in the Bible who is referred to as a 'son of God': "He [King David] is the one who will build a house for my Name, and I will establish the throne of his kingdom forever, I will be his father, and he will be my son" (2 Samuel 7.13-14).[3]

---

[1] *The Ghost in the Gospels*, Leon Zitzer, page 249
[2] *The Jewish Annotated New Testament*, Levine and Brettler, page 92
[3] Bible, *New International Version*, page 512

Leon Zitzer speaks in great detail to the many inconsistencies in the gospel stories relating to the arrest of Jesus: "The original Barabbas incident implies that Jewish leaders were not looking for Jesus and it implies that Jesus would have had a good reason to surrender to the Romans, making it all too likely that Judas' role was to help in this regard. Judas did not betray Jesus to the priests and they did not betray Jesus to the Romans. Judas and Barabbas together help establish what the priests really did and what the priests really did helps to establish that Judas was not a traitor. All the pieces interlock in a very tight web and the evidence supporting this forms a wide net that covers almost everything we have in the Gospels. It requires that we do very little rewriting of the Gospels. Most of what is in them is accurate – we have just been looking at it through the wrong lens. This is nominal reconstruction of history. As far as I know it is the only interpretation of the Gospels that accomplishes this. And last but not least, it is such a simple theory. There is no need to resort to a dozen or more theories to explain the contents of the Gospels. One thing happened in history and one simple theory unlocks it".[1]

The gospel of *Mark* states that Jesus was escorted to the home of the High Priest where he was questioned and found guilty by a unanimous vote: "They took Jesus to the high priest; and all the chief priests, the elders, and the scribes were assembled" (Mark 14.53).[2] A Jewish person charged with a crime that could result in the death penalty required a thorough investigation, serious deliberation and at least one vote less

---

[1] *The Ghost in the Gospels*, Leon Zitzer, page 143
[2] *The Jewish Annotated New Testament*, Levine and Brettler, page 91

than unanimous by the Sanhedrin, the official Jewish Court of Law: "One witness is not enough to convict anyone accused of any crime or offense they may have committed. A matter must be established by the testimony of two or three witnesses" (Deuteronomy 19.15).[1]

There were witnesses, false witnesses: "Some stood up and gave false testimony against him, saying, *We heard him say, 'I will destroy this temple that is made with hands, and in three days I will build another, not made with hands'.* But even on this point their testimony did not agree" (Mark 14.57-59).[2]

Another misrepresentation of tradition was the meaning of a person tearing his robe: "Then the high priest tore his clothes and said, *Why do we still need witnesses? You have heard his blasphemy!* All of them condemned him as deserving death" (Mark 14.63).[3] The tearing of a person's robe was/is an expression of sadness and emotional pain not of anger toward someone who had supposedly violated Jewish Law: "Then Jacob tore his clothes, put on sackcloth and mourned for his son many days" (Genesis 37.34).[4]

The gospel of *John* states that Jesus was taken to the home of the retired high priest Annas immediately after being arrested: "So the soldiers, their officer, and the Jewish police arrested Jesus and bound him. First they took him to Annas, who was the father-in-law of

---

[1] Bible, *New International Version*, page 326
[2] *The Jewish Annotated New Testament*, Levine and Brettler, page 91
[3] *The Jewish Annotated New Testament*, Levine and Brettler, page 92
[4] Bible, *New International Version*, page 66

Caiaphas, the high priest that year" (John 18.12-13).[1] The Roman soldiers would have had no reason to take Jesus to the home of Annas.

The charges supposedly brought against Jesus by Jewish officials were very serious and would have required a thorough investigation. Also, the Sanhedrin was required to give every person being tried for a capital crime the opportunity to present a defense, including time to find and bring forward witnesses who might testify on his behalf.

As mentioned earlier, this court did not meet on short notice, not at night and not in a family home. Also, every one of the twenty-three members of the Sanhedrin would have written, and read to the court, the basis for his decision before the case was finalized and the verdict given to the accused. Also, the court's final statement of guilty was always deferred to the following day, though never during Passover or on any holy day. Even more telling is that the court never convened during Passover to conduct any criminal proceedings. These are but a few of the many discrepancies in the gospels as well as in today's Christian traditions and teachings.

Nowhere in any of the epistles is there any indication that the authors of the epistles were the least bit unhappy with Judas after the arrest and crucifixion of Jesus. This is not logical if Judas betrayed Jesus: "All the early translators of the Bible, including Tyndale, were constrained to translate that neutral word in connection with Judas as 'betray', though they translated the same word differently and neutrally when it appeared in other places in the New Testament".[2] "One of the

---

[1] *The Jewish Annotated New Testament*, Levine and Brettler, page 190
[2] *The Ghost in the Gospels*, Leon Zitzer, page 67

most impressive of all the clues we have is this: 'Betray' as the word for his deed is a mistranslation. It is not what the Greek Gospels say. With one exception at Luke 6:16, they all use a neutral word".[1] "The word *paradidomi* can also mean surrender, but you don't have to know that to figure this out. I only discovered this was a possible meaning after I solved the rest. The neutral meaning of *paradidomi* tells us that Jesus was sending Judas as an emissary to accomplish something for him".[2]

"Just as startling is that Mark's Judas does not have one literary feature you would expect in a story of treason. No one has been able to explain this. Mark is actually quite famous in scholarly circles for not presenting any motive in Judas or any conflict between him and Jesus that would make the betrayal understandable, nor does he relate any stinging condemnations from fellow disciples aimed at Judas for this supposedly infamous act".[3]

"There is only one thing I can think of that it could logically be: Jesus was surrendering and he was asking Judas to act as his agent to get the authorities to pick him up. It was all very innocent on Judas' part. He was helping Jesus to surrender. And why would Jesus do this? To save the life of an innocent man who had been arrested by mistake in his place – Jesus Barabbas. We are back to Barabbas again. He is the linchpin of the whole affair. The story of an innocent Jew arrested by the Romans would have spread like wildfire in Jerusalem. Jesus and his group would have heard about it too. Moreover, Jesus would have realized it was

---

[1] *The Ghost in the Gospels*, Leon Zitzer, page 124
[2] *The Ghost in the Gospels*, Leon Zitzer, page 126
[3] *The Ghost in the Gospels*, Leon Zitzer, page 125

really he the Romans were looking for. My guess is that Jesus already knew about his impending arrest for some time as gossip about these things circulated. So now a Jesus Barabbas has been arrested and a crowd is demanding his release because of a complaint this is not the man the Romans wanted. How do you think Jesus would have reacted? Doesn't it make sense that he would surrender to save this wrongfully arrested man? (It was thinking about this that made me realize what purpose Judas served, even before I discovered [William] Klassen's book.) Still, it might have been quite a struggle for Jesus to decide what to do. He has a major mission to preach about the coming kingdom of God. He could have chosen to escape. He could run from the Romans, hide out in Galilee, temporarily giving up his mission of preaching, and let an innocent man die in his place. He could not know if the Romans would let Jesus Barabbas go. It is even possible that the Romans held Barabbas as a hostage until the right Jesus was found, though I cannot prove this. Everything the Gospels relate about that last night in Gethsemane confirms that Jesus was sweating a great decision and that he did not share his trouble or his final decision with any of his disciples (who would have vehemently opposed his surrender) except one – Judas, the disciple he loved and trusted the most, the one who would do anything his rabbi asked, anything to help him. Jesus' agony must have been intense. Should he continue the big mission of preaching the kingdom of God, or act to save one man's life, which would likely mean his own death? What a choice. The one thing we can be certain of is that Jesus decided to surrender. It is clear from the presence of Roman soldiers at Jesus' arrest (John 18.3,12) and the ultimate fact of the crucifixion that this was a Roman affair from beginning to end. *The priests never had him in any official capacity. They never arrested him. Jesus was always and only under Roman arrest".*[1]

---

[1] *The Ghost in the Gospels*, Leon Zitzer, pages 126-127

Chapter 22

Pilate was the most brutal and abusive Roman governor in Judean history

Pilate was the fifth Roman governor to rule the city of Jerusalem. He served from 26 C.E. to 36 C.E. and had a reputation for being very cruel and biased against the Jews. He would not have hesitated to execute anyone who created any disturbance among the large crowds that always gathered for holy day celebrations. He was notorious for his extreme cruelty, more so than any other Roman governor in Judea during that era.

Pilate ordered the torture, massacre and crucifixion of thousands of Jews and other residents of Judea. The Romans continued to use crucifixion as a method of capital punishment until 404 C.E.

Pilate routinely executed those suspected of inciting a riot or who publicly spoke out against him. His cruelty fueled a cycle of increasing violence throughout the country. This forced the Roman military to continually increase the number of troops assigned to Judea.

Pilate was eventually recalled to Rome because of his many atrocities committed against the Jews. Philo, a first century writer, had this to say about Pilate: "Philo generally describes Pilate's administration as one characterized by 'his venality, his violence, his thefts, his assaults, his abusive behavior, his frequent executions of untried prisoners, and his endless savage ferocity'".[1]

Pilate would have had little concern for any reason that the Jewish people may have had to arrest any Jewish man: "So the soldiers, their officer, and the Jewish police arrested Jesus and bound him. First they took him to Annas, who was the father-in-law of Caiaphas, the high priest that year" (John 18.12-13).[2] His soldiers would not have stopped at the home of Annas or Caiaphas with Jesus in custody.

According to one of the gospels, Jesus told Pilate that his kingdom 'was not of this world'. However, Pilate would not have considered Jesus a political threat. Jesus had a relatively small following and his teachings were of no concern to Pilate.

It is extremely unlikely that Pilate considered Jesus a revolutionary or a 'messiah' who was trying to liberate Judea from the Romans. Surely Pilate realized that Jesus' actions were directed against other Jews – the *merchants* and the *moneychangers*.

This was not an act of rebellion against the Romans: "Yet Rome did not place numerous troops in Judea and did not, until 66 [C.E.], consider the population threatening".[3]

Pilate had a long-established reputation for his total disregard for the wishes of the Jewish people. He would not have tolerated any actions that might have escalated into a riot. Nor would he have hesitated to

---

[1] *The Anchor Bible Dictionary*, Pontius Pilate, volume 5, page 398

[2] *The Jewish Annotated New Testament*, Levine and Brettler, page 190

[3] *The Jewish Annotated New Testament*, Levine and Brettler, footnote, page 511

execute anyone for causing a disturbance in the Temple, especially a man who had been a servant or slave a few years earlier.

The gospels indicate that the Jewish crowd pressured Pilate into releasing Barabbas: "Now at the festival the governor was accustomed to release a prisoner for the crowd" (Matthew 27.15).[1] There is no historical evidence that indicates Pilate, or any other Roman governor who ruled in Judea, ever granted clemency to any prisoner who ignored a governor's orders or was guilty of any crime.

The author of the gospel of *Matthew*, or later editors, decided to make Pilate less responsible for the death of Jesus. Pilate washed his hands and said: "So when Pilate saw that he could do nothing, but rather that a riot was beginning, he took some water and washed his hands before the crowd, saying, *I am innocent of this man's blood; see to it yourselves.* Then the people as a whole answered, *His blood be on us and on our children!*" (Matthew 27.24-25).[2] This second statement is extremely prejudicial and has been used by at least some people as an excuse to persecute Jewish people.

The gospels do not agree on who told Pilate that they wanted Jesus crucified. Three of the gospels state that it was the entire Jewish crowd: "The governor again said to them, *Which of the two do you want me to release for you?* And they said, *Barabbas.* Pilate said to them, *Then what should I do with Jesus who is called the Messiah?* All of them said, *Let him be crucified!*" (Matthew 27.21-22).[3] "Pilate spoke again to the

---

[1] *The Jewish Annotated New Testament*, Levine and Brettler, page 51
[2] *The Jewish Annotated New Testament*, Levine and Brettler, pages 51-52
[3] *The Jewish Annotated New Testament*, Levine and Brettler, page 51

crowd, *What then, do you want me to do with the one you call the king of the Jews?* They shouted back, *Crucify him!*" (Mark 15.12-13).[1] "*I will therefore have him flogged and release him.* Then they all shouted out together, *Away with this fellow!*" (Luke 23.16-18).[2]

However, according to the gospel of *John* it was not the crowd who wanted Jesus crucified: "When the chief priests and the police saw him, they shouted, *Crucify him! Crucify him!* Pilate said to them, *Take him yourselves and crucify him; I find no case against him.* The Jews answered him, *We have a law, and according to that law he ought to die because he has claimed to be the Son of God*" (John 19.6-7).[3]

In Israel today it would be unconscionable for any Jewish person, or group of Jewish people, to condemn anyone to death in a gas chamber, especially a fellow Jew, regardless of his or her crime. Many thousands of Jews were killed in gas chambers and their bodies burned during the Holocaust of World War II. For Jews today, death in a gas chamber would be a totally unacceptable form of punishment for anyone for any crime. Two thousand years ago, the Jews had this same attitude toward crucifixion – the typical form of capital punishment used by the Romans.

Holocaust is a Greek word meaning 'burnt offering' and originally referred to the burnt animal offerings in the Temple, prior to the destruction of the Temple in 70 C.E.

------

[1] *The Jewish Annotated New Testament*, Levine and Brettler, page 92
[2] *The Jewish Annotated New Testament*, Levine and Brettler, page 147
[3] *The Jewish Annotated New Testament*, Levine and Brettler, page 191

The Roman soldiers followed Pilate's orders and proceeded to execute Jesus as a common criminal. Jesus gave his life to save Barabbas's life.

According to Christian tradition, Jesus was thirty-three years old when he died. However, since the year of his birth cannot be established, his age when he died also cannot be established. The thirty-three years was very likely selected to draw a parallel between Jesus and King David: "Then David rested with his ancestors and was buried in the City of David. He had reigned forty years over Israel – seven years in Hebron and thirty-three in Jerusalem" (1 Kings 2.10-11).[1]

There is evidence indicating that the apostle Judas did not commit suicide as stated in the New Testament: "Throwing down the pieces of silver in the temple, he departed; and he went and hanged himself" (Matthew 27.5).[2] He very likely was distraught since he had participated in his brother's arrest even though it was only upon Jesus' request. It is quite possible that Judas returned to the Temple and paid restitution – *thirty pieces of silver* – to those who may have suffered any financial loss as a result of Jesus' actions in the Temple earlier in the week.

Judas had to have been very depressed and angry with the Romans, as well as himself, when the Romans severely whipped and executed Jesus. He surely regretted having turned Jesus over to the Roman soldiers even though Jesus had asked him to. It would have been quite understandable for Judas to have taken his own life, if in fact he did commit suicide.

---

[1] Bible, *New International Version*, pages 553-554
[2] *The Jewish Annotated New Testament*, Levine and Brettler, page 51

The second story about the demise of Judas does not agree with the first: "Now this man acquired a field with the reward of his wickedness; and falling headlong, he burst open in the middle and all his bowels gushed out" (Acts 1.18).[1] This statement makes no sense at all. It states that he fell, not that he committed suicide. And, what possible connection could there be between Jesus' arrest, Judas buying a field and then falling to his death? Unless, this was to show that Judas went on to lead a normal life and later died in an accidental fall.

The first epistle of *Paul* was written a few decades after Jesus' death. This is the earliest writing of the New Testament. Nowhere in any of Paul's writings does he blame Judas for the death of Jesus. *Epistles* is Greek for *letters*.

Leon Zitzer, a Jewish writer and historian, recently published his book *The Ghost in the Gospels*. In this book he speaks to the relationship between Jesus, Jewish officials, the Romans and others during the last week of Jesus' life and the following few weeks and years.

As he traces back through the gospels to the days and hours before and after the arrest of Jesus, he describes very clearly that the basic teachings in Scriptures do not condone or support the supposed animosity between Jesus and the Jewish officials: "There is a very good possibility that the well-known problems and/or contradictions are not in the Gospels, they are in the world view scholars bring to and impose on the Gospels. Academic scholarship is the problem, not the Gospels. (1) If we are to believe the traditional interpretation of the Gospels, the priests put Jesus on trial, hand him over to the Romans to finish the job, and

---

[1] *The Jewish Annotated New Testament*, Levine and Brettler, page 200

apparently there is no opposition to this. Where was the popular Jewish reaction against such an act? Where was the Pharisaic protest? These are legitimate questions both because the historical context tells us that other Jews would not have stood for such an injustice and because the New Testament itself speaks against the possibility of an unopposed priestly railroading of Jesus. Just as Pharisees came to the aid of Peter (Acts 5:34-40) and Paul (Acts 23:6-9) (this New Testament evidence is also an indication that, in the 1st century, Pharisees regularly participated in the Sanhedrin, the Jewish high court), and just as Pharisees protested the execution of Jacob/James, the brother of Jesus, (Ant. 20.9.1; most scholars believe that Josephus' mention of 'the most equitable of the citizens' is a reference to the Pharisees), so too Pharisees would have done as much for Jesus, if the priests had done to Jesus what tradition and scholars allege. They would have saved him or at least complained after the fact if they were too late. They would have launched a protest so loud and vigorous on Jesus' behalf that it would have reverberated onto the historical record somewhere".[1]

---

[1] *The Ghost in the Gospels*, Leon Zitzer, page 23

Part Four

The early years of Christianity

(33 C.E. and forward)

Chapter 23

Paul taught outside of Judea

After the death of Jesus, the apostles selected by him continued to be very Jewish in all aspects of their lives. As mentioned earlier, this becomes apparent in *Acts:* "Day by day, as they spent much time together in the temple, they broke bread at home and ate their food with glad and generous hearts, praising God and having the goodwill of all the people" (Acts 2.46-47).[1]

There is information about James and the other apostles outside of the Bible. Some of this information can be found in the writings recently excavated from caves near Qumran, approximately thirteen miles east of Jerusalem. These documents were written by the Dead Sea Sect during the decades before the Romans destroyed the Jewish nation. These writings, and those of Flavius Josephus, give historians a wealth of documentation concerning the events that took place during those tumultuous years.

The epistles of the 'apostle' Paul are among the earliest writings of the New Testament. Paul was known as Saul or Saulus during his lifetime. The New Testament writers, or more likely those who amended the writings later, used the name Paul rather than Saul or Saulus to identify him more closely with their own values and beliefs.

---

[1] *The Jewish Annotated New Testament*, Levine and Brettler, page 203

The writings outside of the New Testament indicate that Paul did not have a close relationship with the 'twelve' apostles. Paul took exception to at least a few of the apostles' religious beliefs and was hostile toward them on more than one occasion.

Simon Peter joined his brother James in declaring that at least a few of Paul's teachings were contrary to Jewish teachings: "An increasing number of Jewish scholars believe that Christianity's real founder was a first-century Jew, Paul".[1] Paul acknowledged that Jesus lived and taught the Conservative Jewish laws and customs: "But when the fullness of time had come, God sent his Son, born of a woman, born under the law, in order to redeem those who were under the law" (Galatians 4.4-5).[2]

Paul's teachings were in many ways *not* those of Jesus or the 'twelve' apostles. Peter, the brother of James and Jesus, taught traditional Jewish law: "But when Cephas [Peter] came to Antioch, I opposed him to his face, because he stood self-condemned" (Galatians 2.11).[3] The word 'Cephas' is Greek for *the rock*.

Paul's version of religion was a blending of Greek theology, Roman customs and Jewish Scriptures. He had a history of disregarding some of the Jewish laws whenever it helped him gain converts to his version of Judaism.

Paul and his teachings had been repeatedly condemned by James, the apostle Peter and many others in the Jerusalem Jewish community.

---

[1] *Jewish Literacy*, Rabbi Joseph Telushkin, page 126
[2] *The Jewish Annotated New Testament*, Levine and Brettler, page 339
[3] *The Jewish Annotated New Testament*, Levine and Brettler, page 336

After the death of Jesus, the apostles continued to be in close contact with many of the Jewish people in Judea.

In spite of his differences with the Jewish establishment, Paul's writings indicate that he considered himself a Jew, at least during the early years of his ministry: "It is now perfectly understandable that Paul would admit at Acts 13:28 that there was no Jewish death penalty. It makes perfect sense that, of all the figures in the New Testament, Paul would be the one to retain a glimmer of consciousness that the priests had intended and declared *no harm* towards Jesus. He knew this because he had worked for the high priest. And this is not the only thing that can now be explained for the first time. This also clarifies why Paul in his letters manifests no overriding hatred for fellow Jews or Jewish leaders and why he never makes Jewish responsibility for Jesus' death a feature of his beliefs".[1] "This is a highly noteworthy aspect of his letters which scholars have long been aware of but have never accounted for. I am saying it is very simple: He knew that no Jews, not even Jewish leaders, had done anything bad to Jesus. So blaming Jews is not an issue for Paul and never comes up in his writings, which is remarkable when you consider how important this theme is in the Gospels and even in Acts (though not in any of Paul's remarks recorded in Acts). The only Pauline reference to Jews killing Jesus is at 1 Thessalonians 2:14-16".[2] "It just does not fit everything else we have from him. The other reason given is that if you take out this comment about Jewish responsibility in 1 Thessalonians 2:14-16, then what comes before and after this makes

---

[1] *The Ghost in the Gospels*, Leon Zitzer, pages 242-243
[2] *The Ghost in the Gospels*, Leon Zitzer, page 243

better sense together; the comment itself sounds like an interruption, an insertion put in later".[1]

Paul had Roman citizenship: "The police reported these words to the magistrates, and they were afraid when they heard that they were Roman citizens" (Acts 16.38).[2] "The tribune came and asked Paul, *Tell me, are you a Roman citizen? And he said, Yes.* The tribune answered, *It cost me a large sum of money to get my citizenship.* Paul said, *But I was born a citizen*" (Acts 22.27-28).[3]

By trade, Paul was a tent maker: "There he found a Jew named Aquila, a native of Pontus, who had recently come from Italy with his wife Priscilla, because Claudius had ordered all Jews to leave Rome. Paul went to see them, and, because he was of the same trade, he stayed with them, and they worked together – by trade they were tentmakers" (Acts 18.2-3).[4]

For the Jews, genealogy has remained an issue through the centuries, with more or less emphasis, depending on the religious and political persuasion of those in positions of power and influence.

The Peter who was Paul's traveling companion, was not Simon Peter, the brother of Jesus and James. He was Peter Magus, *a friend of Rome.* A later writing identifies Peter Magus as a person not related to Peter the apostle: "However these things may be, the basic treatment of the confrontation between Simon Peter and Simon *Magus* in Caesarea,

---

[1] *The Ghost in the Gospels*, Leon Zitzer, page 243
[2] *The Jewish Annotated New Testament*, Levine and Brettler, page 232
[3] *The Jewish Annotated New Testament*, Levine and Brettler, page 243
[4] *The Jewish Annotated New Testament*, Levine and Brettler, page 234

where the Pseudo-clementines correctly locate it, can be shown to be more historical than the patently more fantastic presentation of it in the Book of Acts. The *Recognitions* also clear up Acts' lack of precision about Simon *Magus'* place of origin, which is identified as Gitta in Samaria. This is also confirmed in Eusebius".[1]

The New Testament contains the *First Letter of Peter* and the *Second Letter of Peter*. These epistles were very likely not written by the apostle Peter as the Catholic Church has always taught: "Finally, the sophisticated Greek of the letter is unlikely to have been written by a presumably uneducated Galilean fisherman whose primary language was Aramaic. The letter's skillful blending of allusions to the Hebrew Bible (Tanakh) with allusions to Greco-Roman literature and the religious language of the Hellenistic world suggest an author at home in both Jewish and Greek traditions".[2]

James may have been the leader of the apostles after the death of Jesus, as suggested by the author Leon Zitzer. According to Catholic tradition, the apostle Peter was the first 'church' leader after the death of Jesus. However, it is more likely that it was Peter Magus, the companion of Paul.

The letters written by Paul express many of his values and beliefs that were contrary to those of Jesus and his followers. This is evident in his epistles: "Now it is evident that no one is justified before God by the

---

[1] *James, the Brother of Jesus*, Robert Eisenman, pages 77-78
[2] *The Jewish Annotated New Testament*, Levine and Brettler, footnote, page 443

law; for *The one who is righteous will live by faith*" (Galatians 3.11).[1]
"When they heard it, they praised God. Then they said to him, *You see, brother, how many thousands of believers there are among the Jews, and they are all zealous for the law*" (Acts 21.20-21).[2]

Many of the teachings found in Paul's epistles are most likely only Paul's. They were his own Hellenistic adaptation of the Jewish faith, not the Conservative Jewish values taught by Jesus and his family, friends and apostles.

Depending on his audience, Paul changed the importance he placed on various Jewish laws when he spoke to potential converts in order to win them to his understanding of Jesus' teachings and at the same time preach his own perspective of Judaism: "To the Jews I became as a Jew, in order to win Jews. To those under the law I became as one under the law (though I myself am not under the law) so that I might win those under the law. To those outside the law I became as one outside the law (though I am not free from God's law but am under Christ's law) so that I might win those outside the law" (1 Corinthians 9.20-21).[3] "To the weak I became weak, so that I might win the weak. I have become all things to all people, that I might by all means save some" (1 Corinthians 9.22).[4]

---

[1] *The Jewish Annotated New Testament*, Levine and Brettler
  pages 337-338
[2] *The Jewish Annotated New Testament*, Levine and Brettler, page 241
[3] *The Jewish Annotated New Testament*, Levine and Brettler, page 302
[4] *The Jewish Annotated New Testament*, Levine and Brettler, page 302

Paul wrote his own theology, much of which was contrary to basic Jewish teaching. He wrote what he believed Jesus' teachings and beliefs should and would have been had Jesus been Greek-educated, as he himself was: "In all cases the gospel authors have woven Jesus' opponents as characters into a dramatic narrative which is controlled by their purposes in writing the story rather than by a desire or ability to reproduce faithfully the historical events of Jesus' life. Thus the Pharisees undergo mutation [as can be seen in the New Testament] for dramatic and theological purposes and are often attacked as Jesus' opponents".[1]

The Orthodox Jews were always known for their literal interpretation of Scriptures, not the Pharisees. The New Testament book *Acts of the Apostles* is incorrect in stating the opposite concerning Paul: "They have known for a long time, if they are willing to testify, that I have belonged to the strictest sect of our religion and lived as a Pharisee" (Acts 26.5).[2] The Pharisees did not teach a literal interpretation of the laws in Scriptures and were generally not considered the strictest party.

Many of Paul's writings were shared among the writers of the gospels. Each of the gospels demonstrates a gradual increase of slander against the Jewish people. The term *the jews* is used in a disparaging way a total of sixteen times in the gospels of *Mark*, *Matthew* and *Luke*, while in the gospel of *John*, which was written approximately a century later, it appears seventy-one times.

---

[1] *The Anchor Bible Dictionary*, Pharisees, volume 5, page 295
[2] *The Jewish Annotated New Testament*, Levine and Brettler, page 247

Paul's claim that the ancient writings in the Jewish Scriptures state that the Messiah was destined to suffer is not true. As at least one modern day Jewish writer stated, such a prophecy does not appear anywhere in the Old Testament: "This tradition has no external historical support".[1] For the Jewish people, salvation generally referred to the gaining of national freedom and spiritual renewal, not individual eternal salvation.

Paul re-defined Abraham's teachings concerning the Law: "For the promise that he would inherit the world did not come to Abraham or to his descendants through the law but through the righteousness of faith" (Romans 4.13).[2]

Paul explained Jewish teachings in such a way as to bring his own beliefs into the non-Jewish world: "As regards the gospel they are enemies of God for your sake" (Romans 11.28).[3] And: "For we hold that a person is justified by faith apart from works prescribed by the law" (Romans 3.28).[4]

The Jews had developed a strict procedure for killing animals that were to be eaten, especially those that were to be offered as sacrifice in the Temple. Paul taught against the Jewish dietary laws as they applied to the holy days and the Sabbath: "Therefore do not let anyone condemn you in matters of food and drink or of observing festivals, new moons, or

---

[1] *The Jewish Annotated New Testament*, Levine and Brettler, footnote, page 191
[2] *The Jewish Annotated New Testament*, Levine and Brettler, page 262
[3] *The Jewish Annotated New Testament*, Levine and Brettler, page 278
[4] *The Jewish Annotated New Testament*, Levine and Brettler, page 261

sabbaths" (Colossians 2.16).[1] "I know and am persuaded in the Lord Jesus that nothing is unclean in itself; but it is unclean for anyone who thinks it unclean" (Romans 14.14).[2] "Eat whatever is sold in the meat market without raising any question on the ground of conscience" (1 Corinthians 10.25).[3]

The following statement certainly was not true: "So he went in and out among them in Jerusalem, speaking boldly in the name of the Lord" (Acts 9.28).[4] This was not the case: "All who ever saw our temple are aware of the general design of the building, and the inviolable barriers which preserved its sanctity. It had four surrounding courts, each with its special statutory restrictions. The outer court was open to all, foreigners included; women during their impurity were alone refused admission. To the second court all Jews were admitted and, when uncontaminated by any defilement, their wives; to the third male Jews, if clean and purified; to the fourth the priests robed in their priestly vestments. The sanctuary was entered only by the high-priests".[5]

Paul criticized the Jewish officials for not associating with non-Jews and for not allowing non-Jews to enter the Temple courtyard. This would not have been the case for the converts and non-Jews who accepted all of

---

[1] *The Jewish Annotated New Testament*, Levine and Brettler, pages 367-368
[2] *The Jewish Annotated New Testament*, Levine and Brettler, page 283
[3] *The Jewish Annotated New Testament*, Levine and Brettler, page 303
[4] *The Jewish Annotated New Testament*, Levine and Brettler, page 218
[5] *Josephus, Life Against Apion, Volume I, Book II*, Thackeray, pages 333 and 335

the basic precepts of the Jewish faith. Though, it would have been the case for anyone, including converts, who openly disregarded the laws concerning the sanctity of blood.

Paul's teachings regarding blood violated the most basic laws and sacred traditions of the Jewish people. There are many writings in Scriptures that address the respect that was and is absolutely required of every Jewish person concerning blood.

The sacredness of blood was at the very heart of many of the Jewish laws regarding marriage, Temple admittance, religious purity, dietary restrictions and other related issues: "This is a lasting ordinance for the generations to come, wherever you live: You must not eat any fat or any blood" (Leviticus 3.17).[1] "Anyone who eats blood must be cut off from their people" (Leviticus 7.27).[2] "But you must not eat the blood" (Deuteronomy 12.16).[3] "But be sure you do not eat the blood, because the blood is the life" (Deuteronomy 12.23).[4]

The intentional violation of the sanctity of blood was considered a direct affront to God. The Roman and Herod violations of the sanctity of blood within the Temple were among the major issues that precipitated the First Jewish War.

Paul also taught against the legitimacy of the Jewish hierarchy, their legal system and even of a 'Chosen People': "In that renewal there is no longer Greek and Jew, circumcised and uncircumcised, barbarian,

---

[1] Bible, *New International Version*, page 168
[2] Bible, *New International Version*, page 175
[3] Bible, *New International Version*, page 316
[4] Bible, *New International Version*, page 316

Scythian, slave and free" (Colossians 3.11).[1] "For the law brings wrath; but where there is no law, neither is there violation" (Romans 4.15).[2]

Paul also contradicted Jewish law and tradition when he stated that circumcision was not necessary: "Rather, a person is a Jew who is one inwardly, and real circumcision is a matter of the heart – it is spiritual and not literal" (Romans 2.29).[3] "Is this blessedness, then, pronounced only on the circumcised, or also on the uncircumcised? We say, *Faith was reckoned to Abraham as righteousness*" (Romans 4.9).[4] For Paul, this philosophy would have made it easier to recruit men to his congregations because prospective male converts would not have to undergo the pain of circumcision.

[1] *The Jewish Annotated New Testament*, Levine and Brettler, page 369
[2] *The Jewish Annotated New Testament*, Levine and Brettler, page 262
[3] *The Jewish Annotated New Testament*, Levine and Brettler, page 259
[4] *The Jewish Annotated New Testament*, Levine and Brettler, page 262

Chapter 24

Paul lost his Temple privileges

The author Robert Eisenman in his book *James, the Brother of Jesus* points out many instances where the New Testament writers incorrectly recorded people's political affiliation and religious statements. The New Testament writers, or those who revised the writings later, very likely did so to support their own version of history and their own interpretation of many of the Jewish laws.

The Jews had great pride in their heritage. Jewish fathers passed their beliefs and traditions on to their sons, who in turn passed them on down through the generations. It was through a man's sons that he himself would be remembered, as well as being assured the fulfillment of God's promises: "I will establish my covenant as an everlasting covenant between me and you and your descendants after you for the generations to come" (Genesis 17.7).[1]

Later in his ministry, Paul was attacked by a large number of Jewish people and forced out of the Temple. One of the major issues the Jewish officials had with Paul was that he taught the Gentiles who converted to Judaism that they did not need to adhere to several of the Jewish laws, including the dietary restrictions and circumcision.

---

[1] Bible, *New International Version*, page 24

During the course of his ministry, Paul was brought before the Sanhedrin several times because so many of his teachings were contrary to Jewish Law: "Five times I have received from the Jews the forty lashes minus one. Three times I was beaten with rods. Once I received a stoning" (2 Corinthians 11.24-25).[1] In spite of the lashing, Paul continued to teach the Jewish religion.

At some point, the Pharisees brought the issue of Paul's teachings before a Sanhedrin council. The council decided that Paul's teaching no longer conformed to even basic Jewish law. The Sanhedrin had determined that Paul was a blasphemer, no longer a member of the Chosen People. Because of this, Paul was excommunicated. Paul then used his vendetta against *the jews* as part of his theology. With his separation from the Jewish community, Paul was forced to re-evaluate his own 'salvation' theology.

The 'apostle' Paul's writings speak of the many confrontations he had with James, the brother of Jesus. One of these confrontations happened when Paul came to the Temple to celebrate a feast day and to preach his own beliefs. James met him there and told Paul that he needed to observe one month as a Nazirite/Nazorite (self-imposed penitential living) in atonement for past transgressions, including having violated the sacredness of the Temple. Instead, Paul attacked James. During this altercation James accidently fell or Paul pushed him from the Pinnacle of the Temple and left him for dead. James survived the fall, but sustained serious injuries, which included both of his legs being broken.

---

[1] *The Jewish Annotated New Testament*, Levine and Brettler, page 329

The crowd within the Temple immediately mobbed Paul in support of James. They were determined to apprehend Paul since he had already been excommunicated and had entered the Temple grounds illegally. Paul's friend (or possibly nephew) Julius Archelaus saw Paul's life was in danger and immediately asked the Roman officials for troops to protect Paul.

The Roman troops rescued Paul and immediately brought the crowd under control and escorted him out of Jerusalem, to Caesarea, a Roman stronghold on the Mediterranean coast: "Then he summoned two of the centurions and said, *Get ready to leave by nine o'clock tonight for Caesarea with two hundred soldiers, seventy horsemen, and two hundred spearmen. Also provide mounts for Paul to ride, and take him safely to Felix the governor*" (Acts 23.23-24).[1]

It is doubtful that the Roman soldiers were traveling to Caesarea just for Paul. It is more likely that this was a routine rotation of military troops and Paul was invited to travel with them.

James survived this attack and was carried to Jericho where he recovered from these injuries. Many of the Zealots also retreated to Jericho at this time because of the escalating violence in Jerusalem. Sometime later, James had another altercation with Paul.

Paul presented God as a vengeful God: "How much worse punishment do you think will be deserved by those who have spurned the Son of God, profaned the blood of the covenant by which they were sanctified, and outraged the Spirit of grace? For we know the one who said, *Vengeance is mine, I will repay.* And again, *The Lord will judge his*

---

[1] *The Jewish Annotated New Testament*, Levine and Brettler, page 244

people. It is a fearful thing to fall into the hands of the living God" (Hebrews 10.29-31),[1]

Paul condemned the laws in Scriptures when he stated: "But law came in, with the result that the trespass multiplied" (Romans 5.20).[2] And: "Therefore, since we are receiving a kingdom that cannot be shaken, let us give thanks, by which we offer to God an acceptable worship with reverence and awe; for indeed our God is a consuming fire" (Hebrews 12.28-29).[3]

---

[1] *The Jewish Annotated New Testament*, Levine and Brettler
pages 419-420
[2] *The Jewish Annotated New Testament*, Levine and Brettler, page 264
[3] *The Jewish Annotated New Testament*, Levine and Brettler, page 425

Chapter 25

Paul continued to teach outside of Judea

It was sometime between 62 C.E. and 67 C.E. that the Sanhedrin officially excommunicated Paul and forbade him from entering the Temple or any synagogue, from possessing or reading Scriptures and from participating in any Jewish religious function. Paul had thus been formally rejected and excommunicated by the Jewish authorities. With his excommunication, Paul lost all legal claim to Judaism even though he had been teaching the Jewish faith in synagogues and people's homes in several countries outside of Judea, albeit his own version of Judaism.

With his excommunication, Paul no longer had a stake in a Jewish nation or traditional Jewish culture. Also, since he was no longer a member of the Jewish community he was free to incorporate Greek theology and myth as well as Roman culture into what he then considered his own Roman church.

Paul, with his excommunication, was no longer a member of the Chosen People and had little concern for a Jewish nation. This can be seen in his letters. Paul denied Judea's right to independence and acknowledged the legitimacy of Roman domination and taxation: "Let every person be subject to the governing authorities; for there is no authority except from God" (Romans 13.1).[1] "Pay to all what is due them

---

[1] *The Jewish Annotated New Testament*, Levine and Brettler, page 280

– taxes to whom taxes are due, revenue to whom revenue is due, respect to whom respect is due, honor to whom honor is due" (Romans 13.7).[1]

After Paul was excommunicated by the Jewish authorities, his writings increasingly demonized the Pharisees even though he himself claimed to have been a Pharisee. However, it is more likely that Paul was a Sadducee since early in his ministry he was employed by the priests in the Temple who were usually, if not always, Sadducees. The gospel writers, or more likely those who made changes later, followed Paul's lead in slandering the Pharisees.

Paul spoke out against the first command in Scriptures which, according to Jewish interpretation, considered it essential that a man marry and have at least one child. Paul stated: "It is well for a man not to touch a woman" (1 Corinthians 7.1).[2] "So then, he who marries his fiancée does well; and he who refrains from marriage will do better" (1 Corinthians 7.38).[3].

Bias against women can also be seen in Paul's writings in his other epistles: "… but any woman who prays or prophesies with her head unveiled disgraces her head – it is one and the same thing as having her head shaved. For if a woman will not veil herself, then she should cut off her hair; but if it is disgraceful for a woman to have her hair cut off or to be shaved, she should wear a veil. For a man ought not to have his head veiled, since he is the image and reflection of God; but woman is the reflection of man. Indeed, man was not made from woman, but woman

---

[1] *The Jewish Annotated New Testament*, Levine and Brettler, page 281
[2] *The Jewish Annotated New Testament*, Levine and Brettler, page 297
[3] *The Jewish Annotated New Testament*, Levine and Brettler, page 299

from man. Neither was man created for the sake of woman, but woman for the sake of man" (1 Corinthians 11.5-9).[1]

"Let a woman learn in silence with full submission. I permit no woman to teach or to have authority over a man; she is to keep silent. For Adam was formed first, then Eve; and Adam was not deceived, but the woman was deceived and became a transgressor. Yet she will be saved through childbearing" (1 Timothy 2.11-15).[2] "As in all the churches of the saints, women should be silent in the churches. For they are not permitted to speak, but should be subordinate, as the law also says" (1 Corinthians 14.33-35).[3] "Husbands, in the same way, show consideration for your wives in your life together, paying honor to the woman as the weaker sex" (1 Peter 3.7).[4]

With Paul's attitude toward women, it is not surprising that his wife, if he was indeed married, is mentioned only indirectly in the Bible, and only once: "Do we not have the right to be accompanied by a believing wife, as do the other apostles and the brothers of the Lord and Cephas [Cephas/Peter/*the rock*]?" (1 Corinthians 9.5).[5]

Many Christian leaders during the following centuries followed Paul's lead in developing church laws and teachings that perpetuate this same bias against women. This attitude is not reflected in the teachings of Jesus as recorded in the gospels nor in Jewish Scriptures: "A wife of

---

[1] *The Jewish Annotated New Testament*, Levine and Brettler, page 304
[2] *The Jewish Annotated New Testament*, Levine and Brettler, page 385
[3] *The Jewish Annotated New Testament*, Levine and Brettler, page 310
[4] *The Jewish Annotated New Testament*, Levine and Brettler, page 440
[5] *The Jewish Annotated New Testament*, Levine and Brettler, page 301

noble character who can find? She is worth far more than rubies. Her husband has full confidence in her and lacks nothing of value. She brings him good, not harm, all the days of her life" (Proverbs 31.11-12).[1] "*She is clothed with strength and dignity; she can laugh at the days to come. She speaks with wisdom, and faithful instruction is on her tongue. She watches over the affairs of her household and does not eat the bread of idleness. Her children arise and call her blessed; her husband also, and he praises her: Many women do noble things, but you surpass them all.* Charm is deceptive, and beauty is fleeting; but a woman who fears the LORD is to be praised. Honor her for all that her hands have done, and let her works bring her praise at the city gate" (Proverbs 31.25-31).[2]

Philo, a Greek-educated Egyptian Jew, also held very sexist ideas. He lived from 20 B.C.E. to about 50 C.E. and is famous for his lengthy interpretation of the meanings behind many of the stories in the Scriptures.

Following is an example of Philo's attitude toward women: "For as in the roads, one may behold a great variety of living beings, inanimate and animate, irrational and rational, good and bad, slaves and free, young and old, male and female, strangers and natural citizens, sick and healthy, mutilated and perfect; so also in the soul there are motions inanimate, and imperfect, and diseased, and slavish, and female, and innumerable others of the class of evils; and on the other hand, there are

---

[1] Bible, *New International Version*, page 1113
[2] Bible, *New International Version*, pages 1113-1114

motions which are living, and perfect, and masculine, and free, and healthy, and ripe, and virtuous, and genuine, and really legitimate".[1]

In the early Christian Church, in particular for many church leaders, the discrimination against women went beyond 'typical' bias. Origen (185 C.E. – 254 C.E.), a Church theologian, wrote that it was not proper for a woman to speak in church, however admirable or holy she was, because what she said came from female lips and that God does not stoop to look upon what is feminine and of the flesh. He also wrote a synopsis on six versions of the Old Testament.

Ipiphanius (315 – 403 C.E.) was born into a Hellenized Jewish family. He became a Christian and later the Bishop of Salamis, Cyprus. He wrote that the female sex is easily seduced, weak, and without much understanding. He said that the devil seeks to vomit out this disorder through women and that he wished people would apply masculine reasoning and destroy the folly of these women.

John Chrysostom (347 – 407 C.E.), the Archbishop of Constantinople, preached against Christians participating in any Jewish holy day celebrations and made it known that he hated Jews. He also expressed his attitude toward women. He stated that women's bodily beauty is nothing less than phlegm, blood, bile, rheum, and the fluid of digested food. He said that if you consider what is stored up behind those lovely eyes, the angle of the nose, the mouth and cheeks you will agree that the well-proportioned body is merely a whitened sepulcher.

---

[1] *The Works of Philo*, translated by C. D. Yonge, page 48

Women in many Middle Eastern countries in ancient times were required to draw water from wells or streams and to go to the marketplace while most of the men were at work in the fields or elsewhere. This was to reduce the amount of time that the women would be seen in public by the men of the city or village. The women and older girls were required to wear full-length dresses and veils whenever they appeared in public. Supposedly, this was to prevent men's lustful thoughts and any subsequent inappropriate actions.

The attitude of the early Catholic Church leaders toward the 'higher virtue' of celibacy and the accompanying rules to hide women's sexuality continued to expand over the centuries. One likely reason the men (the Church hierarchy) decided women should never be allowed in the priesthood was that they believed women by their very nature were temptresses. Catholic women who joined religious orders and dedicated their lives to the service of their communities were eventually forced to live in convents to avoid becoming a 'temptation' to men, including the parish clergy.

Money and power within the Catholic Church leadership was also a factor in the changes in Church law that prohibited women from joining the priesthood and the law that required priests to remain celibate.

Later, the Catholic Church allowed nuns to go back into society in limited ways. Even then they were required to wear unattractive clothing to minimize their feminine features. Their uniforms were typically long black dresses and head coverings that concealed their hair.

The dress requirements and socially acceptable choices for women changed considerably in the Western world during the nineteenth and early twentieth century. One of the major factors for this change was the rapid increase in industrialization within many of these countries.

The United States military entered World War I in 1917 and World War II in 1941. Subsequently, many men were drafted into the armed services, which decreased the number of men in the work force. This, coupled with the dramatic increase in the demand for war supplies, made it necessary for many more women to work in the factories and offices.

During this era it became increasingly acceptable for women in the United States to speak at public gatherings. With the passage of the Nineteenth Amendment to the United States Constitution on June 4, 1919 and the ratification of that amendment on August 18, 1920, women in the United States gained the right to vote.

Hopefully, cultural and legal changes throughout the world will someday allow women equality in all areas of society, including organized religion. All members of every religious establishment have the obligation to re-evaluate their own beliefs and teachings and acknowledge the bias against women that is written into the New Testament and Christian history.

They also have a social responsibility to encourage equality and inclusiveness for women on all levels and a sense of wholeness within their respective religious establishments and society in general.

Paul, a Roman citizen, wrote his own religious and political perspective into his letters. Much of this bias against *the jews* was later incorporated into the New Testament, some of which can be seen in the gospel of *Matthew* (Matthew 27.24-25) where the author, or a revisionist later, stated that Pilate washed his hands of any responsibility for the fate of Jesus.

As stated earlier, these statements appear to have offered an excuse for many people to persecute the Jewish people repeatedly during the past two thousand years. Sadly, this portion of the gospel continues to be read in Catholic and other Christian churches throughout the world.

This bigotry against the Jewish people is very likely one of the insertions made in the New Testament by Christian leaders, decades or even centuries after the death of Jesus, at least in part, to pacify the Romans. The Jewish people had always been taught: "The child will not share the guilt of the parent, nor will the parent share the guilt of the child" (Ezekiel 18.20).[1]

These writings further alienated Jewish people in spite of the fact that it was the Jewish people, their history and their culture that provided Christians with the Bible and a belief in one God: "In the generations following Jesus and Paul, Judaism and Christianity moved in two very different directions with regard to the observances that characterized Second Temple Judaism.

Rabbinic Jews maintained circumcision and expanded the dietary and Sabbath laws. Rabbinic Judaism also developed fuller systems of law to deal with marriage, civil matters, and criminal law, all the while maintaining the memory of laws concerning matters of purity and sacrifice that were no longer practiced following the Temple's destruction. These came to be recorded in the first great literary monument of rabbinic Judaism, the law book known as the Mishnah.

---

[1] Bible, *New International Version*, page 1418

Christianity, by contrast, moved in the direction of Galatians 5.2 and Mark 7.19b: foods were declared clean, circumcision was disregarded, and the Jewish holy days, Sabbaths, and other observances were replaced by distinctive Christian rites such as baptism. The writings of the early church thinkers take on a tone that is entirely different from the legal style of the Mishnah. And Judaism comes to be seen by some Christians–unfairly–as a *legalistic* religion".[1]

[1] *The Jewish Annotated New Testament*, Levine and Brettler, footnote, page 518

Chapter 26

Christians distanced themselves from Judaism

James and the other apostles parted ways with the followers of Paul because of serious differences in their beliefs and values. It is Paul's teachings that have prevailed in Roman Christianity, not those of James and his followers.

At one point Paul vigorously denied the Jewish belief that observing the Torah's laws and Temple rituals made a person righteous in God's eyes. He stated that people could be saved only if they followed the laws in the Torah perfectly and that God would damn people for any violation whatsoever. Furthermore, since no one could do that, these laws must be seen as a curse, not a blessing. He then taught that to be saved, everyone must set aside the laws in the Torah: "For all who rely on the works of the law are under a curse; for it is written, *Cursed is everyone who does not observe and obey all the things written in the book of the law*" (Galatians 3.10).[1]

The Jewish people rejected virtually every element in Paul's reasoning process. While they advocated observance of the Torah, they also recognized that people would inevitably violate at least a few of these laws: "Indeed, there is no one on earth who is righteous, no one

---

[1] *The Jewish Annotated New Testament*, Levine and Brettler, page 337

who does what is right and never sins" (Ecclesiastes 7.20).[1] Well before Jesus and Paul, Judaism had worked out an extensive process for *teshuva* (repentance).

"As long as the small sect of Christians differed from their fellow Jews only with regard to certain beliefs about Jesus, they remained part of the Jewish community. **But once Paul dropped the Torah, and dropped any legal requirements for converting to Judaism, Christianity ceased being a [Jewish] sect and became a separate religion.** From the perspective of Christianity, this made Paul into a great hero, Saint Paul. Most Jews find it hard to regard him with equal adulation".[2] Unfortunately, Paul's claim that God damns people for violating any Torah law has led many people in the Western world to believe that the God of the Hebrew Bible is a harsh, vengeful figure.

Following is a quotation that addresses a Jewish scholar's response to believers in Jesus in ancient times: "Complicating the study is the question of *how* to read each source: Is it stylized rhetoric, symbolic language, or a reflection of lived reality? Were boundaries between groups apparent, or were they erected by later religious thinkers, trying to tame a messy social reality? Christ-followers, both Jew and Gentile, must have had different kinds of relationships with different kinds of Jews in different places, at different times. The dashing of hope for Jewish self-rule after the Bar Kochba revolt (132–35) [132 C.E. to 135 C.E.], coupled with the replacement of Jewish church leaders in

---

[1] Bible, *New International Version*, page 1124

[2] *Jewish Literacy*, Rabbi Joseph Telushkin, pages 128-129. Bold type has been added by the author for emphasis

Jerusalem with Gentile bishops made it very difficult to be both a loyal Jew and a Jesus-follower in Judea. This tells us nothing about the Diaspora, however, and how Jewish and Christian neighbors regarded each other in cities like Antioch and Rome".[1]

Numerous versions of the New Testament were developed during the first few centuries of Christianity. As shown in *The Anchor Bible Dictionary*, these versions included the Syriac, Latin, Coptic, Armenian, Georgian, Ethiopic, Arabic, Nubian, Persian, Sogdian, Gothic, Old Church Slavonic, Anglo-Saxon and Old High German. Many of these writings gave conflicting accounts of people and events. Each contained somewhat different theological doctrines and varying degrees of re-written history.

Most Christian holy days are set using a solar calendar. However, the lunar calendar is used to set the dates for Easter Sunday and Ascension Thursday. Easter is always the first Sunday after spring's first full moon. Ascension is celebrated forty days, plus the intervening Sundays, after Easter. Christians celebrate the Last Supper on the Thursday before Easter. The Jewish day begins at sunset. Thus, using the Jewish method of time-keeping, the Last Supper was on Friday, the evening before the Sabbath, the same day he was crucified.

Over time, many of these manuscripts were blended together, edited, revised and officially declared The New Testament: "The tags 'Old' and 'New' institutionalized the Christian habit of Jewish

---

[1] *The Jewish Annotated New Testament*, Levine and Brettler, footnote, page 577

denigration. More than that, the creation of a New Testament amounted, in [Helmut] Koester's words, to the creation of 'an authoritative instrument ... that would establish Christianity as a separate religion'".[1] The New Testament was so named to show superiority over Judaism, in effect stating that the Old Testament was only a backdrop for Christianity. The Roman ruler Tertullian, about 200 C.E., was the first official to use this term 'New Testament'.

For many Christians, in centuries past, Judaism was thought of as an antiquated and irrelevant religion.

---

[1] *Constantine's Sword*, James Carroll, page 146

Chapter 27

The First Jewish War cost thousands of lives

Rome's oppressive policies progressively increased tensions in Judea: "Many of the Roman governors in that era who were appointed to office overseas clearly regarded the job as an opportunity to enrich themselves and wield great power with little control from distant Rome. So it was that from 44 C.E. a whole series of thoroughly unsuitable governors seem to have deliberately gone out of their way to provoke the Jews into rebellion".[1]

Judea and the nearby countries were impacted by a drought that began in the year 45 C.E. This resulted in widespread famine and starvation that lasted several years. During this time Judas, quite possibly the brother of Jesus, preached in northern Syria and is credited with the conversion of Queen Helen.

Queen Helen's husband, King Agbarus, had several wives; each queen lived in one of his several Persian kingdoms. King Agbarus had given Helen both Mesopotamia and Parthia for her to rule.

After Helen's conversion, she came to the aid of the Jewish people by sending them considerable funds for the purchase of grain from Egypt. Later, she moved to Jerusalem with her two sons Izates (Isaac)

---

[1] *The Dead Sea Scrolls Rediscovered*, Stephen Hodge, page 59

and Monobazus and completed two seven-year terms of Nazirite-type lifestyle.

From all indications, the 'twelve' apostles and their early followers remained true to the Jewish faith and were never banned from the Temple. Judas, again possibly the apostle Judas, was arrested and beheaded in 45 C.E. or 46 C.E. by Herod of Chalcis for preaching the same Judaism that Jesus had taught more than a decade earlier. Judas was buried in Berytus, Phoenicia (Beirut, Lebanon).

Later, Rome tried to conquer Adiabene, a province which had been under the rule of Queen Helen for some time. Helen took this opportunity to have the Jewish people join her in the fight against Roman aggression. In response, the Romans called for additional troops from Caesarea. These troops had to cross the Beit Horon Pass in order to reach Jerusalem and then Adiabene. Caesarea was a Mediterranean port city rebuilt by Herod the Great. This city functioned at various times as the Roman administration headquarters for the Roman authorities in Judea.

Queen Helen's son Izates led his mother's troops and the Jewish men in an attack on the Romans at this mountain pass. Izates' forces were not able to stop the advance of the Roman army and Izates was killed. Nonetheless, this gave some Jews a renewed hope that they might finally unite and drive the Herods and Romans out of Judea. Very recently, in 2007, archeologists uncovered a memorial in Jerusalem honoring Queen Helen for her kindness toward the Jewish people in their time of need.

H. St. J. Thackeray translated and published *The Works of Josephus*, the writings of Flavius Josephus ben Matthias (Yosef ben Mattityahu in

Hebrew). These writings are an invaluable resource for the history of that era. However, as a theological source, they may be less accurate or objective.

Josephus was from an upper-class family. He was educated and well versed in both Jewish law and Greek literature. His writings indicate that he had likely spent at least some time 'in the wilderness' with the Essenes. He helped manage the Jewish affairs of Galilee. During one of his trips to Rome, he pled the cause of a few Jewish priests. In 66 C.E., he spoke out against the Romans in an effort to prevent a Jewish revolt.

However, riots within the Temple courtyard continued to become increasingly violent: "After the death of Herod, sovereign of Chalcis, Claudius presented his kingdom to his nephew Agrippa [Marcus Julius Agrippa], son of Agrippa [Agrippa I]. As procurator of the rest of the province (Tiberius) Alexander was succeeded by Cumanus; under his administration, disturbances broke out, resulting in another large loss of Jewish lives. The usual [very large] crowd had assembled at Jerusalem for the feast of unleavened bread [Passover], and the Roman cohort had taken up its position on the roof of the portico of the temple; for a body of men in arms invariably mounts guard at the feasts, to prevent disorders arising from such a concourse of people. Thereupon one of the soldiers, raising his robe, stooped in an indecent attitude, so as to turn his backside to the Jews, and made a noise in keeping with his posture. Enraged at this insult, the whole multitude with loud cries called upon Cumanus to punish the soldier; some of the more hot-headed young men and seditious persons in the crowd started a fight, and, picking up stones, hurled them at the troops. Cumanus, fearing a general attack upon himself, sent for reinforcements. These troops pouring into the porticoes, the Jews were seized with irresistible panic and turned to fly from the Temple and make their escape into the town. But such violence was used as they pressed round the exits that they were trodden underfoot and crushed to death by one another; upwards of thirty thousand perished, and the feast was turned into mourning for the whole nation and for every household into lamentation".[1]

The Zealots had become increasingly determined to force the Romans out of Judea. In 66 C.E. they burned Herod's palace which contained all of the Temple debt records and served as living quarters for a large number of Roman soldiers. In retaliation, the Roman military advanced against the Jews. They did not draw any distinction between Pharisees, Zealots, Essenes, Herodian Jews, Christian Jews or any other Jewish group or sect. The lives of all Jews and Jewish converts within Judea and all of the neighboring countries that were under Roman control were in danger.

After the death of James in 67 C.E. tensions and rioting continued to escalate not only in Jerusalem, but throughout Judea. Some of the Zealots demanded that priests no longer offer sacrifices on behalf of Herod or the Romans or any other non-Jew.

According to Josephus, there was a corresponding rise in religious fanaticism fueled by self-styled visionaries and messianic prophets. He wrote that some Jews led their desperate followers into the desert, promising them redemption through repentance while others incessantly

---

[1] *Josephus, The Jewish War, Volume II, Book II,* Thackeray, pages 411 and 413

preached against Rome and urged the people to take up arms against their overlords. Even the priesthood was not free from discord. Many of the priests seized the tithes that might otherwise have gone to the poor.

The Jews did not have a full-time army. They enlisted the common people and their slaves to form a militia whenever necessary. When they did fight, it was quite often a guerrilla style of warfare. Thousands of Jews and their recruits lost their lives fighting the Romans. The only advantage the Jews had at this time was their determination to rid Judea of the Romans.

Unlike the Jews, the Romans had a constant flow of soldiers available to them. The Romans had full-time soldiers who were well-armed, well-trained and well-paid. In spite of this, the Zealots, who typically had minimal or no military training, continued to fight the Romans. After several years of war throughout Judea, the Zealots were forced to retreat to Jerusalem. As the city of Jerusalem fell they retreated to the Temple.

The Temple had a huge store of food supplies set aside for emergencies. The Zealots burned these food supplies in an effort to force all of the Jews within Jerusalem during this siege to join their fight against the Romans.

In the year 70 C.E. the Roman emperor Vespasian commanded four legions for the final assault on Jerusalem. At this point, Josephus was considered by most Jews to be a traitor. He assisted the Roman general Titus during the last months of the war, including the final assault on Jerusalem.

Josephus wrote many details of the Roman war against the Jews: "The total number of prisoners taken throughout the entire war amounted to ninety-seven thousand, and of those who perished during the siege, from first to last, to one million one hundred thousand. Of these the greater number were of Jewish blood, but not natives of the place; for, having assembled from every part of the country for the feast of unleavened bread [Passover/Pesakh], they found themselves suddenly enveloped in the war, with the result that this over-crowding produced first pestilence, and later the added and more rapid scourge of famine".[1]

The First Jewish War ended in 70 C.E. with the Romans totally destroying the city's defensive walls that encompassed the old portion of the city. They also destroyed the Temple, except the Western Wall (Wailing Wall or Kotel) which still stands today: "The army now having no victims either for slaughter or plunder, through lack of all objects on which to vent their rage – for they would assuredly never have desisted through a desire to spare anything so long as there was work to be done – Caesar ordered the whole city and the temple to be razed to the ground, leaving only the loftiest of the towers, Phasael, Hippicus, and Mariamme, and the portion of the wall enclosing the city on the west: the latter as an encampment for the garrison that was to remain, and the towers to indicate to posterity the nature of the city and of the strong defenses which had yet yielded to Roman prowess".[2]

By the end of the war, the Romans had killed nearly all of the Jews within the city of Jerusalem who could not or would not leave and many

---

[1] *Josephus, The Jewish War, Volume IV, Book VI*, Thackeray, page 299
[2] *Josephus, The Jewish War, Volume IV, Book VII*, Thackeray, page 307

other Jews throughout the Roman world. This marked the end of the Jewish State and the end of Herodian rule in Judea. Judea was then re-named Syria Palaestina. Jerusalem was no longer the capital. Vespasian returned to Rome after he destroyed the Temple and declared that *he was Christ, the savior of the world, the savior that had been promised in Hebrew Scriptures.*

An eminent sage, rabbi Johanan ben Zakkai, escaped from Jerusalem shortly before the military's final assault on the Temple. He pretended to be dead as his friends carried him and many sacred Jewish writings out of Jerusalem in a casket. In the years that followed, he went on to share his wealth of knowledge and wisdom.

By the year 73 C.E. all pockets of resistance had been eliminated. Also, Rome declared that the half-shekel (two denarii) annual Temple tax paid by every adult Jewish male was from that time on a penal tax to be paid by all adult Jews, men and women alike, and was to be used to rebuild the Temple of Jupiter in Rome.

The First Jewish War cost the lives of many Jews: "The aftermath of the destruction of Jerusalem and the slaughter or enslavement of hundreds of thousands of Jews must have left deep wounds in the country".[1] Even though the Roman army killed many of the Jews in Jerusalem in the final year of the war, many had lost their lives due to starvation or fighting each other for the last of the food.

The majority of the treasures taken from the Jewish people and the Temple during this war were sent to Rome to finance the ten-year building of the famous/infamous Colosseum: "Josephus said that the

---

[1] *The Dead Sea Scrolls Rediscovered*, Stephen Hodge, page 61

whole facade of the Temple, 150 feet square, was covered with gold plates, as were the entrances and the portico. Titus would bring a huge solid-gold menorah to Rome as his greatest piece of war booty; its image can still be seen on the Arch of Titus near the Colosseum. In the Holy of Holies, every inch of wall surface was overlaid with gold. Josephus says that after the sack of Jerusalem in 70 C.E., gold from the Temple flooded the market, so much so that 'the standard of gold was depreciated to half its former value".[1] "Following this tragic event, in which thousands of Jews were killed or exiled, the survival of Judaism was in doubt. New leaders were needed to preserve the Jewish traditions as well as to interpret the Torah for a changing world. The conflict inherent in Matthew's Gospel may reflect this competition for survival, thereby explaining the harsh attitude exhibited toward the Pharisees, who were the forerunners of the rabbis. Matthew's Gospel thus may provide a look into the tensions that existed between Jewish Christians and traditional Jews following 70 CE.".[2]

After the destruction of the Temple, the Jewish fortress at Masada was the last stronghold to fall to the Romans. But then a few years later, in 73 C.E., the remaining Zealot survivors managed to overpower the Roman guards in the Masada armory. They again took control of the fortress. These nine hundred Zealots held the fortress for several months. When they realized they were about to be overrun, they mutually agreed that rather than risk 'pollution' (coming into physical contact with

---

[1] *Constantine's Sword*, James Carroll, page 97
[2] *The Jewish Annotated New Testament*, Levine and Brettler, footnote, page 2

blasphemous idolaters) they would commit mass suicide. To accomplish this, they used a lottery system to select one out of every ten men. These men killed the women and children, then, each man killed nine other men. The remaining men again selected one out of every ten men. These men then killed another 90% of those remaining. The killing lasted for two days, until only one man remained. He then killed himself.

This procedure of mass suicide/killing had been used at another fortress a few years earlier by Josephus and his followers: "Josephus later wrote that he manipulated the ensuing lottery so that he would be among the last two to survive. He then persuaded the other surviving soldier to go with him and surrender. Josephus charmed the Roman general, Vespasian, who appointed him to record the war's progress".[1] Josephus became a spy and military recorder for the Roman army. The man with Josephus was executed.

Josephus wrote a very lengthy account of the events that transpired during this era, especially the Roman military activities in Judea and the resulting repercussions for the Jewish people. The Romans honored Josephus by placing many of his writings in Rome's main library. He received many rewards for his services to Rome, including Roman citizenship. Josephus honored two Roman emperors by assuming their family name, Flavius. Josephus had betrayed his countrymen and his Jewish faith. Nonetheless, his version of those tumultuous times became the accepted version of history within Christianity and most Western non-Jewish cultures. His writings, as with Paul's, were written from a

---

[1] *Jewish Literacy*, Rabbi Joseph Telushkin, page 139

very Roman perspective and with considerable bias against both the Conservative and the Orthodox Jews.

Much of the identity of the Jews was centered on the Temple and their genealogy system. The genealogy records that had been collected over the centuries and stored in the Temple were destroyed. Many of the genealogy records that had been kept in the Jewish homes had already been destroyed prior to the destruction of the Temple during the many battles and wars in Judea and neighboring countries. This left the system of hierarchy and the very identity of just who was and who was not legally Jewish in question.

For the Jews, genealogy has remained an issue through the centuries, sometimes with more or less emphasis depending on the religious and political persuasion of those in positions of influence and power. It is this separateness that made it possible for their society and culture to survive. It has been through them that much of the world has come to share a belief in one God as well as many of the moral and legal teachings found in the Bible.

Some of the Greeks and Romans who were open-minded to the teachings of the Jewish religion eventually adopted a Jewish lifestyle. Nearly all converts to Judaism since that time have been those who married a Jewish person and completed the necessary admittance requirements.

Even today, not all Jews agree on the convert issue. Recruiting converts has never been a completely accepted part of the Jewish culture: "… the influence of the priest-teachers had the effect of preserving the tradition of racial exclusiveness in practical life, so that purity of stock continued as the token of aristocracy, family records were guarded jealously, and the separation of classes by reason of blood taint as established by Ezra remained in effect for centuries thereafter".[1]

---

[1] *Marriage Laws in the Bible and the Talmud*, Epstein, page 167

Chapter 28

Greek culture found its way into an early translation of Scriptures

The Romans destroyed the Temple in Jerusalem in the year 70 C.E. Several years later, the gospel of *Mark*, as with the other three gospels that followed, was written to teach others in their local communities about Jesus' life, his teachings and the circumstances of his death.

Only the approximate dates of the writings of the gospels are known. All of the gospels were written after Paul had been excommunicated from the official Jewish community. The gospel of *Mark* was very likely written between 70 C.E. and 75 C.E., after the destruction of the Temple. The gospel of *Matthew* was written between 75 C.E. and 80 C.E. The gospel of *Luke* was written between 80 C.E. and 85 C.E.

As each of the gospels was being written, they became increasingly hostile toward the Jewish establishment. It would have been the normal transition of events for the Jewish officials, as well as some of the people who did not know Jesus, to counter this hostility with similar recriminations.

It is very likely that the 'Christian' community that produced the gospels credited Jesus with setting down many moral guidelines even as they continued to develop their own laws decades after his death. This not only gave them a single person as a role model and patriarch, but it also gave them a voice for their own teachings. As mentioned in an earlier chapter, this was the case with Moses when he was given credit for the many laws found in the Torah that had actually been developed by a whole community during his life time and by many generations long after his death.

The *Letter of James* indicates that Jesus taught Jewish beliefs and traditions: "You will do well if you really fulfill the royal law according to the scripture" (James 2.8).[1] The *Letter of James* does not contain anything derogatory against traditional Jewish law. Most, if not all, of the congregations represented in the gospels saw themselves as Jews. There was no comparable Greek or Roman religion that subscribed to the majority of the beliefs contained in Judaism, especially the belief in only one God.

During the past two centuries, there have been many people who have researched history in an effort to find a more realistic view of Jesus and his life: "Throughout the scholarship from the 1830's until our time, there has dominated the theme of the 'recovery' of the Jesus of history. The resultant convictions range from the view that only a limited quantity of material is historically authentic respecting Jesus to the view that virtually nothing is historically authentic about him".[2] "Jewish Christians, like those who celebrated the Eucharist as a Passover meal, and Christian Jews, like those who'd continued worshipping in the Temple until its destruction or revering Jerusalem until its final

---

[1] *The Jewish Annotated New Testament*, Levine and Brettler, page 431
[2] *Judaism and Christian Beginnings*, Samuel Sandmel, page 341

obliteration, disappeared from this story and from history, if only over a very long time".[1]

It is doubtful that the gospel writers, at least not the writer of the first gospel, the gospel of *Mark*, intended to portray Jesus as a Hellenistic Jew who had set aside or disregarded the Jewish laws regarding the sanctity of blood. Catholic doctrine states that during Jesus' last meal, he changed wine into his blood, which the apostles proceeded to drink. Jesus was not a Hellenistic Jew who had set aside or disregarded the Jewish laws regarding the sanctity of blood.

For Jesus to have changed wine into blood at the Last Supper, and then have the apostles *drink the blood*, would have been *absolutely abhorrent* and repulsive to everyone within the Jewish community including those who shared that meal with Jesus. The apostle James, after Jesus' death, stated that it was immoral to drink blood: "Therefore I have reached the decision that we should not trouble those Gentiles who are turning to God, but we should write to them to abstain only from things polluted by idols and from fornication and from whatever has been strangled and from blood" (Acts 15.19-21).[2]

The gospels state that, during the Last Supper, Jesus changed bread into his body and then asked the apostles to eat it. To eat human flesh would have been considered cannibalistic by most, if not all, people in Judea especially those within the Jewish community. Such an act would have been unconscionable for Jesus and his followers, especially considering that Jesus, just before his death, had confronted those who

---

[1] *Constantine's Sword*, James Carroll, page 145
[2] *The Jewish Annotated New Testament*, Levine and Brettler, page 229

were desecrating the sacredness of the Jewish Temple and all that it stood for. The gospel accounts of the Last Supper are examples of history re-written, or, at the very least, misinterpreted to create later theology within a Roman/Hellenistic church.

The writings of Josephus mention Jesus and even speak of him as the Messiah. Most modern scholars regard the passage as not having been written by Josephus, but interjected later: "Josephus' importance to the Christian world derives from a Slavonic edition of his works, in which he wrote of Jesus, *'And there arose a man, if you could indeed call him a man'*. If this passage truly was written by Josephus, it would be the only relatively contemporaneous passage outside of the New Testament (aside from Tacitus's notation of Jesus' crucifixion) that speaks of Jesus. But virtually all scholars today believe that the paragraph about Jesus was inserted later by a Christian writer, and is definitely a forgery".[1]

Ancient records indicate that the belief in an afterlife for more than royalty dates back at least to the Egyptian First Dynasty, 3100 B.C.E. to 2890 B.C.E.: "Assuming that the kings reached the next life on the other side of the horizon, what were they going to do there? Possibly, the pharaoh would continue his royal role; we have no Egyptian proof for this, but Gilgamesh, once dead, joined the gods of the underworld to help run the place. If the early pharaohs were believed to continue their kingly functions in the afterworld, the sacrificial burials make a kind of sense. After all, if a king's power only lasts until his death, he must be obeyed during his life, but there is no good reason to follow him into death. If, on the other hand, he's still going to be waiting for you on the other side,

---

[1] *Jewish Literacy*, Rabbi Joseph Telushkin, pages 139-140

259

his power becomes all-encompassing. The passage to the undiscovered country is simply a journey from one stage of loyalty to the next".[1]

---

[1] *The History of the Ancient World,* Susan Wise Bauer, page 64

Chapter 29

Multiple translations led to several versions of the Bible

The Mediterranean area had become a hub of international trade during the Roman occupation. Several languages were used in Judea/Palestine during this period of history including Hebrew, Aramaic, Greek and Latin. There were also various dialects within these languages. As mentioned above, many Hebrew words oftentimes did not translate well phonetically into other languages. Since they were originally written, the gospels and epistles have been rewritten and translated into many languages and have undergone many changes along the way, including some very notable changes, within the past few decades.

Not all Bibles have the same verses in the *Book of Sirach*. Various manuscripts add verses 5, 9, 16, 17, 18, 21 and 2b-3. The *King James Bible* does not have verses 36 through 105 in the book *2 Esdras* in the Old Testament, even though these verses have been restored from ancient sources.

Many theologians today acknowledge that some of the writings in Scriptures are myth: "The Book of Tobit is a tale reflecting a large measure of ancient folklore. ... The account of Tobit is fiction, not history. ... Judith is a patriotic book, with literary qualities of a high order and an ending that qualifies it as being among the best of all horror stories. Judith is fiction; the use by its author of Jewish history known from the Bible is marked by either freedom or recklessness about such matters as chronology".[1]

The majority of the Old Testament quotations used in the New Testament are based on the Greek Septuagint translation of Jewish Scriptures. There are fifteen books in the Old Testament that some Churches do not recognize as being 'canonized' (not completely accurate or not historically authentic) and refer to them as 'Apocrypha'. The writers of the New Testament also used many styles of writing, including prose, poetry, narrative, direct address and what some readers today consider to be myth or legends to tell their stories. These fifteen books very likely each fall into one of these categories.

The gospels and epistles were based on oral stories that had been shared and passed down by relatives, friends and new members of this emerging religious sect. Given human nature, these stories were told and retold with at least some degree of exaggeration to make them more memorable, dramatic and exciting to their audience. This led to at least a few changes in the stories.

The people who put these stories into written form, and those who re-wrote them later, also made changes that incorporated some of their own theological and political convictions and aspirations. However, at least some changes were made unintentionally: "**Unintentional Scribal Errors**. Accidental alterations are often characterized as errors of the eye, of the ear, or of memory and (unthinking) judgment. First, those

---

[1] *Judaism and Christian Beginnings*, Samuel Sandmel, pages 59-61-62

involving oversight include (1) confusion of letters that have similar appearance ... ; (2) mistaken division of words ... ; (3) misreading of abbreviations or contractions; (4) metathesis, or interchanging the order of letters or words; (5) mistaking a less familiar word for one more familiar to the scribe; (6) haplography ("single/simple writing"), the omission of one word when it occurred twice, or two or several words (even a sentence or more – cf, Luke 14:27) that are dropped as the scribe's eye jumps from one group of letters to a similar group of letters farther down the leaf, thereby resulting in the failure to copy what lies between the two words that have a similar ending; (7) dittography ("double writing"), repetition of a letter, word, or passage because the scribe's eye went back to what had already been copied; and (8) simple misspellings due to carelessness and failure to notice the error. ... Second, unintentional errors of the ear, occurring when scribes produced copies from dictation, include (1) itacism, ... which is an interchange of various vowels and diphthongs that were similarly pronounced, ... ; (2) interchange of certain similar-sounding consonants or combinations of letters ... ; and (3) failure to emphasize or hear a rough breathing mark. Finally, unintentional errors resulting from a momentary lapse of memory include (1) the use of a synonym for the word in the exemplar ... ; (2) a change of word order; (3) and unconscious assimilation to the similar wording of another biblical passage or liturgical formulation that is better remembered than the wording the scribe has just seen in the exemplar; ... (4) unconscious harmonization with a word, phrase, or grammatical formulation in the immediate context of the passage then being copied. In addition, errors due to poor judgment may be included here, though – like certain cases of harmonization – some may deem them intentional".[1]

Some changes in the Bible were made intentionally: "**Intentional Scribal Alterations**. Changes made intentionally by scribes as they copied texts were motivated, in virtually all cases, by a desire to improve the text or to correct it in accordance with what they believed to be its true reading. ... It is the thinking scribe who is more likely to make intentional alterations in the text, inevitably in good faith and out of worthy motivations, including occasional changes made to introduce or promote a viewpoint not in the text being copied. As a class, intentional alterations are far fewer than accidental ones, yet they can exercise far more influence in the transmission process. The categories of intentional scribal changes include (1) alterations in grammar, spelling, and style, including the spelling of proper names; (2) intentional harmonizations to bring the passage being copied into conformity with one similar or parallel (such as a parallel in the synoptic Gospels), or with an OT [Old Testament] quotation (sometimes expanding it to include more of the source or conforming it to the LXX) [early Greek translation of the Old Testament written in Egypt c. 250 B.C.E.], or with a liturgical passage in the Church lectionaries, or even to bring a passage into conformity with a translation known to the scribe or found in a bilingual ms [manuscript]; (3) clarification of perceived geographical or historical discrepancies, such as references to time or place, or to authors of OT quotations; (4) conflation of varying readings present in two or more mss [manuscripts]

---

[1] *The Anchor Bible Dictionary*, Textual Criticism, volume 6
  pages 416-417

accessible to the scribe, yielding a full text; (5) addition of logically appropriate material, such as expanding "Jesus" or "Lord" to the "Lord Jesus Christ"; and (6) theological or ideological alterations, usually involving minor changes in the interest of the Virgin Birth, the omniscience of Jesus, the trinity, or asceticism, to mention a few examples, as well as extensive additions of material, as found, e.g., in mss of the so-called Western text".[1]

The gospel of *Luke* contains a serious contradiction with Christian tradition. Christians teach that Jesus ascended into heaven forty days after his resurrection from the dead. However, the gospel of *Luke* states that Jesus ascended into heaven the same day he rose from the dead: "But on the first day of the week, at early dawn, they came to the tomb, taking the spices that they had prepared. They found the stone rolled away from the tomb, but when they went in, they did not find the body" (Luke 24.1-3).[2] "Now on that same day two of them were going to a village called Emmaus, about seven miles from Jerusalem, and talking with each other about all these things that had happened" (Luke 24.13-15).[3] "That same hour they got up and returned to Jerusalem; and they found the eleven and their companions gathered together" (Luke 24.33-34).[4] "Then he led them out as far as Bethany, and, lifting up his hands,

---

[1] *The Anchor Bible Dictionary*, Textual Criticism, volume 6, page 417 (fourth century manuscripts from Nag Hammadi, Egypt found in 1945)

[2] *The Jewish Annotated New Testament*, Levine and Brettler, page 149

[3] *The Jewish Annotated New Testament*, Levine and Brettler, page 150

[4] *The Jewish Annotated New Testament*, Levine and Brettler, page 150

he blessed them. While he was blessing them, he withdrew from them and was carried up into heaven" (Luke 24.50-52).[1]

The gospels do not mention Joseph's religious convictions or affiliation. However, according to the gospels, Joseph was an artisan, a trade that included carpenters and other craftsmen. Thus, his religious beliefs, and those in his household, were likely similar to those of the Pharisees.

Jesus also very likely adhered to and taught the same beliefs as the Pharisees who advocated *living by the spirit of the Law* more so than by *the letter of the Law*. In one of Jesus' speeches he addressed the punishment he advocated for a person who maliciously caused another person to lose his eyesight in one or both eyes or for causing the loss of another person's tooth: "You have heard it said *An eye for an eye and a tooth for a tooth*. But I say to you, Do not resist an evildoer. But if anyone strikes you on the right cheek, turn the other also" (Matthew 5.38-39).[2]

Jesus did not advocate a literal interpretation of Scriptures as did many of the Sadducees. Jesus was certainly not a member of the extremely traditionalist Dead Sea Sect or the Essene sect. Jesus' teachings show that he subscribed to Oral Law, as did most Pharisees, not the literal interpretation of the Written Law as did the majority of the Sadducees.

---

[1] *The Jewish Annotated New Testament*, Levine and Brettler, page 151
[2] *The Jewish Annotated New Testament*, Levine and Brettler, page 12

The writer of the gospel of *Mark* was a Jewish man with a Greek education. His gospel was completed several years after the end of the First Jewish War, at least forty years after the death of Jesus.

This gospel served as a major source of information for subsequent gospel writers. The gospels of *Matthew*, *Luke* and *John* presented progressively more Greek and Roman attitudes as they explained the teachings of Jesus and his apostles.

The gospels of *Matthew*, *Mark* and *Luke* clearly state that Pilate ordered the execution of Jesus and his soldiers carried out those orders. However, the gospel of *John* contains a substantial increase in the bias against the Jews by stating that it was *the jews* who executed Jesus: "They cried out, *Away with him! Away with him! Crucify him!* Pilate asked them, *Shall I crucify your King?* The chief priests answered, *We have no king but the emperor.* Then he handed him over to them to be crucified" (John 19.15-16).[1] For the Jewish people to say that Pilate or Caesar was their king was absolutely not true. The Jews despised Roman rule. The gospel of *John* demonizes the Jews by stating: "Since it was the day of Preparation, the Jews did not want the bodies left on the cross during the Sabbath, especially because that Sabbath was a day of great solemnity" (John 19.31).[2]

---

[1] *The Jewish Annotated New Testament*, Levine and Brettler, page 192
[2] *The Jewish Annotated New Testament*, Levine and Brettler, page 193

Chapter 30

The Jewish people fought for independence from Rome one last time

The Essenes, Zealots, Messianic Sadducees and sicarii must have realized for many years that they were fighting a losing battle. But, they continued to resist Roman domination and Hellenistic influence and repeatedly tried to gain their independence: "In 117 [117 C.E.], under the Emperor Trajan, the Jews of Egypt and Cyrene (in what is now Libya) had risen in insurrection against the Romans, as had the Jews of Cyprus; those insurrections were repressed after much slaughter on both sides. Very little beyond the bloodshed is known of the uprisings".[1]

Several years later there was again an outcry by the Jewish people who still remained in Palestine: "In his twenty-one-year reign, Hadrian proved a cautious and conservative man, a middle-ground emperor, not much loved but not particularly feared. His biggest war came not from aggression, but from an error in judgment; he tried to build himself a new capital city overtop of the ruins of Jerusalem and even planned to put a temple to Jupiter on the site of the Second Temple".[2]

---

[1] *Judaism and Christian Beginnings*, Samuel Sandmel, page 248
[2] *The History of the Ancient World*, Susan Wise Bauer, page 743

The Zealots led a final revolt against the Romans in an effort to reclaim their independence: "The revolt might have been the outgrowth rather of the ongoing Jewish desire for independence from Roman rule".[1]

In 130 C.E. Hadrian decided to rebuild Jerusalem as a Roman colony. The Jews revolted again. The Bar-Kokhba/Bar-Kochba revolt, 132 – 135 C.E., is often referred to as the Second Jewish War. During this war thousands of Jews died and the Romans lost one full legion of soldiers: "Fifty of the Jews' strongest fortresses were destroyed by the Romans, and nine hundred and eighty-five of their most important settlements razed. Five hundred and eighty thousand Jews were slaughtered in battles and skirmishes and countless numbers died of starvation, fire, and the sword. Nearly the entire land of Judea lay waste".[2] "Hadrian's suppression of the Bar Kochba revolt was accomplished with relentless cruelty, and Hadrian figures in Rabbinic literature as an arch villain. Having suppressed the rebellion in 135 [135 C.E.], he rebuilt Jerusalem, naming it Aelia Capitolina for himself, Hadrianus Aelius".[3]

From that time on, all Jews were forbidden by the Roman authorities from being within eyesight of Jerusalem, except for once a year when they were allowed inside the city on pilgrimage to the Kotel, or Western Wall. 'Wailing Wall' is generally a non-Jewish expression. A few of the remaining Zealots and Essenes who escaped the wrath of Rome during the Second Jewish War very likely moved to today's Iraq,

---

[1] *Jewish Literacy*, Rabbi Joseph Telushkin, page 145
[2] *Jewish Literacy*, Rabbi Joseph Telushkin, page 146
[3] *Judaism and Christian Beginnings*, Samuel Sandmel, page 249

Iran and India. Some of the old Jewish laws and traditions can be seen even today within Islamic and other Eastern religions.

The destruction of the Temple, and the many thousands killed, was devastating for the Jewish people. Membership within the Sadducee sect, the Essene sect and the Dead Sea Sect continued to decline over the next few centuries until they dropped from history altogether. The descendants of priests continued to be identified as Cohen, Kohanan, etc., which designated their priestly heritage.

The Jewish people who did survive the wars against the Romans struggled to maintain a cohesive community. By the third century, the Jewish people had re-established acceptance within many Roman communities. The Jewish people from that time forward referred to themselves collectively simply as Jews, not as Pharisees or Conservatives or liberals. Today there are again several sects within the Jewish community. As with Christians, some are more Orthodox, others more conservative, while others are more liberal.

Chapter 31

A few Christian bishops refused to yield
to the demands of Constantine

The fourth century saw major changes in the Christian communities. These events began with the Roman general Aurelius Valerius Diocletian. He was a commoner who had been declared emperor by the soldiers he commanded: "In 284 [284 C.E.], his claim was widely recognized, and he immediately applied what would prove to be his administrative genius to the task of drawing order out of the chaos into which the empire had fallen. In 285, Diocletian divided the empire in half, assigning the more vital and less conflicted East to himself, and taking the title Augustus. ... As for the West, he designated as his fellow Augustus one of his fellow generals, Maximian. ... Maximian named a general of the legions in Gaul, Constantius, who ruled from a capital at Trier. ... Meanwhile, Christianity had grown, but slowly, with most of its converts being drawn from the lower classes of the Mediterranean world. ... From the early informality of a house-based network of communities that had sprung up in the generations after the Gospels were written down, and partly because those texts, once canonized, served as an organizing structure, the early Jesus movement had developed, probably by the mid to late second century, into something we can call the Church. It had imitated the highly efficient political system of the empire, dividing itself into dioceses and provinces, with local bishops serving as ecclesiastical equivalents of regional governors".[1]

Christianity, like Judaism, was a religion of One God. This created problems for those serving in the military: "Church members who were in the army, in particular, could face impossible pressures to drop incense in the bowl or put an offering of a bird on the fire. The religion of Mithras, a Persian god, had become popular in the military, and as the army's power grew – there were half a million men under arms by now – Christian soldiers found themselves pressed by their officers to participate in that cult, too. In general, they refused. The Church remembers this refusal as having resulted in a long tradition of martyrdom in ancient times, but in fact, violent oppression of Christians was relatively rare and sporadic".[2]

Constantius died in 305 C.E. and was succeeded by his son Constantine: "Thus begins the remarkable story of the reign of the man who transformed the Roman Empire, the Church, and the place of Jews. … When the power of the empire became joined to the ideology of the Church, the empire was immediately recast and reenergized, and the Church became an entity so different from what had preceded it as to be almost unrecognizable. It goes without saying that the conversion of Constantine, for Church and empire both, led to consequences better and worse – although not for Jews, for whom, from this, nothing good would come".[3]

---

[1] *Constantine's Sword*, James Carroll, page 166
[2] *Constantine's Sword*, James Carroll, page 167
[3] *Constantine's Sword*, James Carroll, pages 170-171

Constantine realized it was to his advantage to unify his countrymen as much as possible: "If Constantine was to succeed in imposing authority on a restless Roman populace whose loyalties were divided among contending tetrarchs, he needed a political base within the city. His arrival behind the standard of Christ would have instantly given him one – among Christians. They were a minority, but a well-organized one, and no claimant had the allegiance of a majority. Fierce Christian devotion to a conqueror whose miraculous conversion proved the truth of their faith would have made Christians powerful political allies. ... As seen in Constantine's originating piety, that supreme deity would have been associated with the sun, and pagans would have recognized, with reason, their own solar cult in such Christian practices as orienting churches to the east, worshiping on 'sun day', and celebrating the birth of the deity at the winter solstice. That Christian piety commonly included pagan practice and superstition would have been part of the broad appeal of the Gospel among the least educated. Constantine's famously converted army, for example, was made up of unlettered peasants and barbarians, and it is unlikely they would have grasped essential matters of their new religion. Indeed, to the Teutons and Celts among them – and an army mustered from Trier would have drawn heavily from such tribes – the cross of Christ as the standard to march behind would have evoked the ancestral totem of the sacred tree far more powerfully than it would have Saint Paul's token of deliverance. Such an association may have figured in Constantine's instinctive grasp of the cross as a sign to rally to, since his army of barbarians, which grew with every conquest, was the first population he had to unify".[1]

In 324, Constantine defeated Licinius, another Roman general. That was his last rival. Constantine then pressured some of the bishops. He told them to settle their differences in conflicting teachings and unify the Church.

A gospel referred to as the gospel of *Thomas* was proposed and probably partially written. This was to be a gospel that would consolidate and replace the gospels of *Matthew*, *Mark*, *Luke* and *John* in order to eliminate the many obvious contradictions and inconsistencies. However, this effort was short-lived: "Bishops vied with each other for influence, and worshipers openly disagreed on the meaning of their worship. In addition to the Donatists, there were Docetists and Manichaeans and Arians with their cat's cradle of disputes about ways in which Jesus was man or God, and about the nature, substance, and personality of God".[2]

The following year Constantine increased pressure even more on the uncooperative bishops to unify Christianity. He demanded they hold a council in Nicaea (now Iznik, Turkey): "Thus, the now absolute and sole Caesar, demonstrating an authority no one had ever exercised before, summoned the bishops of the Church to a meeting over which he himself would preside: *Wherefore I signify to you, my beloved brethren, that all of you promptly assemble at the said city, that is at Nicaea …* Two hundred and fifty of them came. He would not let them leave until they had begun to do for the Church what he was doing for the empire. This

---

[1] *Constantine's Sword*, James Carroll, pages 182-183
[2] *Constantine's Sword*, James Carroll, page 186

meeting was the Council of Nicaea, the first Ecumenical Council of the Church. It took place in 325, only a year after [the battle of] Chrysopolis. In response to the emperor's mandate, the bishops did, in fact, agree to a formulaic statement of belief, defining especially, and in explicit terms, how Jesus is God. They did so unanimously – well, almost unanimously. Those who dissented [with the contents and editing of this new, official, 'canonized' version of the New Testament, primarily those who adhered to the more Jewish teachings and traditions] were exiled by Constantine".[1]

The heresy to be religiously different was then declared treason, a civil crime. This led to overt persecution of the Jewish people. The Christians quoted this new canonized Roman-approved New Testament to show that *the jews* had refused to accept Jesus as the promised Messiah and furthermore, that they were directly responsible for the death of Jesus. The teachings of the Roman Christian (Catholic) Church changed dramatically during this period. The Jerusalem Christians were pushed to the sidelines: "Following the edict by Emperor Theodosius that declared Christianity the official religion of the Roman Empire in A.D. 380, versions of Christianity that did not agree with that of the newly empowered hierarchy of bishops were ruthlessly persecuted and their teachings destroyed".[2]

Soon after this: "In 388, a Christian mob, led by the bishop in Callinicus, a small city on the Euphrates [River], attacked and burned a synagogue, destroying it utterly. They also destroyed the chapel of a

---

[1] *Constantine's Sword*, James Carroll, page 189
[2] *The Woman with the Alabaster Jar*, Margaret Starbird, page 66

Gnostic sect, despite the fact that its leaders had just agreed, under pressure from the emperor Theodosius, to accept Nicene Christianity. ... the bishop of Milan declared himself ready to burn synagogues 'that there might not be a place where Christ is denied'. A synagogue, he said, is 'a haunt of infidels, a home of the impious, a hiding place of madmen, under the damnation of God Himself'. To order the rebuilding of such a place, once it had been burned, was an act of treason to the Faith. Theodosius yielded, but insisted that the Christians of Callinicus had to restore the sacred articles of worship they had plundered. He would rebuild the synagogue himself. Ambrose rejected this, too. The principle had to be established that the destruction of the 'vile perfidy' of Jewish worship was a righteous act, in no way to be punished. Ambrose challenged the emperor to his face, during Mass at the cathedral of Milan. Rosemary Radford Ruether describes the scene: 'Coming down from the altar to face him, the bishop declared that he would not continue with the Eucharist until the emperor obeyed. The emperor bowed to this threat of excommunication, and the rioters at Callinicum went unadmonished'".[1]

---

[1] *Constantine's Sword*, James Carroll, page 207

Chapter 32

Mary Magdalene left Judea after the death of Jesus

Much of the history of the early Christians was destroyed in the first few centuries after the death of Jesus: "The Coptic scrolls were hidden at Nag Hammadi in about A.D. 400 during a period in which the orthodox Christian church (having been declared the official church of the Roman Empire by the Emperor Theodosius) began persecuting and destroying the documents of sects it deemed heretical. These scrolls were preserved in jars similar to those containing the scrolls of the Dead Sea Caves near Qumran in the Judean desert. Found in the 1940s and '50s, they have opened up a whole new era of research into the early centuries of Christianity. The prominence of Mary Magdalen [Magdalene] in the four canonical Gospels is strengthened in many of these apocryphal documents. The Coptic scrolls, many of which are second- and third-century parchments, predate the existing copies of the canonical Gospels by centuries!".[1]

Shortly after Jesus' death, Mary Magdalene, pregnant with Jesus' daughter Sarah, left Jerusalem. A few years later, circa 42 C.E., Mary Magdalene and her daughter moved to France: "The early French legend records that Mary 'Magdalen,' [Magdalene] traveling with Martha and

---

[1] *The Woman with the Alabaster Jar*, Margaret Starbird, page 54

Lazarus of Bethany, landed in a boat on the coast of Provence in France".[1]

Margaret Starbird, in her recently published book *The Woman with the Alabaster Jar*, gives some insight into the life of Mary Magdalene after the death of Jesus: "I know of no way to prove beyond a doubt that the 'other Mary' was the wife of Jesus or that she bore a child of his bloodline. But it is possible to prove that belief in this version of the Christian story was widespread in Europe during the Dark and Middle Ages and that it was later forced underground by the ruthless tortures of the Inquisition".[2]

Margaret Starbird also wrote: "The belief that Jesus was married and had heirs was indigenous to Provence. Mary Magdalen [Magdalene] was believed to have lived on their soil and to have been buried there, along with her brother, her sister, and several close friends. The legends and place names of Provence confirmed these beliefs".[3] "In 1209 the Vatican launched a crusade against the entire region of Provence".[4] "Perceiving danger in allowing the rumor of Jesus' marriage and alleged bloodline to circulate, the Church of Rome moved quickly and firmly in the thirteenth century to ensure that it was the mother of Jesus, not his wife, who was venerated by the faithful".[5] Given the hundreds of years of Christian teaching and traditions to the contrary, it is not surprising

---

[1] *The Woman with the Alabaster Jar*, Margaret Starbird, page 51
[2] *The Woman with the Alabaster Jar*, Margaret Starbird, page 27
[3] *The Woman with the Alabaster Jar*, Margaret Starbird, page 76
[4] *The Woman with the Alabaster Jar*, Margaret Starbird, page 75
[5] *The Woman with the Alabaster Jar*, Margaret Starbird, page 79

that many people today find it difficult to believe that Jesus was married and that his wife Mary Magdalene gave birth to their daughter shortly after he died.

Conclusion

Moral lessons that have been drawn from Scriptures have served as stabilizing factors in many societies through the centuries. However, it appears that at least a few of the biblical stories are cases of history re-written to meet later theological and political agendas. As a result, phrases taken from the Bible have been used to justify discrimination and encourage bias and hatred toward people of different ethnic and religious beliefs, especially the Jewish people.

There have been many conflicts, and even wars, that have resulted from people's religious bias. However, Christian theology continues to evolve even today to meet the needs of an ever-changing society. This is reflected in the wide variety of beliefs in the many different Christian churches in the world today. There are members in both the Roman Catholic Church and the Jewish community who are reaching out to each other to improve relations between them.

Most people, when they select a book to read, will typically read the entire book. However, this is not the case with the Bible. According to a recent survey a very low percentage of people, including Christians, have read the entire Bible, from start to finish.

For a better understanding of history and Christian theology I strongly recommend everyone who teaches religion or quotes phrases from the Bible take the time to read a Bible from beginning to end, including the introduction, footnotes and comments.

Questions addressed in this book

According to early Jewish tradition, how old is the universe?

In the story of Noah and the Flood, where did the people believe so much water had come from?

What became of the Hebrew lost tribes?

When were the Scriptures first consolidated, edited and canonized?

What were the major differences between the Jewish sects – the Sadducees, the Pharisees and the Essenes?

Why did the Jews hate the Herods so much?

What is the explanation for the differences between the two nativity stories?

Why was Mary Magdalene regarded by some as a prostitute?

When was each of the four gospels of the New Testament written?

When did the Romans discontinue crucifixion as capital punishment?

Permissions

Permissions are in the order of appearance.

Scripture quotations taken from The Holy Bible, New International Version NIV. Copyright © 1973, 1978, 1984, 2011 by Biblica, Inc. Used by permission. All rights reserved worldwide.

Essential Judaism – Reprinted with the permission of Pocket Books, a Division of Simon & Schuster, Inc. from ESSENTIAL JUDAISM by George Robinson. Copyright © 2000 George Robinson.

Excerpts from pp. 266, 267, 434, 435, 513, 574, 599 [554 words] from BIBLICAL LITERACY by RABBI JOSEPH TELUSHKIN. COPYRIGHT (C) 1997 BY JOSEPH TELUSHKIN. Reprinted by permission of HarperCollins Publishers.

Numerous excerpts [pp. 69 – 428: 2401 words] from JEWISH LITERACY by RABBI JOSEPH TELUSHKIN, COPYRIGHT (C) 1991 BY RABBI JOSEPH TELUSHKIN. Reprinted by permission of HarperCollins Publishers.

Index

CPSIA information can be obtained
at www.ICGtesting.com
Printed in the USA
FSOW03n1026290317
32314FS